MUSIC CITY READER 2005

Savana!
Thanks for the
support!
Randy

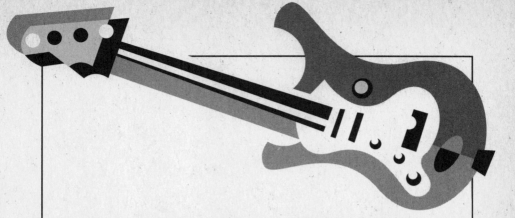

MUSIC CITY READER 2005

Great Writing on Country & Bluegrass Music

Edited by
Randy Rudder

Music City Books

Copyright © 2005 by Randy Rudder

Publisher's Cataloging-In-Publication Data
(Prepared by The Donohue Group, Inc.)

Music City Reader 2005 : great writing on country & bluegrass music / edited by
Randy Rudder ; foreword by Doug Kershaw.

   p. ; cm.
  ISBN: 0-9769745-0-9

1. Country music—History and criticism. 2. Bluegrass music—History and criti-
cism. 3. Country musicians—United States. 4. Bluegrass musicians—United States.
I. Rudder, Randy. II. Kershaw, Doug. III. Davis, Francis. IV. Hume, Martha. V.
Cooper, Peter M., 1970- VI. Stubbs, Eddie. VII. McCall, Michael. VIII. Cantwell,
David. IX. Sweetland, Phil. X. Kingsbury, Paul. XI. Wilkinson, Alec, 1952- XII.
Goldsmith, Thomas, 1952- XIII. Hickey, Dave. XIV. Berrier, Ralph. XV. Morris,
Edward, 1935- XVI. DeMain, Bill. XVII. Shave, Nick. XVIII. Filene, Benjamin.
XIX. Cardwell, Nancy, 1958- XX. Allen, Bob. XXI. Wynn, Ron.

ML3524 .M87 2005
781.642 2005929882

Music City Books
2496 Port Kembla Dr.
Mt Juliet, TN 37122
www.musiccityreader.com

Cover and book design: KerseyGraphics

CONTENTS

Foreword . . . . *viii*

Acknowledgments . . . . *xv*

"God's Lonely Man" (Johnny Cash) *1*
By Francis Davis
From *The Atlantic Monthly*

"Is Loretta Lynn Country Music's Scarlett O'Hara?" *11*
By Martha Hume
From *The Journal of Country Music*

"Proud to be a Redneck Woman" (Gretchen Wilson) *25*
By Peter Cooper
From *The Tennessean*

"James Henry "Jimmy" Martin
(August 10, 1927—May 14, 2005)" *31*
By Eddie Stubbs
From *Bluegrass Unlimited*

"From Down-home to Big Time" (Fan Fair) *37*
By Michael McCall
From *The Nashville Scene*

"Iris DeMent: All That Living Will Allow" *45*
By David Cantwell
From *No Depression*

"Kris Kristofferson: The Hemingway of Songwriters" *59*
By Phil Sweetland
From *American Songwriter*

Contents

"The Celebrity Two-Step" (Brad Paisley) 67
By Paul Kingsbury
From *The Journal of Country Music*

"The Ghostly Ones" (Gillian Welch and David Rawlings) 81
By Alec Wilkinson
From *The New Yorker*

**"Through Fifty-Year-Old Eyes: Ricky Skaggs
and the State of Bluegrass"** 97
By Thomas Goldsmith
From *Bluegrass Unlimited*

"His Mickey Mouse Ways" (Waylon Jennings) 105
By Dave Hickey
From *Texas Monthly*

"Rhonda Vincent: Enjoying the View" 113
By Ralph Berrier, Jr.
From *Bluegrass Unlimited*

"The Big Show" (Tim McGraw) 119
By Edward Morris
From *The Journal of Country Music*

"Dwight Yoakam: Hillbilly Redux" 133
By Bill DeMain
From *Performing Songwriter*

"Voice of America" (Mark O'Connor) 143
By Nick Shave
From *The Strad* (London)

"O Brother, What Next? Making Sense of the Folk Fad" *151*
By Benjamin Filene
From *Southern Cultures* (University of North Carolina)

"Lost Notes and Myriad Blessings" (John Prine) *169*
By Michael McCall
From *The Nashville Scene*

"They're Back: Rodney and Douglas Dillard" *177*
By Nancy Cardwell
From *Bluegrass Unlimited*

"Fame From the Tips of His Fingers" (Bill Anderson) *189*
By Bob Allen
From *The Journal of Country Music*

"A Tribute to Texas Songwriters" *201*
By Ron Wynn
From *American Songwriter*

"The Resurrection of Keith Urban" *209*
By Peter Cooper
From *The Tennessean*

"The Art of Inauthenticity" (Sammi Smith) *215*
By David Cantwell
From *The Oxford American*

Contributors *219*

Permissions *221*

FOREWORD

In this book you will find a collection of articles about some amazing country singers, songwriters and musicians. It's a pleasure and an honor for me to discuss them in this foreword. I'm happy to say that I knew a few of these old folks very well. And the others, the newcomers to the scene? I feel a great pride in seeing them shine. It's their turn now. But that doesn't mean I'm about to give up *my* turn! Not yet, not by a long shot. There's room out there for us all.

Reading this book, and learning new things about these talented people, I found myself being carried back to some old memories.

Picture this. It's a Friday afternoon in the late 1950s. It's over 100 degrees and the middle of a Texas heat wave. Hot air rises in waves off the tarred and narrow road that stretches far in the distance. You're about to play an outdoor show at some county fair. And when it's done, you got 18 hours to pack up the equipment, and the band, and hightail it out of Texas, then head north in time to make the Grand Ole Opry for your Saturday night appearance. You *had* to be there, if you were an Opry member. It was known as the Saturday Night Rule. So, you're in a used Ford, maybe a 1952 Coupe. There is no air conditioning. There are still almost no motels in existence. Hotels are the order of the day, standing proud and tall at town centers. The few, short patches of toll road are still in the East, except for a tiny stretch in Kentucky. The United States itself is mainly a country of two-lane highways. There's no by-passing cities and towns; you drive through the heart of each one to get to the other side. The notion of a Silver Eagle bus, or flying to shows on jet airplanes, is still a long way in the future. Someone in the car mentions that their kid is having a birthday party and he'll miss it. Someone else hopes his mother gets well. She's been in the hospital. Maybe, on the next trip through Georgia, he'll finally get to visit her.

As I look at the list of stars in this collection, I know the ones who drove the same two-lane roads as I did. And we did it so many times we knew exactly which little café in what tiny town had the best fried chicken, the cleanest hotel rooms, and the club owner who always paid the band on time. Johnny. Kris. Waylon. Loretta. Jimmy. Bill. Rodney and Doug.

Foreword

The dusty highways may have changed into bustling interstates, and the old cars into custom-built buses worth too many dollars to count, but what hasn't changed is the love that drew us all to country music. It talks as strongly today to Brad Paisley and Tim McGraw as it talked to Johnny Cash, long before Johnny hit Memphis and met up with Luther Perkins and Sam Phillips. It's the kind of music so strong and so from the heart that it drew farm boys off the land, leaving behind them the legacy of their forefathers so they could pursue a dream in Nashville. It drew daughters and sons down from the Smoky Mountains, out from the Ozarks, up from the Panhandle of Oklahoma and the Big Thicket of Texas. It spoke to young men and women in cotton fields and cornfields, kids who worked long hours to save enough money to finally buy that first guitar. This wasn't a rich man's music. It was a Celtic music born of people who had lived the life. In a way, that makes it our own kind of blues. I know I sure heard the call, all the way deep in the swamps of Southwest Louisiana, in the midst of another houseboat *fais do do*.

And I hear that call just as strong today. Maybe stronger.

But sometimes you gotta cover a lot of miles in order to stand backstage somewhere, whether at the Opry, or the Wheeling Jamboree, or an outdoor concert tucked away in the hills of Kentucky, and listen to Jimmy Martin's guitar run on "Uncle Pen." And when you do, well, what are a few hundred miles in an old car, with all the windows rolled down to cool you off, and a million bugs splattered across the windshield? It was suddenly worth all that and more. Hell, you just heard Jimmy Martin play the guitar!

Are there young boys and girls out there now, listening with both ears full-throttle as Keith Urban plays guitar, or Rhonda Vincent plays the mandolin, kids who secretly whisper to themselves, "One day, I'm gonna grow up and play like that."

Of course there are. A lot of them. When I joined the Grand Ole Opry in 1957, along with my brother Rusty, we were the youngest members at that time. I had just turned twenty-one and Rusty was barely nineteen. That was a long time ago, so I've seen a lot of people in a lot of crowds. And yet, every time I walk out onto a stage, I still see them: young faces full of drive and ambition and longing.

And guess what? A few of them are gonna make it.

Foreword

When I read Phil Sweetland's article on Kris Kristofferson, "The Hemingway of Songwriters," I smiled at the notion. I feel not just friendship and camaraderie for Kris (we did our share of partying, I freely admit this), but I feel a pride at all the things Kris has accomplished in his life. You see, when I first met Kris Kristofferson he was a janitor at Columbia Studios, sweeping floors and emptying ashtrays. I wouldn't say he was a typical janitor, but I suspect he was a damn good one. Anything Kris did, he did with his full heart. I am reminded of the night he used his janitorial keys to try to open the tape vault at Columbia so he could steal me a copy of my own demo session. Since I had put every single penny I had into recording the session in the first place, I soon discovered I couldn't afford any tape copies of it! Kris couldn't get the vault opened, but he tried.

And Johnny Cash? It's difficult to even think of John without getting a little choked up over the fact that he's now gone. There went not just a talent but one of the most generous men that ever lived. A lot of careers in Nashville were jump-started by Johnny Cash. Mine was one. I remember the day when John came to me with an offer, back in 1969. He was about to tape his first special, a big television deal that would launch his variety show. Did I want to be on the premiere with the likes of Bob Dylan and Joni Mitchell, or later, as a regular guest on the show? I chose the premiere. I even let Bob Dylan try on some of my outfits. You know why? Bob had brought only black clothes to wear and suddenly thought it might offend Johnny Cash. But none of my outfits fit him (My velvet Edwardian suits? Imagine Dylan in one of *those!*) I convinced Bob Dylan that John Cash was the kind of man who wouldn't even notice.

Will the day ever come when the world can forget it once had the likes of Johnny Cash? I doubt it. But a little bit of him is still alive in Francis Davis' essay.

What about the true-blue songs that were drawn from the soul of Bill Anderson? There was a time the man couldn't turn around without a hit song falling out of his pocket, and these were classic songs, like "Still," and "City Lights." Bill is *still* writing them.

And so is the great John Prine. When was the last time you heard a song with such powerful lyrics as "Paradise,"in which a town in Kentucky is being hauled away by a coal company? Listen to the words of "Hello in There" and tell me you can still be the same after-

Foreword

wards. That's the kind of talent that makes you proud to be in this business. And it's from that same pure, creative center in Prine and Anderson that the likes of Dwight Yoakam pulls out the words to songs like "Guitars, Cadillacs, and Hillbilly Music," and "Streets of Bakersfield."

How many of us remember the first time we ever heard Sammi Smith sing? Remember "Help Me Make It Through the Night"? (By the way, that song was written by the former janitor at Columbia Studios.) As you think of Sammi's incredible, soulful voice, listen to Iris Dement sing "Our Town." Listen to Gillian Welch and David Rawlings sing "Long Black Veil."

It gets passed on, the love and the tradition of country music. There's no stopping it. It might lie low for a time but then it comes back full force, just as it did in the smash film by the Coen Brothers, *O, Brother, Where Art Thou?* (Welch is on that soundtrack, too, by the way, as if you didn't already know.) What Loretta Lynn started with "The Pill," and "Woman Enough," Gretchen Wilson has picked up and carried forward with "Redneck Women." And the Dillards, those talented brothers Rodney and Doug? Who can forget them (along with Mitch and Dean) as the Darlin' boys, on the *Andy Griffith Show*, who lived up in the mountains, and occasionally came to town in an old car, with Denver Pyle as their patriarch? Remember the famous snoring episode in the Darling cabin? Doug says they had to keep retaping since nobody could quit laughing. When you hear those guys sit down and play a song, right along with Sheriff Andy Taylor, it's just as fresh and good and wonderful as the day they taped that show. That's talent, folks. And talent lives on, even in those black and white television shows that make us yearn for the past.

The bluegrass tradition of the Dillards, carried forward by the likes of Ricky Scaggs, keeps alive a tradition far older than country music itself. It keeps alive everything those Celtic ancestors packed into worn trunks in the old country and brought with them to the new country, into the Carolinas and out through Kentucky and Tennessee. Listen to Dwight Yoakam sing "Miner's Prayer" and you'll know what I mean.

The music in itself becomes a family heirloom passed down to other generations.

Foreword

It's been a lot of years since country music moved out of tent shows held in cow pastures and onto the stages at Madison Square Garden or Carnegie Hall. (By the way, I'm proud to say this Cajun has played both those places!) When WWII soldiers left the South and went off into the world, they took their love of music with them. When civilian men and women packed up their belongings in Tennessee and Arkansas and Mississippi and Georgia and went off to work in the automobile and ship-building plants in such far-off places as Detroit and Baltimore, they packed up their love of country music and took that, too. In return, the songs gave them solace. The words and music gave them back their memories of Georgia pine trees, the Mississippi River, Kentucky hollers, the flat level landscape of Texas and Oklahoma, the cool mountains of East Tennessee. The music kept their roots safe while they made a few dollars and paid a few bills and settled down to a new way of life in a strange new part of the country. They were homesick as hell, but the music kept them alive. Buoyed them up.

Music can do this to people.

Maybe it's just the way it should be, then, that today's biggest stars fly to gigs in private jets or drive there on custom-made buses that roll along like little castles on wheels. In the beginning, after all, the Anglo-Saxon bards walked from village to village as they carried their songs to the people. I bet they would've liked a ride now and then in an old 1952 Ford Coupe with no air conditioning! In other words, each generation thinks theirs is the best. But it all changes. We can't stop it, so let's go with it. What's more important is that the tradition is safe. The music is being fostered now by Keith Urban, an Aussie who sings country as picks as good as any American farm boy I ever heard. It's safe with the Gretchen Wilsons, the Gillian Welches, the Brad Paisleys, and the Dwight Yoakams.

And, oh yes, did I mention that there's an article in this book on my competition? That's the fiddler Mark O'Connor. Here's what I think about him: That boy can play the instrument! And what kind of place would this world be if there wasn't room for just one more fiddler?

In the end, we need the best of journalists to carry this history of our music and of our "bards to the page, to help keep it safe for us. In this collection—thanks to the editing skills and good judgment of Randy Rudder—you will find some of the very best writers of the day,

Foreword

all scholars and fans true to the art. Without journalism like this, and without books like this, the future might not remember the day Bill Monroe handed his mandolin over to Ricky Skaggs. Or that the Hemingway of Songwriters was once a hired janitor emptying ash trays for other artists.

Or that there's always room in the world for just one more honest fiddler.

Doug Kershaw

ACKNOWLEDGMENTS

Editing and publishing a book on country music in Nashville, Tennessee seems like cheating. It's almost too easy. Not only is Nashville the capitol of country music; it's also a huge book publishing town. As a result, one has relatively easy access to artists, songwriters, label executives, and publicists, as well as to a number of great music research facilities, such as the Country Music Hall of Fame and Middle Tennessee State University libraries. Furthermore, Nashville is home to book publishers Thomas Nelson and Broadman & Holman, and periodicals like *The Journal of Country Music*, *American Songwriter*, *Performing Songwriter*, *Nashville Scene*, *CMA Close Up*, and *Country Weekly*, so it's easy to see what a turnkey operation it is. You're never more than a stone's throw from a printer, publisher, or magazine.

I consider myself further blessed to have had the acquaintance of several independent publishers and writers in Nashville, all of whom have been ready and willing to share their experiences and expertise. I have attempted to list some of these friends and mentors, without whom this project certainly would not have succeeded. My sincere thanks to:

Maryglenn McCombs, owner of Dowling Press; Emma Wisdom, publisher of numerous works; and Mark Renz, author and publisher of several books on fossil hunting (and my first roommate in Nashville). I couldn't have done it without the knowledge and expertise you all have shared.

Music journalists and scholars Edward Morris, Ronnie Pugh, James Akenson, Don Cusic, Jay Orr, Bill Conger, Wayne Daniel, Bobby Reed, Ted Olson, Beverly Keel, and all the folks from the International Country Music Conference.

Cathie Pelletier, one of the finest fiction writers in the U.S. today. Thanks for sharing your home and wisdom over the years.

Steven Womack, friend and publishing mentor, for all your advice over the years.

Acknowledgments

The faculty in the University of Memphis MFA program, including my thesis director Kristen Iversen, Randall Kenan, Shara McCallum, Cary Holladay, and Barbara Ching.

Valerie Belew and my fellow faculty members at Nashville State Community College. Thanks for taking an interest in my writing and publishing pursuits and for your insights and encouragement.

Dewayne McFarlin at Broadman and Holman. Thanks for your publishing tips.

Sterling Lance, for helping with my bookkeeping and tax preparation and for letting me beat you at golf.

Cathy Gurley, my publicist, for your enthusiasm and direction on this project.

Designer Bill Kersey for a great cover and photographer Jon LeMay for a great photo.

David Benton, Joe Perricone, and Hugh Kirkpatrick for sharing your marketing ideas.

Arnold Rogers, for giving me my first byline.

Dwight and Martha Bratcher, for letting me live in your attic when I was down and out, and for being such good friends.

All the folks at Two Rivers Baptist Church, including Pastor Jerry Sutton, who have encouraged me and ministered to me over the years.

Jerry and Michelle Bailey for taking our daughter overnight when we really needed some couple time.

Eddie and Tammy Garst, for befriending us and welcoming us into your home group.

Clare Rudder, for setting up my office, being my consultant; for sacrificing a lot of lonely nights, and for being my 'help meet' for the past eight years.

My mom, Jane Rudder, for always being my biggest fan.

All my friends back in my hometown of Wellsville, Ohio.

Abigail Jane Rudder for always waiting with a hug and a scream when I come home and just for being so doggone cute.

To all the contributors to this edition for your excellent work. You are all true craftsmen.

And to Jesus Christ, through whom all things are possible.

If the adage, "He is wealthy who has many friends" is true, then I am rich beyond compare, even if this anthology never sells a copy. It was a true labor of love putting it together.

Randy Rudder

GOD'S LONELY MAN
Johnny Cash was a Christian who didn't cast stones, a patriot who wasn't a bully

By Francis Davis
From *The Atlantic Monthly*

In 1956, when he recorded "I Walk the Line" for Sun Records, Johnny Cash became an overnight sensation. But it was his many years of singing as if he knew from personal experience all of humankind's strengths and failings — as if he had both committed murder and been accepted into God's light — that made him a favorite of liberals and conservatives, MTV and the Grand Ole Opry, Gary Gilmore and Billy Graham. A tall piece of timber, Cash was often likened to John Wayne, to whom he otherwise bore only the slightest resemblance. The biggest difference was that Wayne never really lived up to (and probably only dimly comprehended) the democratic ideals he personified on screen — which were more likely the ideals of the directors he worked with anyway. Cash took on a greater variety of roles as a singer than Wayne did as an actor, and both he and the characters he gave voice to admitted their weaknesses. From song to song he was a cowboy or a white outcast who rode with Indians, a family man or a drifter, a believer in eternal life or a condemned murderer with no tomorrows anywhere. His credibility as all of these owed as much to the moral effort involved in endlessly putting himself in others' shoes as it did to his professional savvy in putting a song across.

Waking to the radio last September 12 and hearing that Cash had died in the middle of the night, I remembered thinking about Cash just days after the attacks two years earlier, while watching a nationally televised prayer service attended by the President and the First Lady and featuring a performance by the mezzo-soprano Denyce Graves. It should have been moving — but as I listened to a mannered black diva render an old spiritual as if it were a European art song, it

Francis Davis

was impossible not to think that the occasion called for a more home-grown performance style. If the point was to rally Americans to draw on their inner resources, it would have been a comfort to hear from Johnny Cash, who stood for what Christopher Wren, his first biographer, called "the dignity of the commonplace and the redeeming grace of hard knocks."

I thought of Cash frequently in the weeks and months that followed 9/11, as music written in response to the attacks began to be released. With few exceptions, rock's singer-songwriters lapsed into their habitual pattern of dissent, and country singers beat the drums for retaliation. All of it reminded me of that period in the late 1960s, before public opinion solidified against the Vietnam War, when we heard "The Ballad of the Green Berets" and "I Ain't Marchin' Anymore" — neither side giving any ground — and when Cash became a voice of reason. The lyrics to "I Walk the Line" pledge sexual fidelity regardless of temptation; but whenever Cash performed this song in the early 1970s (as he surely must have at every show), he might just as well have been describing his principled balancing act in opposing our military policy in Southeast Asia while continuing to voice support for our troops. "Singing in Vietnam Talking Blues," "What Is Truth?," and "The Man in Black" — Cash's antiwar songs — weren't among his best numbers, and they didn't really say anything that countless rockers and folkies hadn't said already. They were powerful by virtue of who sang them: not a hippie leading a chant at Woodstock but a country music icon who was risking the sort of ire unleashed last year against Natalie Maines, of the Dixie Chicks, when she told a British audience she was embarrassed that George W. Bush was a fellow Texan.

In 1969 *The New York Times* ran a Sunday magazine article on Cash titled "First Angry Man of Country Singers" — a reference not just to Cash's activism in behalf of prisoners and Indians but also to his having generally made life miserable for those closest to him, a few years earlier, when he was taking huge daily doses of amphetamines and barbiturates. If suicidal habits and self-destructive behavior are the primary definition of "angry," Hank Williams (for one) was years ahead of Cash. But unless you count Woody Guthrie — which the Nashville establishment does not, even though it should — Cash was country music's first protest singer. "Singing in Vietnam Talking Blues" was released as a single in May of 1971, and it isn't much of an

God's Lonely Man

exaggeration to say that his performance of the song on television early that year marked a turning point: If Johnny Cash wasn't buying this war, why should anybody?

That performance was on Cash's own TV show, which aired on ABC from 1969 to 1971. According to his own accounts, Cash fought only two battles with his network bosses, who eventually gave in to him on both. One disagreement arose from his desire to introduce a hymn by declaring his own faith in Jesus. The other was over an appearance by Pete Seeger, whom Cash defended as "a good American as I've ever met." One can imagine the same thing being said of Cash.

In 1975, when an interviewer for *Penthouse* asked him if he was a political radical, he replied, "I'm just tryin' to be a good Christian" — a good Christian, but not a professional one, despite his many songs about Jesus and his tours as a member of his friend Billy Graham's Crusades. He was a Christian who didn't cast stones, a patriot who didn't play the flag card.

Cash's image evolved in tandem with his musical style. The albums that he recorded on the fly at Folsom and San Quentin in the late 1960s made do with a bare-bones instrumentation that recalled his early singles for Sun, and their crossover into pop may have been what convinced him that he was better off without the background choirs and instrumental "sweetening" featured on most of that day's country recordings, including too many of his own. He dispensed with other frills as well. In the late 1950s and early 1960s, around the same time that Frank Sinatra was popularizing the "concept" album, Cash brought the idea to country music. His album jackets often showed him costumed in keeping with a musical theme: he was a farmhand on *Now, There Was a Song!*, for example, and a gunfighter on both *Ride This Train* and *Johnny Cash Sings the Ballads of the True West*. By 1969, however, he had settled on one style of dress. In his frock coat and morning pants, he was "The Man in Black" — a look and a nickname, but also a singular persona. Though he said in the 1971 song of that name that he wore black to remind himself and his audiences of society's injustices, he must have known that it was flattering to him — and made him stand out from that era's rhinestone cowboys.

He was in his late thirties and already had plenty of mileage on him when he was discovered by television: longer hair and the shadows and dents of middle age brought out the character in his face, making him almost handsome. He appeared in a couple of movies

Francis Davis

around this time, but gave what I think of as his finest performance in John Frankenheimer's *I Walk the Line* (1970), for which he merely supplied the score. His songs do such a good job of letting us know what's going on in the mind of the character played by Gregory Peck (a small-town Tennessee sheriff in the grip of a midlife crisis) that it's as if he and Peck were sharing the role. The movie was a flop at the box office, but "Flesh and Blood" — perhaps the single most beautiful song Cash ever wrote, and one whose lyrics could stand alone as inspired nature poetry — reached No. 1 on the country charts.

With maturity Cash grew into his voice. To read his obituaries, one might think that his credibility as a singer depended entirely on his credibility as a man. True, he never developed his upper range to the point where he could trust it, and the dear emphasis he gave every single word would have precluded gliding from note to note even if he had been able to. Among the singers of his own generation he lacked the bravura and the sheer lung power of such country Carusos as Elvis Presley, Conway Twitty, Roy Orbison, Ferlin Husky, and the young Waylon Jennings. We tend not to value deep voices as much as we do high, soaring ones, perhaps because the effort involved in producing a low note is less apparent. Something about hearing a singer go low strikes most ears as a trick, a human special effect. The bass singer does the grunt work in doo-wop and rhythm and blues, sometimes literally. There is a style of country music, however, in which a male singer's descent to a virile low note at the end of a phrase, or for the closing chorus, supplies the same payoff as a soul singer's falsetto — one conveys masculine certainty and the other uncontrollable passion, but each signifies a moment of truth. No country singer was better at this than Cash, and few singers in any field of music have been as expressive or as instantly recognizable.

Cash wasn't usually thought of as a folk singer, but in terms of updating traditional material and writing new songs in the same vein, he was the closest thing to an authentic troubadour to emerge since the end of World War II. "Don't Take Your Guns to Town" (1958), about a headstrong young man who comes to a violent end after ignoring his mother's advice, was based on an Irish ballad that found its way to the American South. "Five Feet High and Rising" (1959), about the devastation caused by a 1937 flood of the Mississippi, was entirely his own creation. Anyone listening to these two songs and unfamiliar with their sources would be hard put to guess which was

God's Lonely Man

traditional and which original. Possibly at the instigation of Seeger and Bob Dylan, Cash performed at the Newport Folk Festival in 1964. It was Freedom Summer, and the festival was a recruiting ground for the voter-registration movement and for leftist causes in general. The presence of a country music star must have raised a few eyebrows. But the organizers must have recognized that Cash virtually defined folk music in his relationship to his primary audience — a country music audience that embraced him because his music reflected their experience, even if his political beliefs occasionally differed from theirs.

Cash was one of the original Sun rockabillies, along with Presley, Carl Perkins, Jerry Lee Lewis, and the forgotten Warren Smith and Billy Lee Riley — like him, southerners who had grown up aspiring to country stardom before anyone had ever heard of rock-and-roll. Yet Bono, Bruce Springsteen, and Tom Petty smiled on Cash as one of their own: they heard something close to rock-and-roll in his music, and recognized it for sure in his independent stance. After country radio turned its back on his generation in the 1990s, in favor of young beefcake cowpokes like Toby Keith and Tim McGraw, Cash attracted the attention of MTV by recording his own versions of songs by groups such as Soundgarden, Depeche Mode, and Nine Inch Nails for Rick Rubin, a producer identified with rap and heavy metal.

For all that, whenever Cash made the Top 40 (as he did with some regularity for twenty years, beginning in 1956 with "I Walk the Line"), it was always with what sounded like a country song, not one that conformed to current pop trends. country music record buyers didn't extend him the same loyalty, nor did the Nashville power brokers. Cash was a posthumous winner in three categories at last year's Country Music Association Awards. *American IV: The Man Comes Around*, his fourth album for Rubin and the last to be released before his death, was named Album of the Year, and his version of "Hurt" — a song written by Trent Reznor, of Nine Inch Nails — won for Single of the Year and Music Video of the Year. But there was an air of atonement to these awards, which were given out in November, less than two months after Cash's death. Not counting his election to the association's Hall of Fame, in 1980 (the equivalent of being kicked upstairs), he hadn't received a CMA award since 1969. The association had completely ignored *American Recordings*, his first album for Rubin and arguably his greatest work, even though it won a Grammy as the Best Contemporary Folk Recording of 1994. Cash was in any case

Francis Davis

never part of the country music establishment, and at the height of his celebrity, in the early 1970s, he towered above it.

Cash wasn't an outlaw — just an outsider, in a way that had nothing to do with stage image. He even seemed a little out of place in the Highwaymen, the country music supergroup he started recording with in the 1980s, which also featured the shaggy Nashville "outlaws" Waylon Jennings, Willie Nelson, and Kris Kristofferson. His singing and the way he carried himself did influence a number of country singers of his generation and slightly younger, most notably Merle Haggard and Kristofferson. But among today's younger country performers, the only ones who sound like they've listened much to Cash are somehow related to him: his daughter Rosanne Cash, his stepdaughter Carlene Carter, and his former sons-in-law Marty Stuart and Rodney Crowell. Where his influence is still widespread is in the work of performers ignored by country stations but likely to be on the playlists of classic rock stations and public radio's World Café — such younger singer-songwriters as Steve Earle and Billy Bragg, along with Bob Dylan and Bruce Springsteen.

In the movie *Taxi Driver*, Cybill Shepherd tells Robert De Niro that he reminds her of Kris Kristofferson's song "The Pilgrim:" "He's a walking contradiction / Partly truth and partly fiction." That song was actually Kristofferson's homage to Cash; but the line from the movie that best describes him is "God's lonely man," De Niro's reference to himself. Cash seemed a man alone even when surrounded by his family on stage, and there was a brooding quality to even his songs about doing right by his fellow man and finding redemption through Jesus.

Cheating songs are a dime a dozen in country, but the one of Cash's that most readily comes to mind may be unique: his adaptation of the traditional ballad "The Long Black Veil," whose narrator chooses to hang for a murder he didn't commit rather than reveal that he was in bed with his best friend's wife on the night in question. His songs about the wild life usually end with someone either serving time or bleeding to death on a barroom floor.

Cash identified with society's victims, but the true measure of his compassion was his realization that some of us become victims of our own dark impulses. The inmates we hear cheering for him on the albums he recorded at Folsom and San Quentin sensed his empathy for them, even though they may have misinterpreted it. According to legend, many of these men believed that Cash was one of them — that he had served hard time himself. In truth his jail time was limited to what he often humorously described as "seven one-night stands" in the 1950s and early 1960s, all after busts for drunkenness or possession when he was popping pills. On both albums the loudest cheers — the most frightening ones — come during "Folsom Prison Blues," when Cash delivers his famous line about killing a man in Reno "just to watch him die." The prisoners we hear whooping at that line took it to be a boast; but Cash once wrote that he had written it after asking himself what was the most unforgivable reason he could imagine for taking another person's life. He was the favorite singer of Gary Gilmore, who was especially fond of "Don't Take Your Guns to Town." It's too bad Gilmore didn't live to hear "Delia's Gone," the opening number on *American Recordings*. No other song I know has ever probed so chillingly the mind of a murderer — particularly the ability of a psychopath to dissociate himself from his own deeds.

For the most part, *American Recordings* presented Cash alone, accompanying himself on guitar. The album's beauty was in its starkness and simplicity, with Rubin producing Cash in much the same way that country blues performers were recorded in the 1930s: just sit the man down and roll the tapes while he sings whatever he wants to — his own songs along with others he knows and likes. In their own way, Cash's interpretations of Leonard Cohen's "Bird on the Wire" and Nick Lowe's "The Beast in Me" (a song actually written for him by another of his former sons-in-law) were just as compelling as "Delia's Gone." Three of the album's new songs rank among the most touching Cash ever wrote: "Oh, Bury Me Not," a variation on an old cowboy lament with a half-spoken introduction in which Cash tells us he senses God's hand in nature more than he does in churches; "Drive On," in which he sings from the point of view of a Vietnam veteran who's leading a normal life though still haunted by his wartime experiences; and "Like a Soldier," a love song presumably addressed either to Jesus or to June Carter Cash, and so gorgeous it hardly matters which.

American Recordings represented an apotheosis, but the albums that followed it were overproduced and unextraordinary; the musicians who accompanied Cash on them somehow managed to sound at once sympathetic and superfluous. Cash was no longer in good voice, and the newer songs that Rubin chose for him (death figured in quite a few) wallowed in a kind of adolescent self-pity that made them all wrong for a performer who, whatever else he was, was always an adult.

Francis Davis

It turns out that some of the best performances Cash recorded for Rubin were passed over for release until after his death, and finally surfaced on the unfortunately titled *Cash Unearthed*, a five-CD boxed set that arrived in stores in November. My favorite of these is Cash's version of Billy Joe Shaver's "If I Give My Soul," in which a man bargains with the Lord in much the same way that Robert Johnson is said to have bargained with the devil at a Mississippi crossroads — except that instead of prowess on the guitar, this man's asking price is sobriety and winning back the love of his estranged wife and son. It's a song full of adult sorrow that leaves "Hun" in the dust.

Whatever his actual relationship to rock-and-roll, Cash was the only surviving performer from its first wave who was still in the thick of things at the beginning of the new century (Chuck Berry, Jerry Lee Lewis, and Little Richard having long ago accepted their fate as oldies acts). Rock-and-roll has been with us for almost fifty years now — an eternity by the standards of popular music, but well short of the average human life-span. Until very recently the only dead rock-and-rollers were the ones who died young — casualties of their own bad habits, of car wrecks and plane crashes, of wronged women and obsessed fans with guns. For all their shortcomings, Cash's last few CDs exerted considerable power by presenting us with something we hadn't really heard before in pop music: a man long past middle age confronting his own mortality, and implicitly asking us to contemplate ours.

Cash made the cover of *Time* following his death, and inside was an eloquent meditation on his career by Richard Corliss. But what really caught my eye was an op-ed piece in the *Philadelphia Daily News*, headlined "Why This Lesbian Loved the Man in Black." The writer, Debbie Woodell, lovingly recalled how she and her brother used to sing along as children to their grandparents' Lefty Frizzell and Eddy Arnold records. "But not Johnny. With Johnny, we listened." There was a tribute to Cash at the Country Music Awards in November, with Willie Nelson, Kris Kristofferson, Travis Tritt, Sheryl Crow, Hank Williams Jr., and the Nitty Gritty Dirt Band all singing his songs and wearing black in his honor. Yet to me, a more meaningful tribute was the Johnny Cash album covers I saw in the windows of a few New York used record stores well into the fall. Many of these shops didn't even carry country music; the owners or employees had brought in albums from their own collections. It reminded me of a scene in the movie

God's Lonely Man

High Fidelity, when John Cusack, playing the owner of a store called Championship Vinyl, faces us and says, deadpan, "My all-time favorite book is Johnny Cash's autobiography *Cash*, by Johnny Cash." Nothing if not ironic, he's aware of the humor in his repetition, but you can tell he sincerely loves saying the name. There are some of us for whom music is a form of religion as well as an addiction, filling the same need in our lives that our President says scripture fills in his. If the point of having Cash record songs by Depeche Mode and Nine Inch Nails was to make it hip to like him again, Rubin needn't have bothered. For us, it's always been hip to like Johnny Cash. You could even say it's one of the definitions.

10

UNSINKABLE: IS LORETTA LYNN COUNTRY MUSIC'S SCARLETT O'HARA?

By Martha Hume
From *The Journal of Country Music.*

To this day, the Appalachian Mountain region of eastern Kentucky is not like other places in the United States. People there believe that the dead walk, and that Bloody Bones might come and snatch the children. Old women divine the future of neighbors and the pasts of strangers. Deep underground, coal miners are said to go crazy and eat coal. High up on the mountaintops, some people talk to hawks and see God. True, everyone has satellite TV now, and wide straight highways offer an easy way out of the hollows. But if you were born and raised in East Kentucky, all you have to do is step out of the house and into the woods to know that the ghosts are walking, that the flickers of light on television are a world of illusions, and that anything—anything at all—can happen any time.

On form, Loretta and Mooney Lynn had about as much chance of succeeding in life as Mr. Ed had of winning the Kentucky Derby. Thanks to a hit movie, two best-selling books, and a body of songs that chronicle the whole story, there are few Americans who don't know that both were born dirt poor, that Loretta was married by age thirteen, a mother of four five years later, and miraculously, a national singing star by the time her oldest child was ready for high school. At the time the Lynns were married in 1949, however, not even Nostradamus would have dared predict that a little more than a half-century later, the sixty-nine-year-old country music queen would be standing on a podium with a twenty-nine-year-old garage rocker from Detroit accepting a Grammy for Best Country Album of the Year.

For when you shake all the stardust off this tale, what you must begin with is an uneducated child from one of the most isolated cultures in the United States who was given in marriage to a man some nine years her senior, a man who was a violent and sometimes brutal alcoholic, who was similarly uneducated and without any job skills to speak of. Add to that a migration to the state of Washington, where the child had no friends or relations; the arrival of four babies; regular—and reportedly mutual—domestic violence; and an income so unstable that there were times when the family had nothing to eat but dandelion greens, and you have a situation that might well have led to murder. But what actually happened was so improbable, so unimaginable, that the lives of Loretta and Mooney Lynn became one of the great legends of the twentieth century.

It's a story that bears re-examination, because the version that was presented in *Coal Miner's Daughter*, the 1980 film about Lynn's life, became so powerful that Loretta herself felt compelled to explain some of it away in a memoir, *Still Woman Enough*, published after her husband's death in 1996. That book, in which she details her late husband's cruelty even as she declares her undying love for him, goes a long way toward restoring Oliver Vanetta "Mooney" Lynn, whom she calls "Doolittle," to his proper and crucial place in her life. But while it may fill in pieces the film left blank or distorted, the book, and very little else that has been written and recorded by and about Loretta Lynn, does not go far in illuminating her art, a body of work that defines crucial aspects of the twentieth-century female experience.

To truly understand that work's importance, Loretta Lynn's songs and her story in all its versions must be examined as a single entity. What emerges is a unified work eerily similar in plot and significance to Margaret Mitchell's *Gone with the Wind*. Both Mitchell and Lynn set their narratives in distinct American sub-cultures—the Civil-War era South and the mid-twentieth century Appalachian diaspora, respectively— that are in the midst of dissolution. Both present women who live up to and are transformed by the challenges of this societal turmoil, which they survive and conquer by dint of courage, resourcefulness, and intelligence. Both stories subject their heroines—each of whom starts out in more or less complete subjugation to male culture—to stormy romance with difficult men, tragic loss, and the consequent adoption of roles of power. These roles, though thrust upon them by circumstance, ultimately lead both Scarlett and Loretta to a completely new place in life that is liberating, yet bittersweet, because the exercise of their newfound power requires sacrifice: Scarlett O'Hara loses her family and the chance of ever having another, and her single-actor status makes her a kind of pariah among women in the post-Civil War South. Similarly, Loretta Lynn loses her chance to be a wife and mother for most of her children's lives, and no matter how much she sings about it, her success excludes her from true membership in the close-knit society of East Kentucky, while her celebrity isolates her from the world at large.

These two creations—one fictional, one real, one descending from the Southern upper economic class, the other ascending from the lowest ranks of poor white America—contain many of the most important elements and contradictions of being female in an evolving America. Scarlett and Loretta are strong women who long for power and independence and yet have so much difficulty coming to terms with it that they are almost deranged when they get it, because the roles they must assume are so different from the roles they were brought up to play. Deracinated, both must re-invent their identities and redefine their femaleness in a changed and alien world.

The major difference is that Loretta Lynn's story is created and narrated by its protagonist. In addition to the description of events presented in the books and the film, the listener is privy to the heroine's inmost thoughts via the songs she writes and records. Thus, we see and more importantly, *feel* her struggle as it is happening. Another important and somewhat puzzling difference is that while Scarlett acts mostly alone, Loretta's achievements have been facilitated by men— her husband Mooney, her original producer Owen Bradley, her most important singing partner Conway Twitty, and now, Jack White. Does this enhance the story's narrative arc or muddy the waters? That's the problem with real life: The edges are blurred and the heroine's thoughts and actions are more complicated than fiction allows. In Loretta Lynn's case, they are extremely complicated: Just as Vivien Leigh's portrayal of Scarlett O'Hara made that character almost real, the persona of Loretta Lynn slips into fantasy all too easily, taking everything and everyone in her path along with it.

I first met her in 1975, when, as a reporter for New York-based

Martha Hume

Country Music magazine, I was sent to interview her en route from Nashville to Houston, Texas, for a date at Gilley's Club. It was my first major interview with an entertainer. I was twenty-nine years old, a whole lot more inexperienced than I thought, and a whole lot more nervous than I had expected to be as I boarded Loretta's bus in a parking lot on Nashville's Music Row late on a fall evening. The star wasn't there yet, but the band had arrived, and Jim Webb, her tall and menacing-looking bus driver who sported a hairdo that would have made Elvis green with envy, stowed me on a banquette near the front along with a pile of Loretta's stuff while the band got settled. Like Loretta, I am a native of the East Kentucky coalfields, but as far as the men on the bus knew at the time, I was a New Yorker. Therefore, I was regarded with palpable suspicion as I was introduced to each one.

"We had a woman on here one time from *Cosmopolitan*," said Webb, accusingly. "You know her?"

"Ah no, I don't think I do."

"We're gonna whip her tail if we ever see her again," said Webb.

"I'm definitely sure I don't know her—I haven't lived in New York very long. I'm really from East Kentucky, just like Loretta."

"You don't look like you're from East Kentucky," said Webb. "What part?"

"McCreary County. We're the poorest county in Kentucky," I answered proudly.

"Never heard of it," said Webb, while, I was sure, dismissing me as a fraud.

"Here comes Mom," said another of the men.

A Volkswagen bug pulled up to the side of the bus and Loretta Lynn, wearing jeans and an oversized T-shirt with a large zero on the front, hopped out of the car. I was introduced as a writer from New York, and Loretta appraised me from head to toe.

"You ain't from *Cosmopolitan* are you?" she asked.

"No, no, "I answered, "I'm from *Country Music* magazine. I've just lived in New York a little while and . . ."

"Well, come on back then," said Loretta, leading the way down the center of the bus and into her room in the rear. She stowed cosmetics in a tiny vanity as the engines revved and the bus began to move. The room, about the size of a pop-top camper, had purple couches running down each wall with an aisle in the middle that led to a console where a stereo tape deck was installed. Still feeling a bit like baggage, I sat on the couch and waited to be disposed of.

"That woman from *Cosmopolitan* said my breasts looked like grapefruits!" said Loretta, abruptly turning to face me. "I don't think they look a bit like grapefruits. Do you?"

"Of course not!" I replied searching my mind frantically for the correct answer. *(Does she think a grapefruit is too big or too little?)* "Maybe oranges." *(Darn! Too small.)* "Ah, Temple oranges, you know, those big ones."

"That's what I think," she replied, and I sighed with relief. "I'm not near big as a grapefruit! Well, ain't you gonna take your clothes off?"

"Beg pardon?"

"Take your clothes off. I'm gonna make the bed."

"Oh. Sure," I said, looking around for a place to undress. There wasn't one. Loretta was staring at me pointedly, and I got the feeling I was being challenged. So I grabbed my nightgown out of the bag, stripped down to my underwear, and threw the gown over my head as fast as I could.

"When these beds is down, there ain't no place to change," she explained, sliding the purple couches forward to meet across the aisle, forming a bed that spanned the room from wall to wall. "Help me put these sheets on and then we can talk."

Not having ever been on a country music touring bus before, I hadn't given any thought to where I would sleep. Now it looked as if I would be sleeping with the star. I wasn't sure what the etiquette should be—not that there was much etiquette left to consider after I'd disrobed in front of her twenty minutes after meeting her.

"I can go out and sit in front if you're tired Loretta. We can talk in the morning, if you want to."

"Naw, honey, just hop on in bed with me. We'll talk all night!"

And so, we put the sheets on the bed, crawling back and forth across the mattress to tuck in the edges. Then we sat cross-legged, making desultory conversation, Loretta still in her jeans and T-shirt, and I in my nightie, feeling very much like I was being kidnapped. Just as I began to relax, the bus pulled to a stop.

"That's Ernest Ray," said Loretta hopping up and heading for the front. I looked out the windows and saw another Volkswagen parked in a pool of light at the far edge of a nearly empty truck stop parking lot. It was about one in the morning by now, and though I didn't think we could have gone far, we seemed to be well off into nowhere.

"Come see the twins!" called Loretta from somewhere in the darkness. I left the room at the back and made my way down the aisle to the front past Webb and the band, feeling more than a little embarrassed to be in bare feet and a nightgown when we'd just met, but it was already obvious from our short acquaintance that you came when Loretta called. I stepped onto the tarmac and walked over to the little car, where she was holding the door open for me to see her twin girls, then about six or seven years old, wrapped in blankets on the back seat.

"That's Patsy and Paiggy," Loretta said, proudly, pronouncing Peggy's name with the long *A* peculiar to East Kentucky and waving her hand toward the children.

Suddenly, the picture that had been forming in my mind of a take-charge woman who dominated the tiny world on her bus like a force of nature shifted into something else. The sight of the little girls, half asleep, blinking in the dome light of the tiny car, not reacting at all to the presence of their mother, was enormously sad. It was somehow evident that Loretta knew the twins as fleetingly as they knew her, that her attempt to claim motherhood was a futile gesture, and that she knew it and knew that I knew it. For just a second, I got the impression of another woman inside her crying, "Look at me. I'm here."

"Gloria, that's my housekeeper, didn't have no one to watch the girls while she carried Ernest Ray over here," explained Loretta as we climbed back on the bus. "Ernest Ray's my baby boy. Ain't he handsome?"

Ernest Ray Lynn, twenty-two at the time, was indeed a good-looking young man. Tall and well built, with his mother's deep blue eyes, he had a rather courtly air about him, at least when he was with his mother, who clearly idolized him and let him know it. Loretta was bringing him along to sing a couple of numbers with her at Gilley's Club, and wanted to brag on him a little more, but right at the moment, Ernest Ray didn't have much to say for himself and was eager to be excused from scrutiny. He faded away to the front of the bus as Loretta and I went back to her room and relief driver Chuck Flynn steered us onto the highway while Webb bunked down for a nap.

It was nearing two AM. I had arrived in Nashville from New York that same day—by now, the previous day—and I was beginning to be very sleepy. Loretta, however, seemed as if she'd just awakened. To my dismay, it appeared that the next item on the agenda was our interview.

Unsinkable: Is Loretta Lynn Country Music's Scarlett O'Hara?

She dimmed the lights in her room, crawled onto the bed, looked at me, and said "OK, what did you want to ask me? You can ask me anything, I don't care!"

I reluctantly pulled my notes and my tape recorder from my bag, put them on the pillow between us, and we began to talk as the bus rolled south into the night. Much of that conversation is reported in the story that was published in the January 1976 issue of *Country Music*, but some of it is not, because when I reviewed the tapes, I decided that parts of what Loretta and I talked about that night were far too personal. At the time, both Loretta and I had what psychologists would call "boundary issues," by which I understand them to mean that we each had a shaky sense of self, easily invaded by another. Whatever the explanation, once Loretta and I discovered what we had in common, which was a lot, we began to read one another like books, each of us bringing her own experience to bear on the other, each understanding the other deeply, if imperfectly.

When we had exhausted my interview questions, our conversation drifted all over creation. We talked about coal mining, and company towns in East Kentucky, what possum tastes like, how to fry a squirrel, and the bloody wars in Harlan when the miners went on strike in 1929. Loretta read my palm, imparting shockingly accurate information about my past, including the fact that I had two children, which I vehemently denied even as she insisted it was true. I finally confessed that I had given up two children for adoption when I was a teenager, something that only my husband and my parents knew at that time. We talked about what it was like to have a baby when you were too young to know where babies came from, how terrifying it was to be in labor all alone and faraway from home, how triumphant the feeling when the baby actually came, and in my case, how the moment when they took the child away was like being stabbed to death. It was hard for Loretta to understand how I could have let my children go to be reared by strangers, and she decided that she'd done the right thing by marrying Mooney when she did, before something like that happened to her. It could have, we agreed, but she would not have known about letting her children be adopted, and she and the child would have had to live forever as fallen people in Butcher Holler.

As the bus and the night and the tape recorder rolled on, our conversation became more serious, veering into stranger and stranger places. Loretta buzzed from subject to subject like a hummingbird,

Martha Hume

and I followed behind like a punch-drunk boxer trying to keep up with the unanticipated challenges of Loretta Lynn in her native habitat.

"Did you ever smoke any of that marijuana?" she asked, apropos of nothing.

"Sure, I tried it," I answered.

"Did it make you tangle?"

"What?"

"You know, tangle? Down there?"

"Oh, *tingle*! Ah, well, ah, sometimes, I guess."

"You got any with you?"

"No way," I answered. "We'd get arrested and it'd be in all the papers!"

"Well, I'm gonna have to get me some of that someday!" she laughed. "Maybe it'll put a little spark in my love life!"

"Do you think you ever lived before?" she asked, caroming off to another subject before the previous one had faded.

"Um, no, I don't think so. Did you ever live before?"

"When I played out in Vegas, there was this man who came up to your room and hypnotized you. I was a Indian princess, standin' on a hill a-lookin' off at my brave. He was on a spotted pony and he had a big feather headdress like a chief. He was goin' off to war and he got killed.

"I'm part Indian you know. I wrote this song about it, 'Red, White and Blue.' You know like I'm a red Indian and a white woman and I'm blue because my man has treated me bad, drinkin' and runnin' around with trash.

"Another time, I was down south somewhere. I was married to a real old man and we was poor. I hated him. He smelled like a hog and he beat me, but I couldn't get away. It was awful.

"Doo, that's my husband, he killed my puppy right in front of me."

"That's awful, Loretta! Why'd he kill your puppy?"

"Pure meanness. I loved that little ole puppy and he didn't want me to have no love. But shoot, there ain't no love in this world anyway!"

"Loretta, you know that's not true. All kinds of people love you—your kids and your fans and . . ."

"Them kids don't even know who I am! I'm tellin' you, I've looked all over the place and there ain't no love to be found! I come in over

Unsinkable: Is Loretta Lynn Country Music's Scarlett O'Hara?

at home and they don't even know I'm there! Them twins don't hardly know me. Sometimes I get on this bus and get in this room and it's the only place I got. It's the only place where I am. My daddy comes in here with me sometimes, but that's all."

"I thought your daddy died, Loretta."

"Oh, he died, but he still comes in here and he cries. We both cry come to that. He's around here right now. Can't you feel him? See, he's a-settin' right up there!"

"Uh, maybe. I'm not sure. Loretta, don't you think you ought to go to sleep for a little while?" I didn't know how to stop this conversation and the little room was feeling very close.

"Oh, honey, I can't sleep. I keep the curtains shut on these windows all the time. Ain't no use to look out. It's the same place it was yesterday and the day before."

Looking for any source of distraction, I grabbed a stack of tabloids from the vanity. "Let's look at these magazines," I said.

"You can read 'em to me," said Loretta, cheering up immediately. "Read ever story about the Kennedys that's in there."

Sure enough, there were several stories about various members of the Kennedy family, and I read them all aloud. Together, we bemoaned their tragic fate and the curse that seemed to have been laid on all of them from birth. Loretta began to feel better, and I slipped away to the front of the bus where Webb had replaced Flynn at the wheel. Driving into the sunrise, I could put the night behind me for awhile. I settled into the buddy seat and looked at the new world.

"She OK?" he asked.

"I guess she is. I think she needs to sleep. We've been talking all night. I think she must be tired or something."

I wondered if I should tell Webb that Mooney Lynn had killed Loretta's puppy or that Loretta seemed to be upset. It appeared to me that this was a woman who was in some kind of trouble. I didn't because I had already been infected by the overwhelming sense of protectiveness that Loretta seems to inspire in everyone around her. Yet our conversation had shaken me. Did she need a doctor? Were her people making her work so hard that she was losing her reason? Was she psychic? Could she read my mind?

It wasn't until years later that I understood that the woman I encountered that long night on the bus wasn't the public Loretta Lynn, but the woman who wrote her songs, and that we were really

Martha Hume

talking about the raw material for those songs. "When the Tingle Becomes a Chill" was released shortly after our trip and became a #2 country hit in 1975 and 1976. "Red, White and Blue" was released in the spring of 1976 and went to #20. This time also coincided with a period when Loretta was thinking seriously about divorce, as she reports in *Still Woman Enough*, and she was feeling used and abused. So the Loretta I encountered that night was a woman whose mind and emotions were in extreme and alarming turmoil; what I didn't understand was that she didn't need a doctor, but a pencil and a notebook.

Loretta Lynn's songs come from direct, unmediated, personal experience. Often, this experience has coincided with wider social issues, which is how she earned a reputation for being a champion of women's rights. What was actually happening when she wrote songs like "Fist City," and "Don't Come Home a' Drinkin' (With Lovin' on Your Mind)" was that she was transcribing the literal details of arguments with her husband. Others might write songs that are drawn from personal experience or based on something that happened to someone they know; many of Loretta's songs *are* what happened. Her art and her life are the same thing.

Although I interviewed Loretta several more times over the next decade, I never again met the songwriter who manifested herself that night on the bus. We finished our trip in relative peace, although I still didn't get to sleep. Loretta and I continued our conversation all the way to Houston. Her curiosity about the world seemed to have no bottom. For the rest of the trip we talked about everything—what it was like to live in New York, the best way to can green beans, what my favorite stories were. I told her the plot of *The Brothers Karamazov* and she guessed who'd murdered Fyodor Karamazov before I got to the end. We talked about her forthcoming book and about George Vecsey, "her writer," who was from the *New York Times* but was a good man anyway. We finished the tabloids, listened to some songs she'd recorded, and after a while, pulled into the outskirts of Houston, where the humongous Gilley's Club was located. It was mid-afternoon by then, but by the time we'd unloaded at the club, checked into a motel for the night, showered, and eaten dinner, it was time to go back to Gilley's for the evening's show. I'd been awake for nearly forty-eight hours.

That night I had two Lone Star beers and passed out cold in Ernest Ray's arms on Gilley's dance floor. No one could wake me up, so he put me back on the bus, carried me back to the motel, and put me in bed. I awoke early the next morning with Loretta sitting by the bed and holding my hand.

"Oh my goodness, honey, we didn't know what in the world had happened to you!" exclaimed Loretta with relief when I awoke. "I was startin' to think you might be one of them heroin addicts from New York City and had gone and overdosed yourself!"

We parted that morning in the parking lot of the motel in Houston, Loretta off to another place on her endless highway, and me back to the city to ponder what had just happened. I never did quite figure it out.

In the years that followed, Loretta Lynn became even more intensely famous. *Coal Miner's Daughter*, the book, was published the following spring and became a bestseller. The film of the same name was released in 1980; a few years later, a young Jack White, born Gillis, would see the movie and decide to become a musician. But while Loretta's persona achieved celebrity icon status, her career floundered during the 1980s. She had no more #1 hits in that decade or the next. Her husband Mooney was aging, and the couple, older and wiser, decided to spend more time together. For a time, Loretta played Branson, Missouri. It was there, in 1993, that Loretta's close friend and singing partner, Conway Twitty, died unexpectedly of an abdominal aneurysm in the same hospital where Mooney Lynn had just undergone bypass surgery. In short order, she also lost two of her brothers, and in 1996, Mooney himself. Emotionally unable to stay at their home in Hurricane Mills, Loretta came to her house near Elliston Place in Nashville and remained in seclusion for a year. It looked like life might have finally brought Loretta Lynn to her knees with the cruelest blows yet.

And then, one day she awoke and told her family to bring the bus around. Loretta had never stopped writing—how could she when writing was all that she had left? But merely writing songs didn't accomplish her purpose. For Loretta Lynn to live, she had to be *heard*. Moreover, she had to be heard by her larger family, the one she had formed over a thirty-year career, her fans. In her mind, her fans deserved to know what it was like when Mooney had died. They needed to know the depth of her grief and she needed them to help her make sense of it. She published *Still Woman Enough* in 2002, and two years later released *Still Country*, her much-anticipated CD. The key word in both releases was "still." Like Scarlett, Loretta perseveres in

Martha Hume

the face of what would kill a lesser woman.

The new music was moving and the book revealing, but sadly, the country music industry had moved on. In 2004, conventional music industry wisdom said that only young singers could attract young fans and young fans certainly wouldn't be interested in songs about death or life back in Butcher Holler. This time, there was no answer when Loretta Lynn knocked on Nashville's doors. And yet, for all the industry's short-sightedness, it must be said that Loretta was missing a key ingredient. Her best work has always required a man she can work off of. Her career could not have happened without the impetus of her husband, and her best songs would never have been written without the continuing friction of their relationship to spark her words. Randy Scruggs, who produced *Still Country*, was not that man—Randy Scruggs is a gentleman.

Loretta needed a man like Mooney who would try to steamroll her, making her mad enough to show him who was boss. Enter Jack White. White, half of the critically acclaimed alternative rock band The White Stripes, had admired Loretta Lynn since he had seen *Coal Miner's Daughter* as a child, and he had dedicated The White Stripes' 2002 CD, *White Blood Cells*, to her. Nancy Russell, Loretta's manager, showed her client the CD and Loretta invited Jack and Meg White to Hurricane Mills for a visit. Jack White, poking around Loretta's house "for something to steal," as he tells it, discovered a notebook of Loretta's songs, and the rest of the story, which culminated in a Top 25 hit on *Billboard's* Top 200 pop album chart and two Grammys, is now history—history that may well be recorded in Loretta's *next* book. Not that she is contemplating another book yet, but who would be surprised if she wrote one? She is most definitely not finished.

"I have three more albums to do with Jack," Loretta told me on the phone from her bus on the way to the Grammy awards ceremony in Los Angeles. "'Course he may not know that and it might make Nancy Russell mad, but I do." In Loretta-speak, that means she has more notebooks full of songs waiting to be recorded. It also means that, even yet, we don't know the whole story.

"Go for it, Loretta," I replied. "Forget this Nashville business. Can you think of one soul in Nashville who would have listened to these songs and cut them?"

Loretta was silent for a moment, and then both of us said, "Nobody" at the same time.

"We just said the same thing at the same time!" said Loretta. "That means we can make a wish. Don't tell nobody what your wish is or it won't come true, OK?"

Loretta and I made our wishes as her bus rolled on toward Los Angeles. Mine came true a few days later when she marched up to claim her first Grammys since 1972. I don't know what her wish was, but I'll bet it comes true too. Loretta Lynn's is a strange, strange world and anything—anything at all—can happen at any time.

24

PROUD TO BE A REDNECK WOMAN

Gretchen Wilson's climb to country stardom is a tale of grit and determination. Just ask the folks from a little redneck town in Illinois

By Peter Cooper
From *The Tennessean*

POCAHONTAS, Ill. - There is nothing to suggest a legacy here.

No ballplayers, no statesmen, no astronauts, no notables have come from Pocahontas. There was a bank robbery in the area once, and that was exciting. But even the tornados have stayed away from this town that's located about 40 minutes east of St. Louis.

Until recently, the most compelling civic event came when an animated movie based on a certain Algonquian Indian princess was released and the town changed its "welcome to" signs to honor the flick.

Mostly, this is a place for farms, for cars skidding down gravel roads, for drinking and farming and more drinking.

"It's what we are," says Mark "Big O" Obermark. "Get up at 5 a.m., milk cows, farm all day, get cleaned up, go out and have a few beers. If that ain't redneck, I don't know what is."

Understand, Obermark knows what is. He has served thousands of bottles of domestic beer to men and women who proudly call themselves "rednecks," and he is a beloved figure in the life of a

Peter Cooper

Pocahontas-reared singer-songwriter who is currently the biggest thing in country music.

She's a 30-year-old named Gretchen Wilson, her *Here for the Party* album sold 100,000 more copies than any other country debut album ever has in its first week, and her "Redneck Woman" single is at the top of the country charts.

"I couldn't be no prouder if she was my own daughter," Big O says. "There was nothing easy for her, growing up. Any time a person lives a rough life like that, people want them to succeed. You know, she was turned down by everybody in Nashville. They had bad taste in music, I guess."

With that, Obermark glanced up, past his interviewer and toward a television set mounted on the wall. The set was tuned, as it nearly always is at Hoosier Daddy's bar, to Country Music Television. There, on the screen, was none other than Gretchen Wilson, tearing around on a four-wheeler in the "Redneck Woman" video, which features cameos by Hank Williams Jr., Kid Rock and even Big O himself.

Then Big O's eyes moistened, as they often do lately. He loves Wilson, and he is simultaneously amazed by her success and surprised that it took her so long. He's been listening to her sing for at least half her life, and she began tending bar at his place when she was 15.

"Her mom was there, and she tended bar for me, too," Big O says. "If anyone gave Gretchen trouble, I grabbed 'em and threw 'em out the door. If I couldn't do it myself, I found someone who could. Anyway, everybody's proud of her here. She's singing what her heart feels."

A key to the city

"It's not the suburbs," Gretchen Wilson said, considering Pocahontas and Pierron and Carlyle and all the little towns of her childhood. "I hadn't been anywhere else, so I figured that's what everywhere looked like.

"There's not much to do, and all of us kids there got into a lot of trouble. You stay out too late, get in fights, play hooky from school. I call that the 'normal stuff' that kids do, but I guess it's not normal."

While Wilson was talking, television cameras recorded her for a forthcoming cable special. Out the hotel room window, the Las Vegas strip was visible: She was in Vegas to perform "Redneck Woman" on the Academy of Country Music Awards, despite the fact that her

Proud to be a Redneck Woman

album was released too late to be nominated for an ACM award.

For the record, Vegas looks nothing like Pocahontas.

"My uncle told me that Pocahontas was wanting to give me a key to the city," Wilson said. "I didn't even know they *had* a key to the city."

The hard tones in Wilson's Midwestern accent are not lilting or refined, and, though pretty, she's a tough-looking lady. She has an easy laugh that serves as a guard-dropper, when she wants it to, but everything in her manner suggests someone who has had to scrap for everything she has. Wilson grew up without a father, bouncing from trailer to trailer with her mother and brother. Her upbringing was hard, but not unusually so for the area.

"If you can grow up in Pocahontas and one day find a job and move to St. Louis, you're doing good," said Justin Hart, a 23-year-old Pocahontas native who attended Wilson's album-release concert May 11 at The Pageant in St. Louis.

Hart is too young to have known Wilson in her youth, but many in the shoulder-to-shoulder Pageant crowd recalled her as a prodigiously gifted singer who carted around karaoke tapes filled with instrumental versions of Patsy Cline and Loretta Lynn songs. A crowd of 350 people from Pocahontas, which is nearly half of the town's population, attended the St. Louis show.

"She was driven from Day One," said Pat Spencer, who said Wilson could silence a clattering bar with her voice even as a kid. "She knew she was going to make it, and we did, too. We all knew."

In retrospect, Wilson's success looks like a sure thing to those who heard her early on, singing karaoke or working with her then-husband in a classic band called Baywolfe. They assumed that the most talented country music singers eventually head to Nashville, where they get weeded out until only the best ones remain. Wilson, of course, would ultimately be declared a winner.

"I thought she'd make it, of course," Big O said. "But then, the first time I went down there to Nashville, I saw how good everybody is. I mean, from one bar to another, everybody's as great as the rest in Nashville, it seemed like."

Add to that the fact that the great ones don't always make it. Nashville is a place where, as Bobby Bare Jr. sings in "Visit Me in Music City"—"The world's greatest living guitar pickers/Can deliver you a pizza or sell you weed."

Peter Cooper

Off the rural route

Gretchen Wilson arrived in Nashville about six years ago only to find her stand-and-sing ethic out of place in a world where many country hopefuls talked of networking and internships and the like. Without a high school diploma or much in the way of savings, Wilson didn't have the option of, say, taking music business classes at Belmont to find out how the industry worked.

"I got here and spent a week walking up and down Music Row, trying to deliver homemade demos, and everybody was like, 'Oh, we can't take that,'" Wilson said. "I thought, 'How does anybody do anything here? How can I get a record deal if nobody listens to my stuff?'"

So she tended bar, lived frugally and tried to figure things out. Many weekends, she'd head back to St. Louis or other Midwestern towns to do shows with Baywolfe. When she found comparatively lucrative work singing demos, she stopped going back home much.

"I'm sure there were conversations back there, around the bar, like, 'Has anybody heard from Gretchen? No? Well, hell, she's been down there for years, I guess it ain't ever going to happen.' I thought about giving up. Absolutely."

When Wilson finally figured out how to get an audience with Music Row power players, one by one, they turned her down.

"I had so many unsuccessful showcases, and I was never really being given a good reason why they didn't want me," she said. "My opinion is that a lot of people were just scared of it."

Fear is a possibility: Wilson does not fit the mold of modern country's female stars, women who are done up to look like prom-night queens rather than rural route handfuls. Surely, Wilson was not being turned down on the basis of her voice, which is a smoky, pliant, expressive instrument that easily ranks with anyone on the country charts.

For years, though, Wilson wasn't writing her own songs, and thus she was left to voice the words and emotions of others. She received encouragement from John Rich, Big Kenny and others in Nashville's now-famous Muzik Mafia collective, and she began co-writing songs that were pictures of her own world.

One of those songs was written just about the time she was preparing to give up her dream of becoming an artist. She wrote it with John Rich, and it was called "Redneck Woman." She played it for John Grady, president of Sony Nashville, who quickly gave Gretchen Wilson what she'd be wanting all along: one shot at the big prize.

Proud to be a Redneck Woman

"Some people look down on me, but I don't give a rip/ I'll stand barefoot in my own front yard with a baby on my hip," she and Rich wrote in "Redneck Woman." Now the anthem of country music's summer of 2004, the song resonates like a rebel yell in a prep school study hall.

"We haven't had a solo female at No. 1 on the country chart in over two years," said Wade Jessen, the director of country charts at *Billboard* magazine.

"This went No. 1 in 12 weeks, which is the fastest climb for a new artist debut single since "Wild One" by Faith Hill a decade ago. For listeners, it's the modern equivalent of Merle Haggard's "Okie From Muskogee." It's, 'Hey, they're singing about me.' "

People from Pocahontas know she really *is* singing about them, and many of them feel delighted and validated and important because of it. At the St. Louis show, people who grew up around Wilson reach from the front row, hoping for a hand-clasp or a wave — for acknowledgment.

"I can't believe I just stood in line for two hours just to get an autograph, when all I used to have to do to talk with Gretchen was walk across the street," said Carrie Spencer, smiling at her husband, Pat, after the show.

There's another song on *Here for the Party* called "Pocahontas Proud," in which Wilson sings "I'm the biggest thing that ever came from my hometown/ And I'll be damned if I'm gonna let 'em down."

To those who haven't been to Pocahontas, that might seem a heady declaration. But - for the moment, at least - Gretchen Wilson is the biggest thing coming out of Nashville, a fact that makes her easily the biggest thing from Pocahontas, a place where there is no legacy.

Check that: a place where there *was* no legacy.

30

JAMES HENRY "JIMMY" MARTIN
(August 10, 1927–May 14, 2005)

By Eddie Stubbs
From *Bluegrass Unlimited*

"Hit Parade Of Love," "Ocean Of Diamonds," "Sophronie," "My Walking Shoes," "Tennessee," "Milwaukee Here I Come," and "Freeborn Man" are but a few of the standards in bluegrass introduced and popularized by one of its greatest singers and personalities, that of Jimmy Martin.

In a professional career that lasted 55 years, Jimmy Martin left a lasting legacy. The music of Jimmy Martin was not easy to play. Nor was it easy to understand Jimmy Martin, the man. A phenomenal rhythm guitarist who had a great ear for a song, a strict band leader, a flashy showman, consummate entertainer, and a stylist who possessed one of the most commercially appealing voices the genre has ever known—these were just some of his noteworthy characteristics. Along the way, he recorded some of the most commercial and radio-friendly bluegrass ever made. He was also one of the most entertaining and complex personalities in the genre's history. In fact, Jimmy Martin was involved in bluegrass almost as long as bluegrass music as we know it has existed.

Born at home near the small community of Sneedville, Tenn., on Wednesday August 10, 1927, James Henry Martin came into the world not long before the Great Depression struck. He came from humble surroundings and the family farmed and raised what they ate. His father died when he was four years old, and Jimmy only received a third grade education.

Martin began playing guitar and singing at a young age and listened every Saturday night to WSM's Grand Ole Opry. His favorite artists were Roy Acuff and Bill Monroe, the latter of whom Jimmy idolized.

Eddie Stubbs

Jimmy realized a dream in late 1949 when he came to work for Monroe as his lead singer and rhythm guitarist. In addition to helping Monroe compose a number of significant autobiographical songs, Martin's strong rhythm guitar and fierce lead voice created a whole new sound and attitude in Monroe's music. That unique and intense style, augmented at various times by fiddlers Vassar Clements, Red Taylor, L.E. White, Charlie Cline, and banjoists Rudy Lyle and Sonny Osborne, would come to be characterized as the "high lonesome sound." Unquestionably, the Decca recordings of Bill Monroe with Jimmy Martin from 1950-1954 rank as some of the most defining work of Monroe's entire career.

Jimmy also appeared as part of Monroe's opening act, the Shenandoah Valley Trio, and sang on their ultra-rare four sides for Columbia Records in 1950. That same year, he played rhythm guitar on Melissa Monroe's first Columbia session.

In between stints with Monroe, Jimmy worked briefly with the Lonesome Pine Fiddlers and later in a short partnership with Bobby Osborne. This duo cut four titles for King Records in 1951, thus being the label's first venture into bluegrass.

After a final stint with Monroe, Jimmy broke out on his own in 1954. He eventually teamed up with the Osborne Brothers in the fall of that year and spent the next 12 months working with them at WJR in Detroit, Mich., appearing on the station's popular show, the Big Barn Frolic. As a trio, they recorded six classic sides for RCA Victor in November of 1954 that included "20/20 Vision," and "Save It! Save It!" In 1956, Jimmy secured a recording contract with Decca Records where he would make a major name for himself.

Martin journeyed to KWKH in Shreveport, La., in very early 1958 to become a member of the Louisiana Hayride. He was warned that he would bomb there, because bluegrass wasn't well known in the station's coverage area, and that he would starve to death. Instead, the two years he spent on the Hayride turned out to be one of the most rewarding periods of his entire career. Some of his recordings were getting into the country music charts, and he was enjoying significant spins on juke boxes, too. Surviving air checks from this period of the Hayride indicate women actually screaming when Martin was introduced at Shreveport's Municipal Auditorium over 50,000 watt KWKH, which at night could be heard in twenty states.

One morning, over breakfast at the 2000 IBMA World Of

James Henry "Jimmy" Martin (August 10, 1927–May 14, 2005)

Bluegrass convention in Louisville, Ky., an almost emotional Jimmy told Marty Stuart and this writer about his days in Shreveport, "Back then, I really had it—I knew I had it, and I know I'll never have it again."

With his two most celebrated band members, mandolin player/tenor vocalist Paul Williams and banjoist/baritone singer J.D. Crowe, Jimmy Martin had found an anointed combination. Together, the three men created a consistent body of first-rate recordings— many destined to become standards.

Jimmy's next base of operations was in Wheeling, W.Va., on WWVA, where he became a member of the World's Original Jamboree in 1960. Like KWKH, WWVA was a 50,000 watt power-house station. WWVA's blanketing night-time coverage sent Jimmy's music into the entire northeastern United States, the eastern half of Canada, and the Maritime Provinces. Like he had in Shreveport, Martin became one of Wheeling's biggest stars. For the first time, he was able to employ a full band with a female vocalist, a drummer, a bass player, and, for a lengthy period, banjo ace Bill Emerson. It was an in-demand act and they were generally working six nights a week. In one summer, they worked an amazing 91 fairs and fire department carnivals. Martin's recorded "Good 'N' Country" music, as it was known, enjoyed consistent airplay, especially over WWVA, and did much to add to his popularity. Interestingly, as Decca began issuing long-playing albums on Martin, they never once used the word blue-grass on the album covers. Jimmy affectionately became known as "Mr. Good 'N' Country Music."

If there was ever a zenith period to Jimmy Martin's career, it would be the Shreveport and Wheeling era which encompassed a five year span. In the opinion of several band members, Martin should have never left Wheeling—he was a big act in a smaller arena and could do no wrong. However, Jimmy felt like he'd paid his dues and he had Nashville and the Grand Ole Opry on his mind. Jimmy moved to Hermitage, Tenn., just to the east of Nashville, in mid-December 1962, where he would remain the rest of his life.

The country music industry was quickly changing in the 1960s, especially in Nashville. Jimmy continued to make some high quality airplay-friendly records for Decca, but like most bluegrass artists, his radio airplay became less and less as the country and bluegrass music industries became more separated. Like other bluegrass acts, the

Eddie Stubbs

multi-day festivals would eventually become Jimmy's major source of income.

Jimmy Martin's brand of music was different than anyone else's. It had a unique bounce and sparkle that sounded good coming over the radio or out of a hi-fi, and it made people feel good. Whether it was fast or slow, happy or sad, something about it spoke to the listener. Martin, like his friend Little Jimmy Dickens, had a penchant for light-hearted and novelty tunes. To many, this approach to material may seem dated, but on stage Jimmy Martin valued an audience's smiles, laughs, and applause that songs like this generated. It was the complete approach to entertainment when going from a song like "I Can't Quit Cigarettes" to the serious inspirational offering of "Shut-In's Prayer." Jimmy would have an audience laughing with one song and crying on the next, then he'd turn around and do a feisty up-tempo tune or instrumental, and change the audience's mood all over again. Adding to all of this were flashy stage costumes and a high energy presentation. There was no mistake, Jimmy Martin knew how to entertain people. When you saw Jimmy Martin and the Sunny Mountain Boys, it wasn't a concert—it was a show!

While many wonderful players came through the ranks of Martin's Sunny Mountain Boys, they would always be expected to "play the show like the records" and deliver what Williams, Crowe, and later Emerson had contributed. Some could do it, while others could not. This became a constant point of contention with both Martin and musicians over the ensuing decades.

A big shot in Martin's career came in 1971, when he was invited to be a part of the Nitty Gritty Dirt Band's *Will The Circle Be Unbroken* album project. The award-winning various artists anthology was extremely well received and introduced a whole new generation to bluegrass and grass roots country music. Jimmy would also participate in volumes two and three of this historic set.

After losing his Decca/MCA contract in 1974, Martin resumed recording a few years later for Gusto where he made a number of albums, including one with Ralph Stanley. It was Moe Lytle, the president of Gusto Records, that bestowed the "King Of Bluegrass" title on Martin, which largely replaced the "Mr. Good 'N' Country Music" moniker.

By the early 1980s, Martin got to the point where he took the late fall and winter months off (typically only working twenty to twenty-

James Henry "Jimmy" Martin (August 10, 1927–May 14, 2005)

five dates annually) in order to pursue his passion for raccoon and rabbit hunting. Like he did with bluegrass music, Jimmy was obsessed with hunting and won many awards to prove it.

Sadly, Jimmy Martin had internal demons that he dealt with. Often, these demons would surface and consequently they had an effect on his personality, his shows, business associates, promoters, his musicians, and his fans. Jimmy was not an easy person to understand. In many ways, he was considered to be his own worst enemy—but sadly, he never realized it. For the most part, you either liked Jimmy or you didn't. There wasn't much middle ground. He was extremely high-strung and would say or do almost anything without reservation. (People would often state, "I love Jimmy's music, but I don't love him.")

No one can deny that Jimmy Martin made an indelible mark on bluegrass music. His contributions were fully acknowledged in 1995 when the International Bluegrass Music Association inducted him into its prestigious Hall Of Honor.

Jimmy's was a rags to riches story. Though he was financially independent, he lived simply. More importantly, he never forgot where he came from. This is clearly evident in the 2003 video documentary, *King Of Bluegrass: The Life And Times Of Jimmy Martin.* For those unacquainted with Jimmy, better than any printed commentary, this documentary portrays the real Jimmy Martin in all facets of his life and personality, from one extreme to the other.

The final concert appearance of Jimmy Martin and the Sunny Mountain Boys took place on October 30, 2004, in Asheville, N.C. There followed a solo appearance by Jimmy at a benefit for Josh Graves on December 11, 2004, at the Gibson Bluegrass Showcase in Nashville. His very last appearance on a stage came on December 18th, 2004. It was a brief and impromptu one where he and Marty Stuart, Ronnie Reno, and Ronnie Bowman performed a few songs together at a private Christmas party at Sputniks, a bar in Hendersonville, Tenn., where they were backed by an electric country band.

Recent years have witnessed a decline in Martin's physical health with numerous hospitalizations. He had quintuple heart bypass surgery in 1997. In mid-2004, he was diagnosed with the largely incurable cancer of the bladder. The condition worsened and in February 2005, his urologist told Jimmy that he didn't have long to live. In his

Eddie Stubbs

final weeks, friends and family rallied around his bedside virtually non-stop, both in the hospital and later at his home. Some who hadn't spoken to Jimmy in many years came to make their peace and to say goodbye. At the end of his life he weighed only about one hundred pounds. For many months, his heart was only functioning at approximately twenty-five percent of what it should as the cancer worsened.

Martin knew that his life was coming to an end. He told many, including several deeply spiritual people, that he was a Christian and that he was ready to leave this world when God called him. Jimmy's wish was to live at least until June so he could perform one last time at the Bean Blossom festival in Indiana, where he'd been the Ambassador for a number of years. Although he put up a tremendous fight, sadly, it was not meant to be.

At the age of 77, Jimmy took his last breath at approximately 8:45 a.m. central time on Saturday May 14, 2005. His death occurred at Alive Hospice in Nashville, just 12 blocks away from the Ryman Auditorium where he first auditioned for Bill Monroe almost 56 years before.

Funeral services were held Wednesday May 18, at the Cornerstone Church in Madison, Tenn., with many former Sunny Mountain Boys providing musical tributes outlined in an accompanying story. Burial followed at the Spring Hill Cemetery also in Madison. Survivors include three sons Timmy, Ray, and Buddy Lee, a daughter Lisa, ten grandchildren, two great-grandchildren, one brother, and five sisters.

Stories about Jimmy Martin the man, his music, and those who worked for him, will abound for years to come. Now that he's gone, all we have left are our memories, but more permanently, his recordings. That body of music will continue to inform, entertain, and educate for generations to come—as well it should. Simply stated, that collection of work is one of the greatest bluegrass music ever made, period.

In spite of his many complexities, short-comings, and his sometimes strange way of doing things, we should be thankful for the life of Jimmy Martin. In the opinion of many, he was a musical genius.

It would be hard to imagine what bluegrass music would've been like had it not been for Jimmy Martin's vital role in its history. Thankfully, we'll never have to wonder.

FROM DOWN-HOME TO BIG-TIME

What used to be Fan Fair has evolved into something bigger, richer and more diverse

By Michael McCall
From *The Nashville Scene*

Nearly everyone in the country music industry still identifies the event as "Fan Fair." But as the city's largest annual musical gathering begins its fifth year as the CMA Music Festival, the hard-to-shake name is about the only connection left between the old, down-home affair and the new, glitzy extravaganza.

Fan Fair, which topped out at 24,000 attendees, was as rural as all get-out, a strange little event tucked away at the Tennessee State Fairgrounds along a run-down, out-of-the-way strip of Nolensville Road where most of the city could easily ignore it. The event epitomized country music back when Loretta Lynn sang about her family and her struggles, then signed autographs and hugged necks until every fan walked away with a piece of her. The crowd left yearning to spend time swapping yarns with her on her bus.

If Fan Fair was as polite as Charley Pride meeting an Alabama radio programmer in 1968, the CMA Fest, which last year drew an estimated 132,000 people, is as citified as can be—a massive, traffic-snarling monster that eats downtown for five days. It's as living-out-loud as a Royal Crown-stoked Big & Rich rolling with Kid Rock in a Nashville strip club, and it represents country music's evolution into Kenny Chesney singing about his dreams and his leisure pursuits after shaking hands with a room full of carefully selected fans in a backstage meet-and-greet. The crowd leaves yearning to share a shot of tequila

37

Michael McCall

with him on his private plane.

The CMA Music Festival is something else, too: it's hugely successful, and it's exactly what Fan Fair needed to become. The economic benefits to the city are enormous, with an estimated $17 million added to the city's tourist trade in 2004. It's the biggest week of the year for Lower Broad nightclubs and many other downtown venues and retail stores, and the massive crowds no doubt lead to return business.

Plus, last year's primetime network TV special was the best tourist advertisement the city has ever had—more than any Monday Night Football telecast or awards program. The broadcast integrated downtown nightlife and city landmarks into the special with an emphasis on showing visitors having a blast. It wasn't Dennis Miller making a yee-haw comment while the screen showed a neon sign in the shape of a cowboy boot. It was groups of young adults dancing and singing and living it up; it was busloads of fans walking through the Country Music Hall of Fame or standing in Riverfront Park with the Cumberland River reflecting the skyline glittering in the background.

Moving the music downtown also saved a unique American event. Whether it was old-fashioned Fan Fair or the spiffed-up CMA festival, no genre of music showcases its artists and celebrates its fans in such an open-armed, mutual embrace. It's just that the relationship between the fans and the artists has changed over the years, and the festival reflects the new dynamic.

At the turn of the century, Fan Fair was in trouble. By 1999, tickets to the June event, which for years had sold out within weeks of becoming available in February, were still on sale when the gates opened. Many longtime attendees grumbled that the biggest stars rarely performed anymore, and even fewer major names showed up at the autograph booths. For the most part, Fan Fair had become a promotional event for record labels to try out up-and-coming acts on the hardcore faithful.

The festival began in 1972 as an outgrowth of the annual Country DJ Convention (which continues today as the Country Radio Seminar). Feeling that the convention focused on business without providing anything for the fans, Loretta Lynn started staging an annual concert and invited the general public instead of performing only for radio insiders. As her show grew in popularity, Lynn added new artists each year, and those she invited all signed autographs and host-

From Down-home to Big-time

ed fan club parties of their own.

Spearheaded by WSM president and CMA board member Irving Waugh, the industry took a cue from Lynn and decided to sponsor an annual music convention for the fans. The event premiered in April 1972, attracting 5,000 people to the Municipal Auditorium, and crowds escalated each year. By 1982, the CMA and the Grand Ole Opry, the event's co-sponsors, moved it to the state fairgrounds.

As the '80s country youth movement turned into its '90s boom, Fan Fair reaped the rewards. For several years, it sold out far in advance, making those who attended each year feel as if they were invited to a special, intimate event. Most of the major stars spent at least a few hours signing autographs in the large, metal exhibit halls. Live music, all of it featuring major-label performers, started at 10 a.m. and continued nonstop until 11 at night. Many fans brought RVs and made friends who they saw again each year.

"There was nothing else like the old Fan Fair, and there never will be anything else like it again," says Hazel Smith, the matriarch of country music journalism, who has been attending Fan Fair for three decades. "There were thousands of people who came every year, and they knew each other by their first names. They camped out together. And, Lord, they loved the music, they loved the artists and they loved each other. But those days are over. Our music has outgrown it. There's so many more fans now, and the event had to change to accommodate them."

Smith can tick off landmark events, like rock producer Mutt Lange attending Fan Fair with rocker Bryan Adams just to meet Shania Twain, with whom Lange had become acquainted by telephone but had yet to greet in person. Within months, the couple were married, and Lange helped Twain become country music's best-selling female act of all time. Beyond that, there was the 1995 onstage reunion of George Jones and Tammy Wynette, performing together for the first time in 15 years, and Garth Brooks signing autographs for 23 hours straight without taking as much as a bathroom break.

Then there were the fans, who in those days were a distinctly colorful lot. Young Music Row hotshots might bemoan their undying persistence or joke about the polyester invasion, but the fans didn't care. They came to throw themselves at the feet of the gods and immerse themselves in the music; they long ago stopped worrying about anyone who looked down their noses at them or their obses-

Michael McCall

sions. Besides, they were amongst friends and fellow believers.

Hazel Smith recalls two stories that capture the uniqueness of the old Fan Fair. One year a fan was in such a rush to get in line at the gate so that she could be among the first to reach the autograph tables, she left her car unlocked, keys in the ignition and engine running. The woman collected scores of autographs, saw dozens of stars perform and lasted until late afternoon before going to her car for a break. It was then she realized what she had done in her haste. Her car sat there untouched outside the gate, still running, but nearly out of gas.

"You think that would've happened at any kind of rock concert?" Smith laughs. "The Fan Fair crowd didn't bother the car at all."

Smith also remembers escorting a first-time visitor through the crowd one sunny afternoon. Coming down the hill from the exhibit halls to the stage, which was set up in front of the grandstands of the Nashville Motor Speedway, Smith saw her guest gawk at someone coming up the other way.

"Oh, those are our Siamese twins," Smith explained while barely batting an eye at the pair, the shorter of whom was pushed along in a grocery cart by the taller one. "They're from Pennsylvania. The funny thing is, only one of them likes country music."

As the man stared, Smith said, "Honey, you're likely to see most anything at Fan Fair!"

Oddly enough, it was Brooks' Herculean autograph-signing session, and the boom that he and Twain detonated, that hastened Fan Fair's demise. Country music no longer earned its bread and butter at county fairs with tinny sound systems set up on flatbed trucks. The era of arena shows, videos and million-dollar stage productions had come to country music.

In the past, top stars like Barbara Mandrell, Ricky Skaggs and Kathy Mattea could spend all day greeting fans, and it would be exhausting but fulfilling. But in the post-Garth era, it would have taken them 24 hours to accommodate all of the fans who had lined up to see them.

"It just got where it wasn't feasible anymore," says Marty Stuart, who experienced the '90s boom firsthand. "I loved Fan Fair as much as anybody ever has, but it got to where the signing sessions went from a few hours to half a day, and you'd still have people yelling for autographs and photos when you had to leave. It outgrew what had made it special."

From Down-home to Big-time

These days, Stuart hosts an annual late night, multi-artist show at the Ryman Auditorium so he can play and talk to fans each year. "There's still some fans who are upset because they miss the old arrangement," he says. "But I have a meet-and-greet session with my fan club, and I have the show, and I ask for their understanding. I do the best I can to entertain them and give them a memorable experience, but it got to where things had become too big to meet every one of them one-on-one. It got that way for all the artists."

In its final years, the old event had lost its luster. Fan Fair no longer sold out. The CMA called a special strategy session to discuss what to do. The board of directors figured it had two options: move and expand it, or kill it. They decided to explore the first option before making a final decision.

The first idea that gained traction was to move Fan Fair to the then-new Nashville Superspeedway in Lebanon. "The attraction was that it would be a good place for RVs and for camping," says Ed Benson, executive director of the CMA. "A lot of country music festivals are designed for campers, so that seemed to be a possibility."

But Mayor Bill Purcell caught wind of the possible move and vigorously opposed taking the festival out of Davidson County. Tony Conway, president of Buddy Lee Attractions, the Nashville talent agency, headed the festival committee.

"We had meetings with the mayor, the Chamber of Commerce, the Nashville Convention and Visitors Bureau, and they were insistent on us considering moving the event downtown," Conway says. "The various departments of the city were unbelievable in their support, and they came to the table with a really attractive plan that would make all of downtown part of the festival's campus."

When the CMA announced the change of name and venue after Fan Fair 2000, there was an immediate uproar. Critics noted that the word "fan" had been dropped out of the name, having been replaced by the CMA logo. Accusations centered on how the festival was now about business and artist promotion, not about connecting the artists and the fans.

"Anytime you make a big change, you're going to face a public relations issue," Conway says. "But, to be honest, I think after last year, that kind of stuff is gone. People had said it wasn't going to be the same. Well, it's not the same. It's better. And I think most everyone has come along to agree with that by now."

Michael McCall

Downtown merchants and nightclubs certainly do. The honky-tonks overflow from Wednesday through Sunday night, with sidewalks packed like Times Square on New Year's Eve. The clubs stay full all day long, with most of them starting music after breakfast and staying open until the 3 a.m. closing time. Lower Broad acts like Jen Jones & The Camaros and John England & The Western Swingers play to wildly receptive audiences packed with both new fans and downtown regulars.

The CMA's current plan targets Middle Tennessee residents as well as tourists. With a network TV special providing national advertising, the CMA wants Nashvillians to know all the ways the event can be experienced. Of the five downtown stages, three are free and don't require event tickets, including stages at the Hall of Fame Park between the Hilton Hotel and the Country Music Hall of Fame, the Fun Zone at the foot of Broadway and the Sports Zone in the Coliseum parking lot.

Tickets for Riverfront Park, with live music coming from a floating stage from 10 a.m. to 5 p.m., cost $14 a day. Coliseum shows, with eight or more country stars performing nightly, cost $30 a night. At this point, field seating is sold out for all nightly shows, as is the Gold Circle seating in the stands. Every Coliseum show could sell out by show time this year.

Part of the appeal, says Conway, is that artists now perform a long set instead of just doing a few songs apiece, as they did at the old Fan Fair. The stage, sound and video is state-of-the-art, which is what the top acts are used to, rather than the lower standard of production of the old event.

While hundreds of artists still sign autographs in the Nashville Convention Center during the festival, few of them are superstars. "We've worked to refocus the expectations of the fans coming in," Benson says. "A lot of fans buying tickets now have no idea that autograph sessions are a part of it. They're coming for a music festival. I wouldn't say we're deliberately trying to downplay the autograph booths in the exhibit hall, but there is more of an emphasis now on the music and the outdoor areas."

As the CMA looks to the future, they are making plans to expand further, eventually incorporating the new symphony hall and baseball stadium into the proceedings while continuing to present music inside the Gaylord Entertainment Center and the Municipal Auditorium.

From Down-home to Big-time

This year, the cable station CMT will tape a concert special at the arena while cowboy singer Michael Martin Murphey hosts a Wild West extravaganza at the auditorium—two events that couldn't have taken place at the old Fan Fair.

"I will always hold a special place in my heart for the old Fan Fair and the fairgrounds," says Smith. "But the new festival isn't only better for the artists and for the business, it's better for the fans. Where else are you going to see that many stars in one night for that price? It would cost them hundreds of dollars to see all these stars in their hometown. I was one of the people who hated to see it change. But now I love it."

44

IRIS DEMENT: ALL THAT LIVING WILL ALLOW

By David Cantwell
From *No Depression*

ingers celebrate the human voice. Their lyrics are words. But animated by voice those words are subsumed into sounds...In most songs the drama or tension results from the fact that the singer moves between word (sense) and note (song). At one moment the song simply "says" something. At another moment the voice stretches out the words—the heart cannot contain!—and the voice moves toward pure sound. Words take flight.
–Richard Rodriguez, Hunger of Memory

Iris DeMent didn't write any new songs, or at least any she was happy with, for close to a decade. In the first half of the 1990s, DeMent released three albums containing 28 original songs that earned her a reputation as one of the best songwriters of her generation. And her singing, which seemed to evoke all the living that mere words can never quite convey, had similarly earned DeMent a spot among the elite vocalists of her time.

Even amidst the dry years, DeMent never stopped singing. But her "writer's block," as it's been termed, became a matter of particular frustration to her audience. One fan would mention that DeMent had sung marvelously in concert, and another would immediately inquire, "Yes, but did she have any new songs?"

All sorts of things can keep artists from creating their art. There are likely as many obstacles that can come between songwriters and new songs as there are songwriters and songs. And it's all the more difficult to discuss because each artist doesn't experience the silencing of creativity in precisely the same way every time it occurs.

During the years of writer's block, Iris DeMent divorced. She

45

David Cantwell

endured both lengthy and brief periods of depression. At times she toured more than she prefers, which left her with too little of what Lucinda Williams once called "cool quiet and time to think." She dealt with hate mail and death threats over her expression of political beliefs. She fell in love and remarried. Now, finally, at age 43, she has a new album of gospel standards, *Lifeline* (due out November 9 on a label of her own invention, Flariella Records). And she's writing some new songs.

When people have asked DeMent over the years why it's taken her so long to put out a new record—and she says she's been asked this many, many times—her pat response has been something like, "I haven't put a record out in eight years because I haven't written twelve songs that I want to make a record of." As pat answers go, that's a fine one.

But the real answers to where Iris DeMent has been all these years, and where she is today, well, that's a long story. It starts in church.

Iris Luella DeMent was born the youngest of fourteen children in Paragould, Arkansas, a tiny town located just beneath the Missouri boot heel, on January 5th, 1961. On January 8th, she attended her first church service. "My mom always prided herself," DeMent says, "on getting her kids to church the first Sunday after they were born."

Both in Arkansas, where Iris' father, Patrick, did factory work at Emerson Electric, and in California, where he moved the family in 1964 after an attempt to unionize the plant failed, the DeMents' life centered on the church. In Buena Park, California, where Iris mostly grew up, she regularly attended several fervent Pentecostal services each week. There, the faithful filled the air with often wordless sounds of praise: sobs, shouts, and moans, as well as the ecstatic "praying in the spirit," more commonly known as "speaking in tongues." The practice has been called "primal speech…a language of the heart" by religion professor Harvey Cox, and it's what Pentecostals believe the Apostle Paul was describing when he wrote of "sighs too deep for words."

The members of the DeMent family often went door to door, as well, or performed in public in an effort to win souls to Christ. "I remember being like six years old," DeMent says, "standing on the corner, shaking my tambourine and some kid would go by on his bike. I'd think, boy, you and I are worlds apart."

All That Living Will Allow

Music was a central part of the family's worship, fostering fellowship among the church members on Wednesdays and Sundays and girding the spirits of congregants at home during the rest of the week. All of the DeMents—eight children remained at home as Iris grew up—sang in church, and did so with abundant strenuousness and joy, as is the Pentecostal way. Many in the family played the piano at home (Iris' father had played the fiddle, too, when he was a young man in Arkansas but put it away when he committed himself to Christ) and occasionally even performed on record. Billing themselves as The DeMent Sisters, a trio of Iris' older siblings provided backing vocals once for a local gospel recording session; another sister was in a gospel group that recorded "I Don't Want to Get Adjusted to this World." "That's how I first heard [that song], when I was just about ten, I guess," she says. *Lifeline* includes her own version of the song, backed by little more than lap steel licks and the strum of her own acoustic guitar.

In fact, excluding one DeMent original, the selections on *Lifeline* are all songs Iris sang in church as a girl or ones she learned from old hymnbooks that her mother had brought with the family from Arkansas.

"The Gospel Ship," for example: "I grew up hearing that song all of the time," DeMent recalls. "But the first time I really remember it was when this lady came to our church to sing. Well, she was probably only about sixteen but to me she was a lady. I was maybe seven. Her name was Sharon Scroggins, and she sang one Sunday morning and was just really, really good. She had this great big beehive hairdo. And she was cross-eyed. And looking back I can see how I should've gone, 'Oh, *this* is weird.' But I was just so taken with her; I wanted to *be* her. I thought it was wonderful that her eyes were crossed.

"She was scheduled to sing again that night, so I spent the afternoon getting my hair up in a bee hive: I borrowed a wig from one of my sisters. Normally I'd sit next to my girl friends at church, but this night I sat up front by myself so I could focus on her. And I sat there and, I kid you not, I crossed my eyes, and she started singing 'The Old Gospel Ship.' I'll never forget it. It was one of those things where you first go, 'Oh, I know this song.' But I *didn't* know the song. *She* knew that song. She could really sing."

So could DeMent's mother, who Iris lists right alongside the Carter Family, Jimmie Rodgers, Loretta Lynn, Merle Haggard, Bob Dylan

47

David Cantwell

and Johnny Cash as her primary musical influences. Indeed, Flora Mae DeMent inspired what is perhaps DeMent's most popular song, the *Infamous Angel* cut "Mama's Opry." She also provided lead vocals to that 1991 album's closing track, the gospel standard "Higher Ground."

"I was lucky like that. I grew up around a lot of really great singers," DeMent says. "My mom, of course, but there was just a lot of *real* voices in our church too; people just opened up and sang. I took it for granted then but I don't hear that a lot any more. There was such a *freedom* in the way we sang in our church growing up."

Even so, DeMent eventually began to question what she'd learned there. She was not the first young person, of course, to reach a place where freedom was the last thing her church represented to her. As someone who had been born into a particular spiritual tradition, as opposed to someone who came to it via an intensely emotional and life-altering epiphany ("I never had that 'born again' moment; it was just the environment I grew up in"), it is perhaps unsurprising that DeMent would at some point begin to examine critically the familiar faith of youth. For Iris, this religious questioning began when she was sixteen. As she puts it, "That's when everything went crazy."

"Crazy in a good way," she adds quickly. "I started reflecting on my beliefs and seeing which ones held up next to my own experience. And when I was able to look at a belief and realize it wasn't true for me anymore, I tossed it. And I had to leave the church because of that. I mean, I left the church in my heart and in my thinking; there was this period when I was there physically but I was not there. A year or two after that I quit going altogether. But even then, the songs still held up for me, they never let me down. I still loved those songs, and I still sang them."

She especially turned to the old songs when she was feeling troubled, a strategy she'd learned from Flora Mae. Iris' mother had always sang gospel songs to help her ease her confusion, or heal a hurt, or give her hope. Her mother sang, DeMent told an interviewer in 1998, in order "to get herself out of a sad miserable place." Today, nearly a quarter of a century after Iris DeMent left the faith of her parents, it's those same gospel songs that she learned at home and at church to which she's most likely to turn to when the sky seems dark and she feels in need of a light to guide her. As she professes in "God Walks These Dark Hills," the new album's closing performance: "God...walks through the cold dark night, the shadows of

All That Living Will Allow

midnight...to show me the way."

"I'm just an ordinary person," she says, "one who was raised to have a conscience—and to check in on it every once in a while and to react out of that place. The old gospel songs help me do that. They *still* help me do that."

The irony is that DeMent's conscience, the roots of her raising, have led her to conclusions in stark contrast to what those raising her might have wished.

Her voice became a little teary, as she went on to say that she would feel like a hypocrite, singing as if everything was right with the world...[S]he went on to say that the tickets would all be refunded, and that if anyone had trouble at all getting their money back, they should contact her directly through her web site. She thanked everyone for coming, said 'Goodnight,' and walked off the stage. At this point, some audience members, myself included, stood up and applauded.

–post to a discussion group at irisdement.com

On March 21, 2003, the day that the United States began its preemptory war against Iraq, Iris DeMent was scheduled to play a show at the Barrymore Theater in Madison, Wisconsin. As show time neared, DeMent sat in her dressing room, struggling to reach a decision. Finally, after the opening act had performed, she took the stage and told the 600 people in attendance that, given the day's events, she had decided not to sing.

"It would be trivializing the fact that my tax dollars are causing great suffering, and sending a message that might makes right," DeMent told the audience according to one press account.

As she explains now, "When I cancelled that show in Madison, I didn't plan to make some big political statement; I was following my own conscience and how I felt. I just didn't feel right singing that night." On DeMent's web site, responses to the singer's small protest against the war were overwhelmingly positive. Even those few in disagreement with her decision seemed to appreciate that she was acting out of deep-rooted personal beliefs. And that might have been end of the episode, except...

"Some right wing radio show picked up on it," she says, "and people who didn't know me or my music at all were writing very threatening things to me. They didn't know me from a hole in the wall, but

49

David Cantwell

I'd been named as one of the new 'enemies' on some extremist show and that's all it took." Hundreds of angry emails began pouring into her web site. Many of them attacked her character, intelligence, and patriotism; others damned her to burn in hell; some included death threats.

It wasn't the first time DeMent found herself embroiled in a minor controversy. In 1997, a Florida state senator, Republican John Grant, heard "Wasteland of the Free," a track from DeMent's third album, *The Way I Should*, on Tampa public radio station WMNF (88.5 FM). Grant was enraged by the song's content—the *Tampa Tribune* said the Senator was especially angered by the couplet, "We got politicians runnin' races on corporate cash/ Now don't tell me they don't turn around and kiss them people's ass." Consequently, Grant led a successful effort to eliminate the station's primary source of funding, $103,000 worth, from the state budget. In response, WMNF listeners helped the station raise more than $120,000 in an emergency fund drive. In 1999, DeMent performed at a benefit concert for the station. The station's state funding has been restored.

Much of DeMent's audience responded to "Wasteland of the Free" enthusiastically. But not all of her fans were appreciative of lines such as, "They say they are Christ's disciples but they don't look like Jesus to me" and "We kill for oil then we throw a party when we win." For example, one fan, upon hearing the song, posted to a discussion group on DeMent's web site that, "I came away disheartened by what I had thought was a remarkably talented person. In music, yes. In thought, character and loyalty—NO."

"I knew the song would stir up controversy and that people might want to respond; that's why I recorded it," DeMent says today. "But I guess I was a little ignorant as to how much of the response would be directed not at the song but at me personally."

The questioning of her character and of her devotion to her country in the wake of the "Wasteland" controversy was, for DeMent, a learning experience about the costs of speaking one's mind, of how easily entreaties that America honor its ideals can be angrily mistaken as attacks on America.

Still, she was unprepared for the reaction to her Madison decision. "I'm telling you, I got mail, vicious mail, like I could've never fathomed. And I'm not some giant entertainer here. By a lot of standards I'm barely on the map. It was very frightening to me, it was very intim-

50

All That Living Will Allow

idating, and it shook me up in a big way. Anybody who thinks you can be the brunt of this sort of hatred and not be affected by it is kidding themselves.

"The whole vibe of this country right now is nowhere near what it was in '96 [when "Wasteland" was released]. What happened then was, yes, I got some hate mail. But mostly it was people who disagreed with me, who stated their case, and I can't complain about that; that's the way it should be.

"But this was a whole different thing," she continues, pausing to make sure she's getting the words right. "It was like...murderous, almost. The place that it came from, I mean. It really made my head spin. It gave me a whole different view of the world we're in these days.

"It would never occur to me to try to crush another human being, to hate them so much you wished them dead. [Those letters] were attacks mostly, I felt, not on my opinions but on my soul. What's so prevalent today—you're evil, you're the enemy—that's a spiritual assault...It's not just that you're discouraged from being different, with people looking at you cockeyed. Now, it's like you're aligned with the enemy. That's a big leap, and we can't give in to it. I mean, to me, it's not anything at all like the Democratic Party that's at stake. It's our *spirit* that is at stake."

DeMent is diligently protective of her privacy, and of her sense of what constitutes a good quality of life, too. ("[I]t's true I don't work near as hard as you tell me I'm supposed to...," she sang on *The Way I Should*. "But I live just the way I want to, and that's the way I should.") That's one reason why, but for a brief stint in Nashville before the release of her debut album, she has continued to live in Kansas City, Missouri, well away from country music's business and celebrity capital. It may also have something to do with her decision to release *Lifeline* on Flariella—basically her own imprint set up through the North Carolina company Deep South, with distribution via Redeye—after pulling out from a deal with New West Records at the last minute this summer. (The process had gone so far as to be announced to some press outlets.)

It's also why she stopped giving interviews at all, for a time, in the wake of the hostile reaction to her Madison decision. "That whole attack reminded me very much of my experience growing up in the church. And there were a lot of good things in the church, and I feel the good things are expressed in these songs [on *Lifeline*], the way I

David Cantwell

sing and feel them. But there was also a very repressive side to that experience. You know, don't speak your mind; don't question anything; go along with the rules. The book's already been written; don't go challenging it. And when I started getting the hate mail it felt like the Pentecostal Church of God all over again to me. And I think I reacted to it in the same way too. I remember when I finally came to that place as a teenager of speaking out and being honest about the fact that I didn't believe a lot of things I was brought up to believe, I went through a period of kind of hibernation. When you step out there on a limb and feel yourself rejected by the people you've leaned on your whole life, it takes some time to absorb all that, to collect yourself and to find your strength again."

> *Sweet Is the melody, so hard to come by*
> *So hard to make every note bend just right*
> — "Sweet is the Melody," Iris DeMent

Who can say exactly why new songs didn't arrive for DeMent during these last eight years like they had in the first half of the 1990s? Since she released *The Way I Should* in 1996, her time has been filled with all of the varied distractions, joyous and sorrowful alike, that any life provides. Then again, who can be certain what an actual "reason" for writing or not writing might even be? Others songwriters, after all, have suffered or enjoyed similar life circumstances to DeMent and have ended up with more songs than they knew what to do with.

All DeMent can say with certainty is that for a long time inspiration did not come calling upon her. It wasn't the first time, either.

"I didn't write a song till I was 25, and I guess I could call all those years writer's block. I always wanted to write songs," Iris remembers. "I used to pray to write songs. When I was little, I'd sit at the piano and wait for a song to come, until my mom would tell me to go outside. I just knew it was *supposed* to happen."

On the other hand, DeMent's standard response when asked why she hasn't put out a new record in so long—"I haven't written twelve songs that I want to make a record of"—doesn't identify the problem as writer's block so much as the songwriter's own impossibly high standards. She's worked very hard at writing songs; she's written some songs; she just doesn't think they're good songs.

"I know people say, 'Oh, it's a craft,'" she continues. "And I know

All That Living Will Allow

for some people that works. But I'm not one of them. I've tried that route. I've done that thing where you sit down every day and write. When I couldn't come up with anything, I'd sit there in my chair and move words around and whatever. And I'd get this...*thing*. But I didn't have any feeling for it, just nothing."

DeMent also has gone years where the problem wasn't merely unsatisfactory songs; the problem was that, mired in depression, there were no songs at all.

"I first had those feelings [of depression] when I was in fifth, sixth grade," DeMent says. "I didn't know what they were at the time, but I would just get very, very sad. I'd be walking to school and start crying. I didn't know what was going on. Times were different then; people didn't talk openly about that stuff. And so from then on, these dark periods would come up now and then. But as far as a long stretch of it, that was new to me.

"And I don't have manic periods, either. I *wish* I had manic periods," she adds, laughing. "But when I come out of depression, I'm so happy to be alive that I am more likely to write. When I feel well, I'm more likely to want to do something creatively with what I'd experienced when I wasn't. But I don't write when I'm depressed. I just feel paralyzed when I'm depressed."

DeMent can at times be her own harshest critic, a tendency that is only compounded by depression and one that, in any event, doesn't always do her any creative favors. She has beat herself up plenty, for example, when the songs didn't come as fast as she or others might have liked.

"There's been times over the last eight years when I've really felt a lot of turmoil over [not writing]. Where I've felt like a failure, like something's wrong with me," DeMent admits. "But I'm over that. I *think* I'm over that. It has its own time, its own reason, and I don't have much say about it, I truly don't. I've accepted that there is a clock that is my own and I don't have to make excuses for it. I'm actually even grateful for it. The way songs come to me, and don't come to me, is its own beautiful, funny, weird thing.

"What I mean is, and maybe I'm letting myself off the hook here a little bit, but I've kind of stepped away from the expectation that, 'Oh, you're a writer, so God damnit, sit down and write. You have to have a record every year or every two years.' I've tried to throw that idea away. That's a business world idea. It doesn't have anything to do with me as

53

David Cantwell

a human being and what I need and what's going on in my life and in this world. I feel free of that now. If I put out a record this year, that's great. If I don't, if I never do, I don't feel crippled by that anymore.

"At the same time, I feel in my heart and my soul that there are more songs that are going to pass through me. You can sense things in life. They don't always have bodies but you can feel them. And when my first song came to me when I was 25, it felt like a presence walked in the room and talked to me. It felt that real. I never had the 'born again' experience, but I've had *that*. The most spiritual experience I've ever had was when I wrote my first song...

"And I still feel that presence. Even in years when I've gone without writing I've continued to feel that presence. And that's what I mean when I say I still believe they are more songs to come through me.

"I *hope* to have a record [of new material] soon," she concludes. "But I've stopped expecting to. I don't know what will happen. I have written a few new songs. We'll see."

> *Nobody knows what it means to me*
> *Nobody knows but my God and me*
> *I've got that old time religion in my heart*
> *And it's way down inside*
> —"I've Got that Old Time Religion in My Heart"

Though it's been eight years since her last album, DeMent didn't just vanish from the face of the earth. To the contrary, she has at times been quite busy. She's contributed tracks to several tribute albums, including one honoring the man she has since married, Iowa singer-songwriter Greg Brown. She sang duets with Ralph Stanley, Steve Earle, and old friend John Prine (who wrote the liner notes for *Infamous Angel*). She performed the folk song "Pretty Saro" in the 2001 film *Songcatcher*. ("I just had one or two lines," she recalls, "but they were terrifying.") And, of course, she's played live sets all over the country.

In other words, no matter what was else was happening in DeMent's life, she kept right on singing. When her soul felt heaviest, the songs she was most likely to sing were the gospel songs she grew up with. As she writes in the liner notes to *Lifeline*: "A few years ago...the hard times came in for a long visit and about the only thing

All That Living Will Allow

that helped was sitting at the piano and singing these songs to myself." Once, when especially troubled, she writes, DeMent called her mother who immediately tossed her a "lifeline": "Iris! You gotta get to a 'peh-yan-uh!'"

"I sit around and play old church songs a lot," Iris says. "For me, it's kind of like looking through a photo album. They take me back to the comforting aspects of my past."

"These songs are a spiritual thing for me," she continues, "but not because they belong to a church or a book or anything. To me, they're like this link I have to where I come from and to my mom and dad— and to the people who came before them. When I go through hard times, I still sit down and sing these songs; I feel like I'm going to make it when I sing these songs.

"How I've kept an important part of my past with me is that I've interpreted [those gospel songs] to suit who I am today," she concludes. "I can sing these songs even more wholeheartedly now than I did growing up. I don't believe in a magic Jesus—I did growing up; I don't anymore. But when I think of Jesus I think of this person that came here and struggled through this life, and was killed in the end, but managed to muster up love and compassion for the world....I think of the human struggle and of someone who is a good example of how to make it through.

"So when I sing [in *Lifeline*'s opening track, 'I've Got That Old Time Religion'] that 'I'm glad Jesus came/ Glory to his name,' I *mean* it."

Does anyone ever complain to her that the writers of the old gospel standards meant to underscore one message and one message only—"For God so loved the world that He gave His only begotten Son, that whoever believes in Him shall not perish but have eternal life" (John 3:16)—and that she's kidding herself if she interprets them in ways other than they were intended?

"Well sure," DeMent allows. "I have a family full of people who would tell me that. If I hadn't grown up with this music, then I probably wouldn't be singing these songs. But they are so meshed for me with the place I come from and the way I learned about...*feeling*.

"So much of what I learned about the world and myself and the people in my world came through these songs. And for me to separate myself from them would be really damaging to me. That may sound a little extreme but I really feel that way. I can't walk away from some-

55

David Cantwell

thing that is such a deep part of me."

"I mean, it's funny," she says later. "I say I'm not a Christian, but I'm not a Christian by what I think is the distorted definition that we all know today. But if I go to my definition, and the one I *think* might have been something *closer* to the original one, then in that sense I guess I am a Christian."

Indeed, the link between the Iris DeMent who writes political protest songs like "Wasteland of the Free" and the Iris DeMent who hears in gospel songs not primarily a formula for eternal salvation but a model for how to live in the here and now—"A new commandment I give unto you; that ye love one another" (John 13: 34)—can be found in *Lifeline*'s one DeMent original, "He Reached Down."

"That's the story of the Good Samaritan, where the man is beaten and robbed and everyone passes him by but the Samaritan, who cares for his wounds and takes him to an inn," she says. "To me [the Samaritan] is the Christian story. It's a story of love and compassion, of non-judgment, of doing for others."

"He Reached Down" is DeMent's attempt to write a gospel song that highlights what she finds most valuable in the New Testament. She communicates this value not only via her lyrics but also through the way the singer's voice conveys human yearnings of innumerable and universal variety, emotions and strivings that mere words are insufficient to contain, just as the inchoate moans of that man left for dead inspired the Samaritan to stop and assist a stranger in need.

"I actually go to church here in town, St. Mark's Union Church…a predominantly black church. It's the first place I've been able to find that kind of lively, soulful preaching style I grew up with *and* that also has a service that speaks to me, that is very free, very accepting of any religions. And of anybody's right not even to have a religion."

"There's a woman in our church, her name is Mother Bohannon. I think she's 85. And every now and then she'll launch into a song and I just come apart. She has a beautiful voice but more than that it's that she just brings up so much emotion and life from so deep down. It's a really wonderful thing."

When asked point blank what she's been up to since 1996, she says: "I got divorced, I bought a house, I remarried, I made some new friends and got back in close with old friends I'd lost touch with, I started working a lot less, eating a little better, resting a little more. I've been gardening. Basically just having more of a home life, something I didn't have much of for a while there."

A big part of this new life is bound up with her 2003 marriage to Greg Brown, a far more prolific songwriter than DeMent but one who grew up in a church environment not unlike his wife's.

"In 1992, at one of the first shows I ever did—I mean, where I left town and went out to the east coast—I was opening for Greg," she remembers, telling the story of the couple's whirlwind romance. "But we didn't actually meet. I listened to him backstage and he says he went out in the audience and listened to me but we didn't actually meet. And then we'd met a time or two at festivals through the years, that sort of thing, but we never spoke together for more than five minutes at a time. Then in July, before we married in November, we did a show together, in Saratoga. We talked a little while, and started seeing each other in late September and got married in November."

"It was very snappy," she laughs. "Not like anything I've ever done before."

During the years when DeMent was waiting for songs that didn't come, her singing was proof of the poet John Milton's faith that "They also serve who only stand and wait." And, we might add, who "only" sing. Fans, critics, the music industry, and DeMent herself have all been disappointed when new Iris DeMent songs didn't materialize, as if her singing wasn't enough of a gift on its own. Much of that expectation can be written off to the perennial and tiresome bias of favoring the second half of the "singer-songwriter" label more than the first. Maybe someday, we'll come to see that DeMent's singing has been her greatest genius all along.

Certainly she's singing better than she ever has, which is saying a great deal. Her singing has always possessed immediacy, and a built-in prettiness, that demanded attention be paid. On *Lifeline*, however, she sacrifices that prettiness, the sweetness, when necessary for something harder, more complex, and beautiful. For example, on "Near the Cross," one of several cuts on *Lifeline* in which DeMent is accompanied only by her own piano, she swallows vowels, stretches syllables, slurs her enunciation, moans, allows her normally soaring voice to speak in breathy, earthbound tones, doesn't always keep perfect time or sing in perfect pitch. Yet every note is perfect.

"Near the cross I'll watch and wait…till the golden strand I reach, just beyond the river," she prays, playing the calming chords she's known practically all her life. It's not just the words of the song but her

David Cantwell

singing of them that reveals how weary she truly is and, at the same time, how deeply at peace. In her rendering, the old hymn is invested with meanings that transcend the limitations of a religious doctrine. Sense gives way to sound, and human desires that are typically inchoate but felt intensely are fleetingly given a specific human voice.

Throughout *Lifeline*, DeMent's vocals sound as deeply felt, as in the moment, as messy and full of life as any singer you care to name. And that's enough. When Iris DeMent sings, no matter who gets the writer's credit, it is, as she says of fellow congregant Mother Bohannon, "a really wonderful thing." And that's enough.

"I'm older and I've gone through some things," she says by way of explaining the emotional depth of her latest recordings. "I didn't play shows really before my first record came out so a lot of my focus was on how to hold it together. Keep strumming, stay on rhythm, what do you say to these people? And so it's only lately that I think I've been able to start relaxing and to just *sing*. I've noticed this around the house, and it's a different thing.

"When I hear Mother Bohannon sing at church, I listen to her and I get really excited. I think, Oh God, no *telling* what I'll sound like when I'm 85. All that living. I'm getting excited about finding out, about learning to turn into sound everything that happens to me. I'm excited about getting at all those changes that are occurring inside me and somehow letting them out in my voice.

"What will I sound like when I've learned to let all that living come out in my voice? All that living!"

KRIS KRISTOFFERSON: THE HEMINGWAY OF SONGWRITERS

By Phil Sweetland
From *American Songwriter*

Few have ever used words better than the novelist Ernest Hemingway or the songwriter Kris Kristofferson. Through divine intervention or just plain luck, these two giants of the American scene brushed past each other one afternoon, in what might have been the perfect setting for their brief encounter. "I even ran into him once, at a bullfight," Kristofferson says in a telephone interview.

There are striking parallels between the lives of the two men. Hemingway (1899-1961), the legendary author of classic American novels like *The Sun Also Rises, To Have and Have Not* and *The Old Man and the Sea*, was as colorful a character in real life as any of those who populated his novels and stories.

He was a bearded, hard-drinking, lion of a man who hunted big game in Africa, covered the Spanish Civil War as a correspondent, and wrote unforgettable novels about both. Papa Hemingway was irresistible to women and uncompromising about his writing, with a genius for communicating a great deal in a few words.

Kristofferson's life and work share many of these traits. It was Hemingway's constant quest to experience life before writing about it that Kristofferson, perhaps more than anyone since Woody Guthrie in the 1930s, has been able to emulate in the field of American songwriting. "I was trying to be like him," Kristofferson says of Hemingway. "I ran in front of the bulls at Pamplona."

At their bullfight meeting, no words were exchanged. "I was trying to do as many different kinds of things as I could, and be a writer,"

Phil Sweetland

says Kristofferson, now 68. "I don't know if it was restlessness or just wanting to experience as much as I could in the time that I had. I got to be a ranger, a helicopter pilot – I was in the Airborne and I did a lot of construction jobs all over the world. Looking back on it, I feel pretty lucky to have done all that."

The Kristofferson Catalog

Kristofferson compositions like "Me And Bobby McGee," "Help Me Make It Through The Night," "For The Good Times," "Sunday Morning Coming Down," and the Gospel-flavored "Why Me" brought a whole new level of frankness to country songwriting, and many of his tunes quickly crossed over to mainstream pop. He has also had successful careers as an artist and a movie star.

Todd Snider, an Americana-styled country artist on the same label as Kristofferson, Oh Boy Records, says, "Hemingway was very sparse in his writing. Kris is like that. He can take four words and say it all."

Bob DiPiero, the writer of George Strait's "Blue Clear Sky" and countless other hits, says, "'My cleanest dirty shirt,' a lyric from Kris's 'Sunday Morning Coming Down,' may be one of the top four most descriptive phrases ever used in a popular song of any genre."

Country star Billy Walker, "The Tall Texan," has been a member of the Grand Ole Opry since 1960 and recorded one of Kristofferson's earliest hits, "From The Bottle To The Bottom," in 1969. Walker says, "I have always loved singing 'For The Good Times.' It brings folks to the dance floor every time. And 'Why Me' (Kristofferson's first No. 1 song as an artist) is as inspirational as 'How Great Thou Art' in my opinion."

Jeffrey Steele, the California native who has become Nashville's hottest modern songwriter with more than 40 Top 5 singles to his credit, was thrilled when Kristofferson recently told him how much Steele reminded Kris of himself in the late Sixties and early Seventies. "At that time in country, Kris was saying things you weren't supposed to say, but I don't think he was trying to be different," Steele says. "He was just writing what was really in his heart and saying it in ways we hadn't heard up till that point."

"For The Good Times" still blows Steele away. "Wow, it's a classic example of how all roads go to the hook!" says Steele, who penned "My Town" for Montgomery Gentry and "Unbelievable" for Diamond Rio. "From the first 'Don't look so sad,' you know it's goin'

Kris Kristofferson: The Hemingway of Songwriters

to a place we've all been in our lives – the end – having to move on and wanting to hold on to what you had forever."

Back in the Day

Kristofferson was born in Brownsville, Texas, in 1936, the son of an Air Force major general. When the young Kris heard Hank Williams sing on the Saturday night radio broadcasts of the Opry, he was hooked.

"Yeah, Hank was my first love," Kristofferson says. "It was love at first sight, the first time I heard him on the Opry. There was just something about him, the voice, the passion, and the heart that he put into it."

Kris began writing songs in the late 40s, and was a Phi Beta Kappa graduate of Pomona College in California as a creative writing major. That earned him a Rhodes Scholarship to Oxford University in London from 1958-60.

"The great thing about getting to be at Oxford . . . was that all I did was read literature," he says. "William Blake (a mystical 18th-century English poet, author and painter who also influenced Jim Morrison of The Doors) probably had the biggest impact on me. He was such a committed artist. Most people did think he was crazy. Blake wasn't published in his lifetime. He said one thing that was really inspirational to me." Kristofferson then quotes the entire Blake centuries-old passage, a call to creative arms, word-for-word: "If you, who are organized by Divine Providence for Spiritual communion, Refuse, & bury your Talent in the Earth, even tho' you should want Natural Bread, Sorrow and Desperation pursues you thro' life, & after death shame & confusion of face to eternity."

After Oxford, Kristofferson served in the Army and piloted helicopters for five years. From time to time, he would mail his songs to Nashville with little success. But a cousin of his platoon leader, Marijohn Wilkin, was a songwriter and publisher in Music City and she gave Kris his first introduction to the country music elite.

Nashville Cats

"Marijohn showed me around the place when I was on leave, still in uniform," Kris says. "I just fell in love with the whole music scene there, especially after five years in the Army. It was such a liberating experience. Marijohn hung out with Mel Tillis and Merle Kilgore and

61

Phil Sweetland

Cowboy Jack Clement. They were all writing stuff and singing to each other, trying to knock each other out."

So, two weeks before he was slated to begin a job as professor of English Literature at West Point, Kristofferson thankfully changed his tune and moved to Nashville. In his scuffling days on Music Row, he worked for a while as a janitor at Columbia Studios and as a bartender. Kris was 29, the same age as Hank Williams was when he died – an irony that has touched Kristofferson ever since.

Kris became fast friends with a fellow Texan, songwriter Mickey Newbury. Newbury was a remarkable talent perhaps best known now for "An American Trilogy," which Elvis later covered. "Mickey had a way of using simple words and simple melodies, just putting them together in a way that would break your heart," Kristofferson says. "He probably had more of an impact on me than any of my peers. He really influenced my songwriting. We never did co-write, and that's really strange, but we were like a tag team. We used to pitch each other's songs."

A turning point came when Roger Miller recorded "Me And Bobby McGee" as a country song in 1969, two years before Janis Joplin's rock version of it became a No. 1 pop hit. "It was huge when Roger recorded that," Kristofferson said. "It was like Bob Dylan cutting my song. When I came to Nashville, Roger Miller was the guy that made country cool. He was just everybody's hero. Mickey pitched him that song."

The way Miller heard the song is classic Kristofferson. "Mickey called me up, and I was in a motel with some strange girl," Kris says with a chuckle. "He said, 'If you can get down to the Ramada Inn in 15 minutes, Roger's gonna fly us to L.A. and he wants to hear 'Me And Bobby McGee.' Roger drove us to the airport. He was driving on the sidewalk half the time – and somehow we made it to the plane. We lived at his house in L.A. for three days. I waited for him to say, 'Show me the song,' but he never mentioned it. Then just as we we're getting ready to go back to Nashville, he asked me to sing it for him."

"Sunday Morning Coming Down," a brutally frank No. 1 hit for Johnny Cash, "was just autobiography," Kris says. "That's another one where I feel the influence of Mickey Newbury."

The song was originally recorded by Ray Stevens in 1969, a vastly underrated performance. Stevens worked 30 hours in the studio to get the tune right, but the single tanked due to poor label support.

The story has another fascinating aspect.

"Burt Bacharach wanted Ray to do 'Raindrops Keep Fallin' On My Head' for the movie *Butch Cassidy and the Sundance Kid*," Kristofferson says. "They wanted Ray to put 'Raindrops' out as his next single, and he wanted to put out 'Sunday Morning Coming Down.' I felt guilty about that." B.J. Thomas' excellent rendition of "Raindrops Keep Fallin' On My Head" went in the movie, and it became an instant classic.

The honors soon started coming Kristofferson's way, much to his own surprise. In 1970, "Sunday Morning Coming Down" was up against Merle Haggard's "Okie From Muskogee" and Marty Robbins' "My Woman, My Woman, My Wife" for the Country Music Association's Song of the Year. Haggard and Robbins were two of Kris's heroes. He didn't think he had a prayer of winning. "I didn't even pay attention to how to get to the stage (at the Ryman Auditorium)," he says. "When they announced that I won, Marty said, 'Well, get on up there!'"

Going to the Movies

His acting career, which has now encompassed more than 80 films, also began somewhat by accident. Dennis Hopper, one of Hollywood's hippie kings in those days, invited Kristofferson to join him in Peru to compose music for Hopper's 1971 film *The Last Picture Show*.

"Dennis ended up putting me in it, and I could speak Spanish," Kristofferson says of the small role he played in the film. "He pulled me in just to hear me sing 'Me And Bobby McGee.' I didn't feel like an actor at all."

By the time Kris returned from Peru his first solo album was out, and soon Kristofferson had a whole new medium to showcase his talents. "When I started performing my own songs, my first gig was at the Troubadour (in Los Angeles)," Kristofferson says. "That was probably a time when people in the movie business were looking for new faces. I got a lot of scripts."

Rough-hewn actor Harry Dean Stanton became a friend. They acted together in Kristofferson's second film, *Cisco Pike*. In his third, he played Billy in *Pat Garrett and Billy the Kid*. He was soon a box-office sensation, acting with Barbra Streisand in *A Star is Born* (1976).

"The success in movies was actually a kind of double-edged sword," he says. "It took the attention away from my music, because

Phil Sweetland

at the time I was getting hottest in movies, my record company (Monument) was going under. The movies helped for about 20 years, when I was either doing a picture or on the road with my band. Now I'm kind of breaking even. I've gotten back into performing music more, and they're paying me more."

Nonetheless, Kristofferson continues to pop up on the big screen these days in an assortment of roles. Two films that are coming soon, due out September 17, are *Silver City* (set in a mythical "New West") and the thriller *Blade: Trinity*, probably the last of the series. Kristofferson (Whistler) has played the revitalized mentor of vampire-slaying Wesley Snipes (Blade) in all three *Blade* films.

The Highway Calls

By 1980, Kristofferson's seven-year marriage to singer Rita Coolidge was over. Five years later, one of the musical joys of his life began when Kris, Waylon Jennings, Willie Nelson, and Johnny Cash teamed up to sing Jimmy Webb's "The Highwayman." This dream team, like Kristofferson's movie career, almost never got started.

"That was (producer) Chips Moman's idea," Kristofferson said. "John (Cash) and Willie were gonna do an album. John had told Willie, 'You've cut an album with everybody on Earth except me,' and Willie told me, 'I think it would be to your advantage to pitch us some songs.' When we sang together, it came off so good in the studio. That's why *The Highwaymen* happened. Every one of those guys was my hero when I first got to town. I got to stand right next to Johnny Cash every night and sing harmony with him – whether he wanted me to or not. He said there was never anybody else who ever had the nerve to sing with him on 'Folsom Prison Blues.'"

Moman also produced Kristofferson's *Repossessed* (1987) album, which Oh Boy reissued this summer as a 2-CD set with *Third World Warrior* (1990). With songs such as "Sandinista" and "They Killed Him," this set shows Kris at his outspoken best, fighting for the underdog as his friend and mentor Johnny Cash always did.

At Cash's memorial service last September, Kristofferson did a superb job as master of ceremonies on what was a terribly painful day for him. He recently spoke of his first meeting with Cash nearly 40 years ago. "It was like shaking hands with a panther," Kristofferson said. "Johnny was supercharged, he was one of the most exciting performers I'd ever seen. He never seemed like a normal human being to

Kris Kristofferson: The Hemingway of Songwriters

me. John was always like a guy who walked off Mount Rushmore."

Mr. Prolific

Kristofferson is something of an elder statesman of songwriting today, though as his recent performances and compositions show, he is singing and writing some of the most touching songs of his career. One includes the line, "the angels were singing a sad country song/It sounded like something of yours."

Some of Kris's new songs include memories of how different the record business is now than when he started. "It was so easy. The whole music business back then was those two streets," he says. "On Music Row, every day you could see all the guys."

He's planning on recording an album of new material next year, likely in Nashville or L.A., and he's also been working on an autobiography for Hyperion Books.

Passing the Torch

In the late 60s, Kristofferson helped found the Nashville Songwriters Association International (NSAI), which elected him to its Hall of Fame and is still going strong today with thousands of members. NSAI has helped countless young writers break into Music Row. What advice would he give to these songwriters?

"If you're in it because you love it and you have to do it, that's the right reason," Kristofferson says. "If you're in it because you want to get rich or famous, don't do it. People often say that my first years in Nashville, when I wasn't getting anything cut, were tough. Hell, those were great years."

Ernest Hemingway, we imagine, would have agreed.

66

THE CELEBRITY TWO-STEP
Great voice, good looks, hot licks, hit songs—will this be enough to make Brad Paisley a superstar?

By Paul Kingsbury
From *The Journal of Country Music*

December 16, 2000

For a new artist, Brad Paisley proved to be surprisingly comfortable and at home in several appearances at the Grand Ole Opry in 1999 and 2000. But on this night he was caught completely off guard, and his composure was put to the test. He had been planning to cut a live track onstage that night for his second album, the follow-up to Who Needs Pictures, *an auspicious, platinum-selling debut that set Music Row abuzz. His producer, Frank Rogers, was there; Paisley had rehearsed; everything was set to go. Then Little Jimmy Dickens and Jeannie Seely came out in matching Mr. and Mrs. Claus suits along with fellow Opry star Bill Anderson to ask Paisley if he would join the Opry, a dream come true for the young traditionalist. And he just lost it.*

"He's in tears, he's a bag of nerves," recalls Rogers, "and he walks off-stage, and I look at him and I go, 'Brad, we're getting ready to cut the gospel song for your record. I know you're emotional, but you've got to pull it together.' And he looked at me, and he goes, 'I'll be on.' And he just had his game face on, and he went back out there during the next show thirty minutes later and absolutely nailed it. We did not touch a word. We did not do anything. That's him singing."

Paul Kingsbury

September 28, 2004

It was a mild fall evening in Nashville, and the occasion was the usual Nashville music-biz party to mark the passing of a commercial milestone, the sort of networking-and-nosh fest that happens several times a month across Music Row to mark #1s, platinum albums, and other such commercial benchmarks. In this case, the party was held on the stage of the Ryman Auditorium, the historic home of the Grand Ole Opry and venerated hall for lovers of traditional country music. It was an altogether fitting place to acknowledge the sales accomplishments of a young singer-songwriter who has been hailed by revered elder statesmen like George Jones, Bill Anderson, and Buck Owens as one of the bright lights for traditional music in the next generation. As he received accolades from his record label, Grand Ole Opry officials, and others, Brad Paisley was his usual relaxed and quippy self.

"This is not something you do by yourself," the then-thirty-one-year-old West Virginian told the crowd of music industry press and well wishers. "You don't ever sell five million albums all on your own. It'd be nice." A beat. "You'd make a lot more." Big laugh. "But you can't do that."

A few minutes later, he added: "This is a surprise to me. I didn't know we'd sold five million albums. It's an amazing thing to . . . uh . . . to retire this early." Another big laugh.

Kidding aside, five million copies sold over three album releases is a significant accomplishment for any recording artist. It's only one of a string of early achievements in Paisley's charmed five-year recording career. In addition to his three platinum albums, he's racked up consistent country award nominations, five CMA awards and one ACM trophy, six Top Five country hits, and four #1 singles. In 2001, when he was officially inducted, he became the youngest current member of the Grand Ole Opry cast.

The question is: Is that enough?

Fifty years ago, becoming a member of the Grand Ole Opry would have clinched one's career in country music. Twenty-five years ago, selling five million albums would have put one right up there with Waylon Jennings and Willie Nelson as a country superstar. In the country music world of 2004, the post-Garth era, however, a platinum album makes you an up and comer, to be sure, but it doesn't put you in the ranks of country superstardom. And becoming a member of the Grand Ole Opry? Depending on what you do with it, it can mean about the same thing as getting a star on the Hollywood Walk of

The Celebrity Two-Step

Fame, or it can be a pleasant way to connect with fans away from all the hoopla of modern celebrity. Either way, though, it doesn't even begin to match the exposure one gets from three minutes with Jay on *The Tonight Show*.

The career of a country music artist of the 21st century is a constant tug-of-war between these two poles of art and artifice, music and star-maker machinery. Brad Paisley tends to downplay his career ambitions ("People have asked, 'Was it your goal to sell five million albums when you started?' No, I just wanted to sell a million albums. *That's* the thing you think about. You'd like to go platinum") because it's just good country manners to be modest about your ambitions. But he's fully aware of Music Row's expectations for someone who's scored three platinum albums out of the gate, as the humorous video (put together by Paisley and his label) that opened the multi-platinum party made plain. The singer was shown sitting at a conference table with a group of local journalists in what seemed to be a high-level media strategy session. "What will it take to boost Brad to the next level?" someone asks. "Steal a horse from a cop!" someone offers. "Dangle Little Jimmy Dickens off a hotel balcony!" another suggests. "Maybe I'm crazy, but why don't we just put out the best album we possibly can?" asks an exasperated Paisley. "That'll never work," someone quickly replies.

At this point the video jump cuts back into a dizzying montage of Paisley's numerous TV appearances and hit-music videos of the past couple of years. Though Paisley makes light of it, that's the crux right there. More TV? Better records? What does Brad Paisley have to do to become the country superstar that everyone has been expecting? What does any talented country artist have to do these days?

The first time I saw Brad Paisley perform it never occurred to me that I was looking at a future platinum-selling artist.

It was the spring of 1999. His first album, *Who Needs Pictures*, was on the verge of being released, and he was doing an acoustic showcase for press at the RCA Label Group offices in Nashville. His debut single, the album's title track, had not knocked me out. To me, it seemed a sappy rather than poignant tale of jilted lover plagued by a photographic memory. I went to the newcomer's showcase because there seemed to be a buzz going around about this guy. The word was that he was more than the standard chiseled pecs, cowboy hat, and voice.

69

Paul Kingsbury

The word apparently was out in force. Paisley drew a full house that day. The label's offices are located on Music Row in a former convent, and the showcase room—the former chapel—was full of journalists hobnobbing and munching free food. After an introduction by Arista Records general manager Mike Dungan, the unassuming twenty-six-year-old came out in clean blue jeans and a pressed shirt. He looked like the squeaky-clean recent graduate of a small Christian college, which he was. He sat down on a stool and began to play his acoustic guitar.

I don't remember all the details of that day the way Paisley or Dungan might. They had something at stake; I didn't. I figured I was just watching one more in the endless parade of singers who work their way through Nashville. So I wasn't expecting much. But Paisley was good, very good. He was poised and sang confidently. Two things stood out. First, his guitar playing was commanding enough to earn him the lead guitarist job in any number of country bands. Second, the songwriting was a cut above the usual Music Row standard, and it was made clear that Paisley wrote or co-wrote all of the songs he played that day.

Paisley definitely had talent. But I felt there was something lacking. He had poise, but he didn't have charisma. And though he sang pleasantly and even with conviction at times, I didn't feel those songs. As I left the showcase that day, I remember telling another journalist I thought Paisley should stick to writing and let George Strait or Alan Jackson sing his songs. He'd do fine, I thought.

Of course, I didn't know the half of it. It's part of Brad Paisley lore now that before that first album ever came out, his publishing company was already pitching a song he co-wrote with producer Frank Rogers. In a single day Alan Jackson, George Strait, and Garth Brooks all put holds on the song, indicating their interest in recording it. But Paisley withheld the song, intending it for his own second album. Bear in mind that the first one hadn't even been released and—given the vicissitudes of the record business—might never be released. That's confidence. The song was "I'm Gonna Miss Her (The Fishing Song)." It became his third #1 hit, and the video—complete with cameo roles played by ESPN sportscaster Dan Patrick, Jerry Springer, and Paisley's future wife, actress Kimberly Williams—won the 2002 CMA Award for Music Video of the Year.

Paisley's well-developed sense of humor has emerged repeatedly

The Celebrity Two-Step

on humorous music videos since and it is no accident, according to Allen Brown, his chief publicist as the RCA Label Group.

"He's a key driver in his videos. He comes up with the concepts, and his sense of humor comes through in all that. He tries to find the right celebrities to fill the roles, and somehow he figures out how to reach these people."

The head of Paisley's record company, RCA Label Group chairman Joe Galante, believes Paisley has a natural charisma that will play a key role as his career develops. "I think the picture of what becomes an Entertainer of the Year is taking place," says Galante. "He's a very funny guy. He's a very handsome guy. He's very self-effacing. That humility translates very well on the screen. I think that somebody will discover somewhere along the line that he's a potential host for an awards show. . . .

"Everything that's happening with him is natural. It's not forced, and I don't think there needs to be a rocket on his tail in order to get this thing done. The problem in country for many years has been things happen so quickly today for so many people, they're not really ready for it, and then they don't know how to hold on to it. And I think Brad's on a natural path to just keep climbing this way."

Music videos and television exposure in general are crucial to this climb. Some time in the eighties or the nineties, country music got caught up in the cult of the televised image that had been so much a part of pop music since Elvis Presley's TV breakthrough launched him to fame and fortune. No doubt the demise of old standby television outlets for country had something to do with the change: *Hee Haw* and The Nashville Network were venues where sincerity generally counted for more than glamour. Though CMT and GAC still exist primarily as an outlet for videos and *Behind the Music* -style documentaries, hard-core country music television outlets have dried up. Today, while the top echelon of country stars **is** still expected to act like a bunch of friends and neighbors, each member has got to look like a million bucks.

Why? The goal is national television exposure in order to sell records and build careers, and the competition is all of America's entertainers, if not the world's. A country artist who looks like Boxcar Willie or talks like Junior Samples has no chance to compete in the land of the TV makeover. Country music publicists fight tooth and nail to get their artists on hit talk shows like *Oprah* or *The Tonight Show*

71

Paul Kingsbury

with Jay Leno, which promise exposure to millions of potential record buyers. It goes without saying that every performance slot on the music award shows is coveted. To land these TV appearances consistently can be the difference between a gold album or platinum, or a platinum album and multi-platinum. For the record label, the stakes are potentially another $5 to $10 million in gross earnings per album title. For the artists, it's literally the success of their career on the line.

In this house of mirrors, Brad Paisley is better equipped than most of his country music peers. A child prodigy on guitar, he's been performing professionally since he was twelve, notably at WWVA's Jamboree USA, Wheeling's long-running counterpart to Nashville's Grand Ole Opry. He's a polished, but relaxed and spontaneous performer; he's comfortable with himself onstage. He also happens to be darkly handsome, trim and physically fit. Since March 2003, he's been married to Kimberly Williams, co-star of ABC-TV's sitcom *According to Jim*, on which Paisley has guest-starred. So he knows more than most country singers about television.

Publicist Allen Brown's job is to work in tandem with Paisley's power-house multimedia booking agents, William Morris & Co., to place their young recording artist on TV. "I think television is very important to bring a career to the next level," says Brown, "but so is maintaining the grassroots. More than anything TV is going to reinforce the image of the artist and create a face that to a lot of people is only something they've heard on the radio."

Talk shows of all kinds are the coveted TV venues. They reach wide audiences, and they allow singers to perform their latest hits and then chat amiably with the hosts. But those opportunities are not plentiful for country artists. "In the last couple of years, the slots that are available for music acts have shrunk," says Brown. "TV and film actors are gonna take priority, and then you also have book authors and other celebrities beyond music. In addition to the music slots having been reduced on those TV shows, realize then you may only have the opportunity of five or six country bookings in an entire year on some of these shows. So the chances are greater you won't get that TV exposure than you do get it. That's why it's a constant work situation."

Given the obstacles, then, Brad Paisley has done astonishingly well in getting his face all over television recently. Few country stars today have made as many different kinds of TV appearances across network and cable television. In 2003 and 2004, he appeared on TV

The Celebrity Two-Step

playing Ricky Nelson on NBC's *American Dreams*, serenading the happy reality-show couple on *Ryan & Trista's Wedding* (ABC), in concert slots for Memorial Day on PBS and at Ford's Theater in Washington on ABC, on widely syndicated daytime chats with Ellen DeGeneres and Sharon Osbourne and he made occasional appearances on his wife's ABC sitcom. He's also had plenty of coverage on CMT, swapping licks on *Crossroads* with popster John Mayer and being profiled by *Inside Fame*.

Paisley claims no interest in acting, but he's more than willing to make time for TV to advance his career: "Not that that's gonna mean that somebody's gonna buy my record," he told me, "but you never know. Everything we can do, I try to do."

Though Paisley puts in the required face time for television, many of his other choices suggest a thoughtful musician motivated by more than simple career advancement. When he signed his album deal with Arista Records, Paisley insisted that Frank Rogers, the Belmont University college pal who had produced his demo recordings, get the nod to be his producer, even though Rogers had never produced a commercially released record. Similarly, for his third album, *Mud on the Tires*, Paisley enlisted his road band to play most of the tracks rather than efficient, on-the-money studio session musicians who play on nearly every Music Row recording. He's also ended each of his three albums with a traditional gospel song and has included instrumental tracks for good measure—definitely not hit-single material. The standard Music Row formula for albums these days is no more than twelve tracks because the record label has to pay mechanical royalties to songwriters and publishers for each copyrighted song on the record. To get sixteen tracks on *Mud on the Tires*, Paisley was willing to forgo songwriting royalties on a couple of his songs.

Perhaps nowhere is Paisley's genuine commitment to music over fame more evident than in his relationship with the Grand Ole Opry, a program at the opposite end of the media spectrum from primetime television. Nearly eighty years old, it was once the most important show in country music. While it hasn't had the power to make careers since the 1960s, its storied history can still convey greatness by association. After being surprised with his Opry membership Christmas present in December 2000, Brad Paisley proudly wore Buck Owens's yellow rhinestone jacket from Buck's *Live at Carnegie Hall* album the night the youngster was officially inducted into the Opry cast,

73

Paul Kingsbury

February 17, 2001. And unlike many current recording artists who have been inducted into the cast, Paisley has taken his membership as a serious commitment, having made 107 appearances between May 1999 and September 2004—close to twice a month. Few platinum-level country singers today appear twice a year at the Opry.

"We look back on our decision to bring Brad into the Opry with a great deal of pride," says Opry manager Pete Fisher. "From the outset he made his management and agents aware that if he was ever available, he wanted to play the Opry. And he's lived up to those words. He makes a tremendous amount of sacrifices to live up to his commitment to the Opry. Many people would expect Brad to spend a little downtime at home when he's off the road and in Nashville. But Brad's just one of those people: He makes his decisions based on principles. It's so easy to focus on and get caught up in short-term pressures, but the artists who endure, it seems to me, are the ones who stand by their principles."

For his part, Paisley doesn't see the smaller paycheck from the Opry—a few hundred dollars in union-scale wages as opposed to tens of thousands for a road gig—as any sacrifice. "I just love it," says Paisley. "I love that feeling of going out there. And the response I get when I walk on that stage is phenomenal, and it's because I think everybody that's there realizes that I love that place. And it's just like what Minnie Pearl said when she said, 'Love them, and they'll love you back.' The audience when they're in that building is the Opry. They're part of the Opry as well.

"It's all about people that probably trekked a long way to get there. Most of them aren't from Nashville, that's for sure, that are sitting in that audience. They have waited, some of them their entire lives to get to see that show. And with that comes a whole different response from an audience.

"The Opry is not about pyrotechnics. It's not about cheerleading, it's not about going out there and putting on a show that makes up for your music, ever. Where so many times out on the road I can feel like that's what I'm doing every now and then. You get that feeling in some of these venues when they're not the right place, when it's not the right venue for country music or for what I do, you get this feeling that I'm apologizing for my music sometimes. Every performer's got those kind of gigs. The Opry is never that way. It's all about walking out there and playing your song and then seeing what they think of it."

The Celebrity Two-Step

In May of 2003, I had the opportunity to drop in on an evening session for Paisley's third album, *Mud on the Tires*—the much-anticipated follow-up to his first two platinum releases and the hit single "Celebrity." Paisley, guitarist Redd Volkaert, engineer Neal Cappellino, and producer Frank Rogers were working that evening in a small overdub studio in west Nashville, laboring on an instrumental—one of two instrumentals slated for the album, which is just about two instrumentals more than were on the last Shania Twain/Faith Hill/Alan Jackson/Kenny Chesney/You-Name-It album. At the time of my visit, the album was due to be mastered in just nineteen days. His record label had lined up everything in expectation of a late July rollout. To get a big sales jump, timing was crucial and the pressure was on.

So what was Paisley doing on a rain-drenched Monday night when he had already lost three or four hours of precious recording time due to a power outage from severe thunderstorms? Noodling around on the guitar, laughing and trading off increasingly bizarre licks with Volkaert.

Spending precious time working on a second instrumental is precisely the kind of thing that hard-core country music fans appreciate about Brad Paisley. While most singers would be obsessing about their vocal takes, Paisley seems to want nothing more in life than to lay down more cool guitar tracks with Redd. Paisley explained that they were calling the instrumental "Spaghetti Western Swing." Given its galloping, *Bonanza*-type tempo and Speedy West & Jimmy Bryant-go-to-outer-space guitar pyrotechnics, the title sounded about right.

Paisley was seated in the center of the room in front of the mixing console, facing Redd. With his Quaker-style reddish beard, blue short-billed cap, little gold hoop earring in his left ear, and husky, tattooed forearms (the one on the left arm is a parrot), Redd called to mind a nineteenth-century sea captain. Though he may have looked like a sailor, the former guitarist for Merle Haggard picks like an A-Team session ace. Maybe better. It turned out Paisley flew Volkaert, whom he's known for a year or so, up from Austin for the session.

Asked after the session if his young friend could cut it as a studio musician in Nashville if ever he had to fall back on his guitar playing, Volkaert responded with a single word: *easily.*

"He's such a great player," Volkaert continued. "To me it's inspiring to see a guy who's that young who's also that eat-up with a guitar.

Paul Kingsbury

I think it's wonderful. Plus, he's doing great as a commercial success. It's wonderful that he's doing that as well as still being a guitar geek, you know?"

Paisley's guitar prowess has become common knowledge on Music Row, since he played all the lead guitar parts on his albums and hit singles. A lightning-fast picker, he's mastered all the pulls, bends, and pops that define the classic country guitar sound, and he's not shy about throwing in clusters of notes that whiz by like a hailstorm of electrified Earl Scruggs banjo licks.

As Paisley and Volkaert swapped little bits of conversation and guitar solos, it became apparent that both of these guys can play pretty much anything that occurs to them. For instance, in between takes, one moment Paisley was doing a quick finger-pick of "Greensleeves" while joking about a killer Mexican guitarist that he and Rogers encountered; the next moment he was falling into the instantly recognizable opening chords and lead lines of Eric Clapton's album-rock standard "Layla." Instantaneously, Volkaert joined him, chipping in perfect harmony lines, playing Duane Allman to Brad's Clapton. They didn't say a word about it, just busted out laughing at how beautifully and spontaneously they stumbled into it. And then they were back to working on the instrumental. Later on, they wordlessly traded riffs on yet another FM-rock staple, the Allman Brothers' "Jessica," laughing as they embroidered the original. The mood throughout the session was loose, spontaneous, and light-hearted. You'd never have known there was a deadline approaching.

Afterwards, Paisley played me a few of the cuts in their rough form, including a shuffle in the classic Ray Price, fiddle-and-steel mold called "Hold Me in Your Arms (and Let Me Fall)" and a moody lovelorn ballad, "Somebody Knows You Now." I told him how much I liked the shuffle. "Yeah I love shuffles," Paisley said. "I think lots of people like shuffles actually. It's just hard to get them on the radio." The ballad, though, was really atmospheric and different for him. I asked if he wrote it. "Yeah, I did." I told him I was impressed. At that, he pretended to swell up with pride like Barney Fife and said in a put-on self-important tone: "Thank you. Thank you. Well, you know, I do this sort of thing all the time. You just take a little old piece of paper, do some thinkin', and there you have it."

I asked him what he was aiming for with this album. With his previous album, *Part II*, he had said he was trying to go farther and deep-

The Celebrity Two-Step

er. "I'm just trying to make an album this time that touches some bases I haven't touched yet, more than anything. And yet doesn't stray too far from what people would expect from me. But I still think there's some things on it that might get people thinking, 'Huh, OK, I didn't know he could do that.'

"I think the main thing is just trying to solidify and grow a fan base. I just like cutting records and trying to see who we can convert. There's nothing I like better than looking online and seeing a comment on a message board from somebody who says, 'I never liked his music until this latest song.'

"You're trying to win as many people over as you can—and balance that with making records you love to make. It's like with that shuffle I played you. I'm pretty sure that's not gonna be a single. But it doesn't mean you don't cut it. Because you know what? It might. And secondly, I want to sing that. I want to do it in my shows. I know that shuffle would be a fun one to do because at soundchecks we're out there playing Johnny Paycheck songs. And I don't even sing at my soundchecks; I let my bass player sing. I just play guitar."

That's Paisley for you. Just when I start to think that he's really calculating, weighing demographics and career moves, he turns the corner and reminds you that at heart he genuinely loves country music.

Still, I asked him about breaking through to the next level of recognition and success, and what it would take. Was he just one big hit song away? His answer was dead serious. "I'm probably two songs away from it. I need just a couple songs in a row that would make people take a little more notice, maybe. May never get 'em. Doesn't matter."

We talked about country music and the long, distinguished careers it's supported: Buck Owens, Kitty Wells, George Jones. I asked him to consider his long-term prospects. "I'd like to do this for a while. But if I can't, then I'll just write songs and play guitar on sessions and whatever people have for me." Then he lightened up and chuckled: "And you know, go to the mailbox." To pick up the inevitable royalty checks that should roll in for a long time to come.

Later he added: "I only write because I picked up a guitar. I only sing because I write. It all leads back to that first guitar in one way or another. And still the most important and the most fun thing that I do is play the guitar on a nightly basis. My sound man jokes that I only sing to get to the next solo. And that sometimes is the case."

Paul Kingsbury

That evening I also spoke with Paisley's record producer, Frank Rogers, who talked a little bit about the game plan he and Paisley had from the beginning. "We kind of a had a three-album plan when we went and got his record deal," said Rogers. "But now that records are taking so long to make, by the time we got to this one, a lot of the songs we had written for the third record were written eight years ago, and Brad's a different artist now. And so it just wasn't as relevant. There are a few things that he's writing now that he wasn't writing back when those records were written. And I think his guitar playing has gotten a little more adventuresome, and we've tried not to hold that back. So I think it's a good natural progression."

What did Rogers think made his friend stand out from the crowd of country artists? "I think it starts with the songwriting. I just think he is truly one of the gifted songwriters out there. Some people struggle at it, and some people have the gift. And he is just a natural writer. His guitar playing is—he's an 'A' session player if he wants to be. I mean, he's that good. I think because he's a great songwriter and a great guitar player, and because his singing style is understated—he doesn't over-sing anything—I think his singing has been overlooked a little bit."

Given Paisley's natural talents, then, what does it take to become a household name? "If I had that answer, I'd be running a record label," Rogers said with a laugh. "I'd like to think it's just consistently doing great songs that are based around what he is but songs that are also unique. It's not doing the same old song. What took George Strait from being just a country singer to being a household name? I don't know. Somewhere between the eighth and the fourteenth record he had consistently great songs and everybody just knew who he was. And then he went to the next level with [the movie] *Pure Country*."

Strait never had any crossover pop hits, did he?

"Nor did Alan Jackson," Rogers replied. "Yes, 'Chattahoochee' was a plateau, and then he had three or four really great records, and there were great songs in there. And then he had 'Where Were You (When the World Stopped Turning).' I think it's consistent great songs that keep him out there that people like, that bring people to his shows. And then every once in a while you'll have that great song that kind of kicks it to the next level."

Released in July 2003, *Mud on the Tires* topped the *Billboard* country album chart two weeks running that August. A year later it was certified platinum. The singles "Celebrity," "Little Moments," and "Whiskey Lullaby," his duet with Alison Krauss, all were Top 5 country hits, with "Lullaby" hitting the coveted #1 spot. Paisley wrote or co-wrote half the album's tracks, and he plays adventurous, fresh-sounding guitar throughout. To my ears, *Mud on the Tires* is clearly Paisley's best album and a substantial artistic leap forward. But it has not yielded the breakthrough single—that one great song—that galvanizes media attention and lifts an album into the multi-platinum stratosphere. (As the *Journal* went to press, "Whiskey Lullaby" won CMA awards for musical event and music video. This was well-deserved recognition certainly, but nevertheless it does not look like the mournful tale of double suicide will be that career-changing song.)

April 24, 2004

Brad Paisley puts on a good concert. I saw him headline a show at the Gaylord Entertainment Center in April 2004, one that was not necessarily his audience. The show was the grand finale to the day's Country Music Marathon race, and it was filled with race participants, many of whom were 1) exhausted and 2) not committed country music fans, let alone Brad Paisley fans.

The crowd mix apparently didn't faze Paisley, who has grown a lot since his first showcase in 1999. He roamed the stage like a seasoned pro, setting up songs effortlessly, it seemed, with relaxed, humorous little stories. His repertoire consisted mostly of the hits from his albums, but he had a few surprises mixed in. He touched on classic rock with strong covers of Dire Strait's "Walk of Life" (a nod to the day's event) and ZZ Top's "Sharp Dressed Man," which he had recorded in 2002 for a country tribute album to the Texas boogie trio. But he balanced the rock quotient by playing his hits "Celebrity" and "I'm Gonna Miss Her" accompanied onstage by Grand Ole Opry pal Little Jimmy Dickens, who seemed proud as a bantam rooster to be backing up Brad while wearing a killer black rhinestone suit and a jumbo guitar that emphasized his diminutive stature.

Throughout the show Paisley appeared fully in control, and the crowd seemed thoroughly entertained. He had stage presence and radiated an appealing low-key charisma. But he seemed most in his element at a moment in the middle of the show, performing his first #1 hit, "He Didn't Have to Be." He sang the song about the love of a stepson for his devoted step-dad with the conviction and care that good country music demands. Then taking off on his electric guitar, he added a new wrinkle to the radio hit, weaving a long,

Paul Kingsbury

majestic, carefully paced solo that first echoed the mood of the song and then deepened it as the coda built in emotion. Shimmering with fused elements of country, rock, and jazz, it seemed like a cry from Paisley's own heart. And with his eyes closed, for a few moments, it was not about hits or ratings or the star-maker machinery behind the popular song. It was about the music, and Brad Paisley seemed transported, doing the thing he loves most in the world.

THE GHOSTLY ONES
How Gillian Welch and David Rawlings rediscovered country music

by Alec Wilkinson
From *The New Yorker*

David Rawlings told me Gillian Welch's life story. She had grown tired of telling it herself. Welch is a singer and songwriter whose music is not easily classified—it is at once innovative and obliquely reminiscent of past rural forms—and Rawlings is her partner. Welch describes them as "a two-piece band called Gillian Welch." I had asked her to talk about her past, and she demurred. Then she said, "Why don't you tell it, Dave?" We were in Asheville, North Carolina; Welch and Rawlings were making a brief tour from Nashville, where they live. They were expected before long on the stage and had things to do to prepare, so I had to wait.

The next day, the three of us were in a car heading east to Carrboro, North Carolina, near Chapel Hill, where Welch and Rawlings had their next engagement. Rawlings was driving. Welch was lying on the back seat, with a blanket over her. It was early in the afternoon, and we were leaving the highway for a restaurant where they knew they could still order breakfast. Welch and Rawlings are nocturnal. A few years ago, they lived in a house that planes flew over. Whenever they tried to record themselves, the microphones picked up the planes. The planes stopped shortly after midnight and started again at six in the morning. The hours of quiet in the middle of the night were the ones they became accustomed to working in. They would take breaks and walk around the neighborhood at two and three in the morning, the only figures abroad. They developed the impression that Nashville was a peaceful city, free of traffic, a paradise, where

Alec Wilkinson

music they loved had been made by people who now were dead but were completely alive whenever they sang on records.

At the restaurant—it was a Denny's—Welch asked for tea. "I don't need a tea bag, though," she said. The waitress regarded her steadily. A moment later, she placed a cup of hot water on the table, and Welch drew a tea bag on a string from her pocket. I thought it was too soon to ask again about her childhood, so I asked Rawlings about his. He grew up in Slatersville, Rhode Island, he said, a former mill town with a river. The mills were textile mills, built on the riverbanks, and they had been allowed to become dilapidated. Rawlings spent a lot of his childhood walking through them. At a friend's suggestion, he began playing guitar in 1985, when he was fifteen. "He was going to ask his parents for a harmonica for Christmas, and he wanted me to ask mine for a guitar," Rawlings said. "That way, we could learn to play and perform at the school talent show, in May." Rawlings pursued a kid who was known as a guitar player for help, and then the boy's father, who had taught guitar. Rawlings noticed that playing guitar "was something I was immediately passable at, or maybe even good at. Which wasn't the case with things such as basketball, which I tried really, really hard at, but it wasn't going to happen. Music, because it was math-based, and I was good at math, I wasn't intimidated." He and his friend learned "Heart of Gold," by Neil Young. They came in second at the talent show, and the next year they won.

Welch excused herself to visit the bathroom. When she came back, she said, "We've been here before."

Rawlings said, "Really?"

"This is the Denny's where they had the film crew," she said.

"The photographer who took the pictures for our third record, Mark Seliger, brought with him a friend who had film equipment," Rawlings said.

"In case we wanted to make a video," Welch said, sipping her tea.

"They came with a 16mm black-and-white camera, and they filmed us at a club."

"Then we drove to Knoxville for a gig, and we stopped here for some food and shot a little film," she said. "They called the cops—state troopers—and they kicked us out."

Rawlings nodded.

"When I got up to go to the bathroom, I realized it's the same place," Welch said.

The Ghostly Ones

We paid the check, and when we got back in the car Rawlings seemed pensive. He tends to brood, and there is an obscurely mournful cast to his thinking. He drove slowly across the parking lot. "The problem with talking about the past is it becomes disturbing," he said finally. "You start thinking of a thousand anecdotes, and your life merely as a collection thereof."

Welch is tall and slender. She has a long, narrow face, high cheekbones, wide-set eyes, a sharp chin, and a toothy smile. She is thirty-six. Her skin is pale, and her hair is fine and reddish-brown. Her carriage is upright, and her movements are unhurried and graceful—her shoulders swing slightly as she walks. She collects hymnals, and handmade shoeshine kits, the kind from which people once made a living on the street. She is inclined toward practicality. As a child, she played the piano and the drums but gave them up because she didn't like being confined to whatever room the instruments were in. Onstage, during instrumental passages, she bends her head over her guitar, like a figure in a religious painting, and plays with a ruthless rhythmic precision. There is a sense of self-possession about her that seems more a matter of temperament than influence. Welch is adopted. Her mother, Mitzie, who is a singer, says she is surprised that Welch became a performer, because performers, in her experience, always have a need to please, and her daughter doesn't seem to.

Rawlings is tall and lanky. He has an oval face, a high forehead, dark hair, a long nose, and dark eyes. His hands are delicate. His manner in conversation varies between an austerity which gives him the air of a Pilgrim and a discursiveness in which he never seems satisfied with something he has said—any observation can always be delivered more emphatically or seen from another point of view or elaborated or clarified or even made more concisely. Because his mind is capacious and lively, his talk is nearly always diverting, but he wishes he were less garrulous. He says almost nothing onstage. He plays with his eyes closed and an impassive expression on his face. He stands on his toes and sways, all of which helps cultivate what Welch affectionately describes as "the Dave Rawlings mystique." One day after Rawlings and I had spent the afternoon listening to tapes of bands he had played in and of Welch's earlier work, and I had filled pages in my notebook with his remarks, he slumped in his chair. "I talk so much," he said ruefully. "I am more as I'd like to be when I'm very sick."

Welch and Rawlings's music is deceptively complex, despite its

83

Alec Wilkinson

simple components: two voices, two guitars, and four hands. The broadest category into which it comfortably fits is country music. In the Country Music Hall of Fame, in Nashville, a video of Welch and Rawlings performing is shown with other videos that are intended to convey the breadth of modern country music. Welch and Rawlings are portrayed as defenders of a faith—old-time string musicians—practitioners of a lapsed form. They initially found a model for their enthusiasms in records made in the thirties and forties by musicians such as Bill and Earl Bolick, who performed as the Blue Sky Boys. Vocal duets unaccompanied by other musicians were eclipsed in the forties by the more forceful sound of bluegrass—the Blue Sky Boys broke up in 1951—leaving duets as one of the few forms of American music not yet completely covered with footprints. The music Welch and Rawlings play contains pronounced elements of old-time music, string-band music, bluegrass, and early country music, but Welch and Rawlings diverge from historical models by playing songs that are meticulously arranged and that include influences from rhythm and blues, rockabilly, rock and roll, gospel, folk, jazz, punk, and grunge. Furthermore, Welch prefers tempos that are languid. A typical Welch song has the tempo of a slow heartbeat.

Welch's narratives tend to be accounts of resignation, misfortune, or torment. Her characters include itinerant laborers, solitary wanderers, misfits, poor people plagued at every turn by trouble, repentant figures, outlaws, criminals, soldiers, a moonshiner, a farm girl, a reckless beauty queen, a love-wrecked woman, a drug addict, and a child. Her imagination is sympathetic to outcasts who appeal for help to God despite knowing from experience that there isn't likely to be any. Their theology is ardent and literal. They are given to picturing themselves meeting their families in Heaven, where mysteries too deep to comprehend will finally be explained. "Until we've all gone to Jesus / We can only wonder why," she sings in "Annabelle," a song about a sharecropper who hopes to give his daughter more than he had but who delivers her to the cemetery instead. A number of Welch's songs are written from the point of view of male characters. "My Morphine," the drowsy, intoxicated lament of a man whose addiction is souring, is the only song I am aware of about a narcotic which creates the sensation of having taken the narcotic. She is accomplished at compressing dramatic events into a few verses and a chorus. In "Caleb Meyer," a man appears, transgresses, dies, and is revived as a spectre

The Ghostly Ones

in the imagination of the woman who slit his throat in self-defense. Welch admires the troubadour songwriters Chuck Berry, Bob Dylan, and Hank Williams, and she writes good car songs. The first song she made big money from was "455 Rocket," which was a hit for Kathy Mattea in 1997, and is about a hot rod. More and more, Welch's songs describe her actual life. "No One Knows My Name" is about her birth parents. "My mother was just a girl seventeen," she sings, "and my dad was passing through, doing things a man will do." Her mother was a college student in New York, and her father was a musician. By the time she was delivered, her adoption had been arranged.

Welch was born in New York in 1967. Ken and Mitzie Welch already had a daughter, Julie, who'd been born in 1961. She and Welch are close; she lives in California, is a graphic designer, and also teaches improvisational comedy. Julie's birth had been difficult, and Mitzie wasn't eager to go through another pregnancy. According to Welch, when they approached adoption agencies "the agencies said no dice because they were entertainers." Ken Welch had been a performer since childhood, in Kansas City. He had begun piano lessons at four, but the teacher soon told his parents that she couldn't do more with him until his hands were large enough to span an octave. "I couldn't reach an octave on a piano, but I could on an accordion," he says. By the time he was seven, he was tap dancing and playing the accordion throughout "Missouri, Kansas, and Iowa, the remains of the old RKO circuit," he says. Eventually, he attended Carnegie Tech, now Carnegie Mellon, in Pittsburgh, where he studied painting. He met Mitzie at an audition. They moved to New York separately. She sold handbags at a store on Broadway, and made twenty-five dollars on Sundays singing in the choir at Norman Vincent Peale's church. She auditioned for Benny Goodman and got the job, but she had only a few weeks in which to learn Goodman's repertoire. She ended up writing lyrics on the palms of her hands and on her fingernails.

As the comedy team "Ken and Mitzie Welch," they appeared in clubs where Lenny Bruce also performed. Bob Newhart was once their opening act. They had their most public success on *The Tonight Show*, when Jack Paar was the host. They performed a slowed-down version of "I Got Rhythm." Mitzie faced the audience and sang, and Ken stood with his back against hers, playing the accordion. By the time the Welches adopted Gillian, with the help of their doctor, Ken was writing music for television shows, and Mitzie was working in

Alec Wilkinson

commercials and on Broadway.

When Welch was three, her parents moved to Los Angeles, to write music for *The Carol Burnett Show*. As a little girl, Welch came home from school one day weeping because she had been reprimand-ed in art class for making a black outline around snow in a painting. This led her parents to enroll her in a school called Westland. At Westland, the students gathered every week to sing folk songs and Carter Family songs, with Welch accompanying them on guitar. "On the tapes from the period, she sounds the same as she does now, except that her voice is higher," Rawlings said.

Welch's parents bought songbooks for her, and, sitting by herself in her room, playing guitar, she made her way through them. When she got to the end, she wrote songs of her own, "about ducks and things," Rawlings said. "Like a kid who writes poems, and they go in a drawer." Welch attended a high school called Crossroads, "where I get way into ceramics and art and stay hours after school building things and they let me," she said. "And I run like crazy—cross-coun-try and track." Welch made the all-state team for the mile and was invited to run in the national trials. "But if I'd gone I'd have got my ass kicked," she said. "They were in Texas, and I didn't do well in hot weather. Really, my sport was cross-country. I discovered that the longer the race, the more I moved up in the field. I don't run that fast—I just go, very rhythmic. I'm endurance."

Welch said that her favorite English teacher had gone to Princeton, so she applied, without telling him. But when he heard that she'd been accepted he told her that she wouldn't be happy there, and she went to the University of California at Santa Cruz instead.

Welch and Rawlings appear often on the Grand Ole Opry. They also perform in clubs in the United States and abroad, where their audiences tend to consist of between a thousand and two thousand people. They play very quietly. Welch sang so much by herself in her room that she never learned to sing above the sound of other musi-cians. Audiences at even the beeriest clubs attend them closely, as if they were at the theatre. Her voice resonates more in her head than in her chest. Its range is not wide—it is more an alto than a soprano—and it has a mournful, vernacular, almost factual quality, as if she were a witness to the scene she is describing. She conveys emotion through dynamics, not vibrato, and by a self-effacing absorption with the nar-rative. What ornamentation she employs comes mainly from bluegrass and brother-team singing—the pounce on certain syllables, the dying falls, the trills, the quick fades and returns, the small tear—though she manages, partly by the solemnity of her bearing, to give the impression of singing without artifice, which in itself is dramatic.

At Carrboro, Welch and Rawlings played in a club called Cat's Cradle. As on many nights of the tour, they shared the bill with the Old Crow Medicine Show, a charismatic, punked-up string band from Nashville. Rawlings sometimes plays with Old Crow. When he does, he is occasionally introduced as Butch Hobson. All of them shared a small dressing room. On the door, in permanent marker, was written, "I Hate This Part of Texas." Welch changed into a full skirt and a sleeveless velvet top. Then she sat on the edge of a small armchair and folded her skirt demurely between her knees and Ketch Secor, the fiddle player from Old Crow, brought out a shoeshine kit and polished her cowboy boots. "It's what the opening act does," he said, "shine the headliner's shoes."

Narrow stairs led to a sitting room in the wings above the stage. Morgan Jahnig, the bass player for Old Crow, came down the stairs and said, politely, "Does the name Jerzy Kosinski mean anything to anyone? It just came into my head."

Welch gathered her skirt and climbed the stairs and sat in a chair. On the pages of a small, lined notebook, she printed a set list in block letters. I went out into the club to listen to Old Crow. From the far corner of the floor, as if through a window, I could see Welch upstairs, seated in front of a mirror, brushing her hair, then turning her head from side to side until it fell to her liking.

Rawlings's account of Welch's past began shortly after we left Denny's. Welch had settled herself on the back seat and said, "I'm still waiting to hear the Gillian Welch story, by David Rawlings." We had arrived at her departure for Santa Cruz when Rawlings paused, as if he had something delicate to impart. "At this point, her family," he said, "they've kept her on a pretty tight leash."

"No boyfriends," Welch said.

"She goes to U.C. Santa Cruz, and when do you start playing in bands?"

"Soon as I get there," Welch said. "The first one was called Penny Dreadful, a Goth band, because that's what my friends were playing. I was very pale, and my hair was very blond from being from California and in the sun all the time. I'm on a bass I borrowed. It doesn't last

Alec Wilkinson

very long. I was not a real creative force in that band."

"At college, though, things deteriorate pretty quickly," Rawlings said thoughtfully. He paused again. "I don't know, Gill," he said, looking opaquely out the windshield at the road. "How accurate do you want this to be?"

"Accurate," she said.

"O.K.," Rawlings said. "So Gill's getting drunk and taking drugs all the time."

"I immediately spin out," Welch said.

"After a very cloistered life," he said.

"I hadn't been a very social person in high school," she said. "I kept to myself. I had friends, but college is so different. You arrive and whatever you want to be you are. The question is, who do you want to be?"

"There are other bands," Rawlings said, as if to return Welch's attention to the story.

"I was the drummer in a psychedelic surf band, Thirteenth-Floor something or other," Welch said. "I don't think we had a singer. We probably had only a handful of gigs, and most of them were house parties. I was always extremely high on acid, and I wouldn't realize that the song had ended, so there were a lot of drum solos."

Welch took classes in art and ceramics and became interested in photography. She moved into a house whose other tenants were members of a bluegrass band that played at a pizza parlor, and she went to all their gigs. "When I discovered bluegrass music, it was like an electric shock that it meant so much to me," Welch said. "I hadn't heard people playing the music I had sung as a kid, and it made me think, I know these songs, and I sound good singing them. I realized this was possible."

"Do you start performing?" I asked.

"A couple of gigs, and they scare me to death."

"And how are they received?"

"Well, I don't think I was singing very loud, and there was no mike," she said. "I sort of go and play them, but everything about how I look says, 'Pay no attention to me.' "

When Welch and Rawlings sing together, their voices fit so tightly that they seem welded. One of their newer songs—it doesn't yet have a title—is almost hypnotically slow and includes several passages sung in unison. Welch says that sometimes she loses the sense of which voice is hers and which belongs to Rawlings.

The Ghostly Ones

Rawlings's ear for harmonic possibilities is impish. He does not always match Welch's phrasing. His line sometimes anticipates what Welch is singing, then meets hers and continues in another direction. He likes intervals that are closer than those commonly used. At certain moments of tension, their voices seem to be leaning against each other, like cards in a card house, which is a bluegrass effect.

Rawlings is a strikingly inventive guitarist. His solos often feature daring melodic leaps. He uses passing tones as signal elements of a solo rather than relying on them merely to bridge chord changes, and there is an obstinate, near-vagrant quality of chromatic drifting to his playing—of his proceeding with harmonic ideas at a different pace and perhaps even in a different direction from the song's changes. He uses double and triple stops and open strings for dramatic effect. Often, he leaves an open string ringing as a drone against which he plays a note that conflicts with the chord the drone refers to. He likes to go as far out on a limb as he can before figuring out how to get back. In Carrboro, he played a solo that seemed as if it were going to skid right off the pavement and recovered itself only at the very last moment. The crowd applauded the simple audacity, and a woman beside me, clearly familiar with his playing, began laughing and shaking her head. "Of course he ends it there," she said to her companion. "Why wouldn't he?" In the dressing room afterward, I asked Rawlings how he would describe his playing, and he said that he simply has a fondness for certain notes and he finds ways to play them. When I asked which notes they were, he shrugged and said, "The ghostly ones."

Rawlings plays a peculiar guitar. It is a 1935 Epiphone Olympic, with an arch top, and f-holes on the face, like a violin, and even when it was new it was a cheap guitar. He may be the only musician who has ever made it his principal instrument. The sound is so unusual that, once when Welch and Rawlings were appearing at a festival where the blind guitar player Doc Watson was also performing, Watson came up to Rawlings while he was warming up and said, "Son, what kind of instrument is that?" In 1997, Rawlings bought a Fender Esquire, an electric guitar, and wanted to use it, so he and Welch got a friend to play drums, and Welch played the electric bass and they began playing clubs as the Esquires. They never announced their performances, and not many people came. They played songs by Neil Young and the Rolling Stones, among others, and Rawlings sang most of them. The Esquires brought to their gigs a complete book of Dylan songs, and

89

Alec Wilkinson

once during each evening the audience was allowed to shout out a number. Welch and Rawlings picked one, then turned to the corresponding page in the Dylan book and played whatever song was on that page. Rawlings says that, for the most part, their playing was "a two on a scale of ten." They last played in 2002.

"The Esquires' big gig was New Year's, because no one would ever hire me and Dave to play New Year's," Welch said. "So we were always free."

The most compelling element of a Welch and Rawlings performance is their deep and, so far as I know, unexampled engagement with each other. Welch's mother and father once asked me if I had ever seen Welch and Rawlings rehearse. I said that I hadn't. "Whatever happens in the ear to people listening profoundly to each other is happening in an extreme fashion between them," he said.

"You know not to interrupt," she said.

"There's a kind of supersensitivity," he said.

"And respect," she said.

"It's like they're breathing together," he said. "They get lost in there."

"We were a little scared," she said.

Parked along the side of the highway here and there on the way to Carrboro were white school buses with "Inmate Transfer Bus" written in black letters beneath the windows, and around the buses were convicts in prison clothes picking up trash. "In the meantime, you're in another band," Rawlings said to Welch.

"Campy seventies covers, which is very funny to do, in my opinion," Welch said. "Late Elvis, Neil Diamond."

"The band's name is Sofa."

"And everyone in it has a persona," Welch said. "I was Oprah von Sofa. Hal, the drummer, worked at a Goodwill sorting station, so he had access to all this wild, psychedelic clothing that people were finally getting rid of. Plaid pants and vinyl belts. I wore my hair in pigtails. It spilled over into my real life. If you've got such great clothes, you don't just want to wear them onstage, and likewise the names. A lot of people just knew me as Oprah. It was very helpful to me to have a costume and an alter ego. In Sofa, I'm sometimes on bass and sometimes on guitar. The bluegrass band moved out of the house, and Sofa moved in. This is the band I actually start doing gigs with. We make a demo, we have posters, we're a slightly working band."

The Ghostly Ones

"Then the next thing, Gill's done with that life, and she's going to live in Wales," Rawlings said.

"The earthquake hit in '89," Welch said. "I was up on campus when it happened, and as I made my way home things got stranger and stranger. People were trapped in their houses, because the roofs had collapsed, chimneys had fallen, cars were smashed under trees, and water mains had broken. They stood on their lawns with their radios on, so you could hear more than one as you passed. By the time I reached home, I was completely shaken up. My bedroom wall was like a spiderweb. In the days after, people couldn't sleep. My best friend, who lived in San Francisco, said, 'You should get out.' We arranged to house-sit for a woman in Wales. We were maybe going to travel around and take pictures."

"But it's a little quiet," Rawlings said.

"We were very out of place," Welch said. "After a couple of months, we got a little bored, then we realized that we had the use of this woman's car. This whole thing ends up in Amsterdam."

"And then there's a conference with her parents, who have long sensed that things are going to need attention," Rawlings said.

"They ask me what do I want to do, and I say, 'I want to do music.'"

"And they say, 'If you're going to play music you're going to have to go to school for it.' "

"Which is funny, because they didn't."

In 1990, a friend of Welch's parents wrote a recommendation for her to the Berklee College of Music, in Boston.

"Her parents make the situation happen. But on the other hand it's in Boston, so they don't have that much control," Rawlings said.

"Just come back to the story," Welch said.

"All right. So Gill goes to Boston, and of course she's useless at Berklee."

"It's a jazz school."

"And she's a primitive."

"I felt like a Martian," she said. "I'm out of my peer group. I have no friends. I'm in my room listening to brother-team music."

"One of her teachers looks at the way she makes a C chord and says, 'If you keep doing that you'll be a cripple in a few years.' But she stays for two years and majors in songwriting, and the songwriting program is just starting to flower."

Alec Wilkinson

Welch and Rawlings began going out with each other at Berklee. They met in a hallway, while waiting to audition for the country-band class. At Berklee, Welch overcame her shyness about performing, she said, "because you had to. In every class, you had to do things in front of about twenty people."

When school was over, Welch said, "I looked at my record collection and saw that all the music I loved had been made in Nashville—Bill Monroe, Dylan, the Stanley Brothers, Neil Young—so I moved there. Not ever thinking I was thirty years too late." At the end of the summer, Rawlings moved to Nashville, too. In Boston, when they played together, they were always among other musicians. In the kitchen of Rawlings's apartment one night, they heard for the first time what they sounded like on their own. "We sang 'Long, Black Veil,' and we stopped," Welch said. "I think we were both a little startled by how natural a blend we were. If you don't sound good together, you can't make it better."

Welch decided that if she wanted a career as a songwriter she would have to make the weekly rounds of songwriters' nights at the clubs. Rawlings was working with other musicians, but he agreed to go with her. "Just sort of to accompany me because you have to sit there and wait, and it's not a good time," she said. When they began arranging her songs, they realized that, "instead of the Stanley Brothers or the Blue Sky Boys, or any of the brother acts we've listened to—lead singers and a tenor—we have a difference," Welch said. "We have a lead singer and a baritone singer." Because Welch was intent on establishing herself as a songwriter, and because their arrangement began informally, and Rawlings was playing with other people anyway, she says it didn't occur to them to name the duet; they performed simply as Gillian Welch.

Almost from the start, people tried to separate them. After about a year, Welch found a manager, Denise Stiff. "I must have had a hundred people say to me, 'Lose the guitar player,' " Stiff said. Rawlings draws too much attention from Welch, they said. Or, he plays twenty notes where ten will do. Or, with a band behind her she could be the next Alison Krauss. As it happened, Stiff represented Krauss, a bluegrass musician, and cared less about having a duplicate of her than she did about trying to discover what Welch and Rawlings required.

For a while, Welch made beds and cleaned bathrooms at a bed-and-breakfast. "That was a good job for me," she said. "You can't lis-

92

The Ghostly Ones

ten to the stereo, because you're moving from one room to another, and the vacuum is too loud; there's no entertainment, so you have to provide it. I would write. Plus, I had a forty-minute drive there and back, and I have always been able to write when I'm driving, if I'm by myself." She brought home tablecloths and napkins to iron. She and Rawlings lived in the same apartment building, and sometimes, if Rawlings needed money, he did some ironing, too.

In 1994, Welch signed a publishing deal, and then devoted herself to trying to get a record contract. Her publisher sent tapes of her and Rawlings to Jerry Moss, at Almo Sounds, in Los Angeles, and in 1995 Stiff and Welch went to L.A. to see him. Welch played for him in his office. Behind his desk, Moss began quietly singing harmony with her. When Stiff heard him, she thought, Those are David's parts. Jerry's heard them on the tapes, and if he's singing them he's missing them. She never again felt uncertain about Rawlings's role. Even so, once Welch and Rawlings were signed to a recording contract the question they heard most often was "Who are you going to get to play guitar on your record?"

One afternoon in Nashville, after the tour had been completed, Welch picked me up at my hotel. I had asked her if she would show me the clubs where she and Rawlings had played Writer's Nights. Welch had written down the names of all the clubs she remembered, and we drove back and forth—it felt as if we were tacking across town. There were twelve altogether, and it took us about an hour and a half to visit them.

"How you'd find them is look in the paper," she said. "If it wasn't a highbrow place, the ad simply said 'Writer's Night,' and if it was a highbrow place you'd see the names of all the writers booked.

"One night, I walked around with the cigar box collecting the money, because there was no one at the door, which says something about how determined I was—do you think our show was worth the money?"

At the end of a side street was a small, two-story brick building with a little sign that said "Pub of Love." "Tuesday nights," Welch said. "Probably forty people." Down by the river, near the Ryman Auditorium, where the Grand Ole Opry was, we stopped in front of a building where there used to be a club called the Silver Dollar Saloon. "One time I came down here to a Writer's Night by myself," Welch said. "November '93. Dave has travelled back to New England for

Alec Wilkinson

Thanksgiving, and I'm here by myself. This night, I'm late, and the guy grudgingly puts me on the list. 'We've got a lot of people,' he says. He works his way through the writers. I'm waiting. The crowd's thinning out. Once the writers play, they leave, and whoever came to see them, their friends, they leave, too. Finally, it gets to be about eleven-thirty, maybe coming up to midnight. The bartender and me are left. The guy says to me, as he's leaving, 'Will you turn off the sound system when you're done?'

"Most of the things that might have been discouraging have their pathetic and funny sides, too," Welch said. "Usually, it was all right. No one kicked me out. They would listen, but they would always say, 'Don't you have any happy love songs?' "

From the old Silver Dollar Saloon, we drove to a part of town called Green Hills. "We're heading for the Bluebird Café, where you'll laugh when you see it, because it's in a strip mall," Welch said. The Bluebird was behind plate-glass windows. We stood on the sidewalk and leaned into the glass, shading our eyes. The room was dark. I could make out some black-and-white photographs of songwriters on a panelled wall, and chairs stacked on tables. "The Bluebird was very important in our coming-up," Welch said. "It was the scene of where I got signed for my writing deal, actually." She moved a step to the side and pointed. "Right there," she said. "Over by the cigarette machine."

Welch is a figure of some controversy, and she wishes she weren't. Some people like to say that as the daughter of musicians in Los Angeles she has no right to play music they regard as reserved for people who grew up in poverty or, anyway, among laborers.

In response, Rawlings likes to bring up Ernest Hemingway. "You read *The Old Man and the Sea*, and you like it," he says. "Then you find out that not only is the man who wrote it not a commercial fisherman, he isn't even a Cuban. Do you not like it now?" Assertions about who belongs in the academy and who doesn't are always partisan, but in Welch's case none can be made confidently. There are complications that involve the issue of identity in a fundamental and enigmatic way. Welch says that the first time she heard bluegrass music she felt stirred as she never had by any other music. She has said that it makes no sense that she plays relic music deeply influenced by a part of the country she did not live in until she was grown. More than a few of her songs, for example, have the harsh modal structure of the ballads sung

94

The Ghostly Ones

in the mountains of North Carolina in the nineteenth century. Her reaction might plausibly reflect her having sung folk songs as a girl and played the guitar at school, and a pleasure that surfaced when she was reminded of it—a sense memory, that is. In any case, to explain the anomaly posed by the difference between her upbringing and her tastes she has told interviewers, somewhat sheepishly, that she has wondered whose blood runs through her veins. She has even considered which musicians might have passed through New York in 1967. She has imagined her father as Bill Monroe, the founder of bluegrass, or as Levon Helm, the drummer in the Band, who was from Arkansas. After all, the first instrument she played was the drums, and now and then she still plays them.

Welch's parents claimed her the day after she was born, and, honoring rules imposed on the adoption, they sent a friend to the hospital to collect her. Over the years, they have learned two things about Welch's mother and father, which they told Welch while she was visiting last Christmas. Her father was not from the South, so far as they knew, but he was a musician; in fact, he was a drummer. And, from an address they had been given, it appeared that her mother, the college student in New York, may have grown up in the mountains of North Carolina.

When Welch and Rawlings arrived in Nashville, they each bought an old pickup truck. Rawlings spent all the money he had come to town with on his. When I asked Welch what kind of truck she had bought, she said, "A 1966 F-100 with a 352 motor, three on the tree, and an eight-foot bed—you could put a whole sheet of plywood in it." Rawlings drives a farm truck from an orange grove in California. It was inherited by someone in Nashville. The California sun dissolved the finish, so the truck is several colors, mainly orange, green, and gray. It looks as if it were covered with lichen. Welch said, "It's a one-piece body, which was a bad idea. If you throw something too heavy in the bed, you can't open the door; it torques."

My last night in Nashville, I went with Welch and Rawlings to a steak house for dinner, and afterward Rawlings drove us to a soft ice cream place on Charlotte Avenue, in Sylvan Park, near the house they had lived in where the airplanes flew overhead. Welch was wearing black jeans and a sleeveless black top, her hair was loosely pulled back, and she had a radiant look. On the way, she sang along with the truck's tube radio, which was playing a Connie Francis song. When Francis

Alec Wilkinson

hit a high note and her voice broke slightly, Welch applauded the effect. Pat Pattison, Welch's songwriting teacher at Berklee, once said to me, "One of the things that Gillian did very well was sing the song rather than the notes. You have singers who have a really great instrument, but you don't feel they're inside the song. When Gillian sings, it's about the presentation of emotion. Even back then, she didn't sing notes; she sang feelings and ideas."

By the time we arrived at the ice cream place, it was closed. The owner happened to see us through the service window. He knew Welch and Rawlings, and he waved. He, too, was a musician.

Welch and Rawlings ordered cones dipped in chocolate, and while we waited for them Welch said there was a path that led from the back of the parking lot through an alley to their old house. The house was damp and dark, and the rooms were laid out shotgun fashion. It was on Nevada Avenue, she said, and they called it the Spaceship Nevada, because the atmosphere inside, with the recording machines and the cables and microphones, was remote from ordinary life. Across the street from the ice cream place was a brick building with signs all over it saying "Whiskey," some of them flashing. Welch said that the tricky thing about working at night was getting to bed before the birds started singing.

The owner handed the cones through the window, and Welch told Rawlings, "I took your advice and had the first bite before the chocolate had dried." To me, she said, "Because it's different every time—it's the humidity, and how the chocolate settles." I wrote that down, because it seemed to typify an acuity of mind that she and Rawlings share. A few days later, I was talking to Welch's mother on the phone. Julie Welch, Gillian's sister, had told me that when Gillian was in high school a television station did a program called "Super Kids," in which they included Gillian as an example of a student who excelled at everything she did. I asked Welch's mother if she remembered the program. "Oh, sure. She was unique. I mean, her lyrics, where does that stuff come from?" she said. "The funny thing is, she got all these awards in school, but I never remember her working that hard. She just sort of loved everything she did." She paused, as if reflecting. "I always think of Gill as paying attention," she said. "Really, what she's done her whole life is pay attention."

THROUGH FIFTY-YEAR-OLD EYES: RICKY SKAGGS AND THE STATE OF BLUEGRASS

By Thomas Goldsmith
From *Bluegrass Unlimited*

It's nearly 4 p.m. on a fall Saturday at Koka Booth Amphitheatre in Cary, N.C. Ricky Skaggs and his powerful Kentucky Thunder band are somewhere close at hand, preparing for the road-life ritual called soundcheck, groundwork for the Skaggs concert that will come later tonight.

From back behind the futuristic stage comes the sound of Scruggs-style banjo, ringing tonefully, rapidly, in the hands of Jim Mills, who wanders out, instrument poised. Award-winning veteran Mills, who is from these parts, greets guitarist Cody Kilby, one of the younger musicians also keeping Kentucky Thunder modern and hot. They pick a little, warm up, play a breakdown that—heard from across the green lawn before the stage—sounds great with no amplification at all. Out front, technicians led by sound engineer Eric Willson connect cords, test mics, move faders, and get ready.

With an actual group tryout of the sound still a ways off, Mills walks out front to sit with wife Kim. His banjo has a little high-tech attachment, the kind of tiny microphone which, blended with a stage mic, allows Mills and other Kentucky Thunder members to achieve the volume needed to keep up with concert acts from other fields. "In order to reach the crowds that we have been playing for, you have to have a pretty powerful system," Mills says, adding that the band gravitated toward a high-tech approach while working on the road with

Thomas Goldsmith

the Dixie Chicks.

Andy Leftwich, the talented young fiddle player, wanders out next, only T-shirted against the increasingly cool fall air. His fiddling is at once hot and technically precise. Leftwich, Kilby, and Mills light into something that sounds like "Teetotalers Reel" as work continues around them. There's a hum or resonance in the system that's bothersome. Trying to locate the problem, Willson listens while rhythm guitarist and mandolinist Darrin Vincent plays an archtop acoustic and sings one of Skaggs' hits, "I Wouldn't Change You If I Could." Tenor singer Paul Brewster, a key Skaggs bandmember for more than a decade, tests his own vocal and guitar mics. At 4:42 p.m., Skaggs emerges, mandolin in hand, in jacket and jeans. The final bandmember to show is bassist Mark Fain, who doubles as road manager. Wasting no time, Skaggs chops a perfect, unforced rhythm on mandolin as the band launches the bluegrass classic "I'm On My Way Back To The Old Home." The music sounds great, but the hum persists.

"Got something for this floor?" Skaggs asks Willson, then suggests moving the large speaker cabinets to the edge of the stage, where they won't resonate so much. Since the hum is located somewhere between E and F, Skaggs suggests a tune in F, "Dim Lights, Thick Smoke and Loud, Loud Music," a honky tonk classic he recorded for his *History of The Future* CD. Skaggs and Mills then pick up acoustic guitars for the gospel tune "I Heard My Mother Call My Name In Prayer," with great trio singing and Mills' wonderful fingerpicking guitar part, the way Earl Scruggs used to do it. The sound is coming together, as Willson turns knobs and makes adjustments on the extensive mixing board provided by the venue. It's time for one more song, and Skaggs elects to run through "Spread A Little Love Around," an affectionate, positive tune from the new record.

It's unlikely that Skaggs, or any artist, gives a great deal of thought to what he plays at sound check. But the tunes he runs through this October afternoon seem to sum up large pieces of his career. "I'm On My Way Back to The Old Home," first recorded by Bill Monroe in 1950, represents the early influence that Monroe and the other founders of bluegrass had on Skaggs. Though recently recorded by Skaggs, "Dim Lights, Thick Smoke..." is exactly the kind of classic honky tonk tune he took the top of the charts in 1980s, when he was a major country music star and a force for returning mainstream country to his roots. "I Heard My Mother Call My Name In Prayer" shows

Through Fifty-Year-Old Eyes: Ricky Skaggs and The State of Bluegrass

once again the strong place that gospel music and Christian faith play in Skaggs' life and music. And "Spread a Little Love Around," a song by Harley Allen and John Wiggins, comes from *Brand New Strings* and is part of Skaggs' belief that bluegrass needs to continue to grow—with new songs and new approaches—to survive.

Located in the prosperous suburb of Cary, the amphitheatre sits about a dozen miles from downtown Raleigh, where the Monroe Brothers, Flatt & Scruggs, and other founding spirits of bluegrass once held forth at radio station WPTF. Skaggs, who as a Kentucky-born child prodigy played on stage with both Monroe and Flatt & Scruggs in the early '60s, turned fifty this year. On the *Brand New Strings* CD, he has turned his considerable energy and creativity to striding forward in bluegrass, while maintaining links to the masters who inspired him.

"My love for that music goes to the core of what I am," Skaggs says in a telephone interview earlier in the fall. "My heart is to educate these young listeners to bluegrass—to Mr. Monroe, to Flatt & Scruggs, and the Stanley Brothers. We have to be diligent to tell the story. That's very important to me.

"But I knew that I absolutely had to come up with some new material that would really, I felt like, stand the test of time. We had to break out the all 'brand-new' material. It's not enough to sing 'Little Maggie' and 'Uncle Pen' and the bluegrass standards—however great those songs may be—over and over again," Skaggs says. "That's not only the road to stagnation for bluegrass, but it's also contrary to the questing, creative way Monroe himself approached music.

"I went to see him one day in the hospital," Skaggs says of a period near the end of Monroe's life in 1996. "He had gotten into his drawer beside his hospital bed and found some paper. He had song titles and he had verses and choruses of, I don't know how many, songs all over his room. I thought, 'Oh, my God, who's gonna finish this stuff?' He was still always trying to write, always trying to create, always coming up with something new." Monroe even expressed enthusiasm for incorporating the jazzy piano of far-reaching bluegrass musician Buck White, Skaggs recalls. "He'd say, 'Buck, I want to use that piano of yours in my music.' And Buck would sit in on an old tackhead piano."

At his half-century mark, Skaggs seems to have several lifetimes of music-making to look back on, in many cases with some of the very

Thomas Goldsmith

top names in bluegrass and country music. In Ralph Stanley's Clinch Mountain Boys of the early 1970s, he picked alongside his teenaged Kentucky partner (and future country legend) Keith Whitley, as well as fiddle master Curly Ray Cline, and the great bassist Jack Cooke. In the Country Gentlemen, his bandmates were Charlie Waller, Doyle Lawson, Bill Yates, and Jerry Douglas. He was part of a legendary line-up of J.D. Crowe and the New South (including Douglas, Tony Rice, and Bobby Slone), before forming Boone Creek along with Douglas, Terry Baucom, Steve Bryant, and Wes Golding. In Emmylou Harris' Hot Band, he joined an historic group whose other members had included singer-songwriter Rodney Crowell, transatlantic guitar hero Albert Lee, and future Music Row leading lights Tony Brown and Emory Gordy, Jr.

But since at least the early 1980s, Skaggs has been his own man, leading a succession of groups which also included some very hot musicians. He enjoyed genuine mainstream country stardom in the 1980s, with just one notable milestone being the Country Music Association's top award, Entertainer Of The Year, in 1985. Perhaps inevitably, changes in country music fashion found Skaggs out of favor and off the charts. But he has forged what must be considered a triumphant return to bluegrass, propelled by 1997's landmark *Bluegrass Rules* CD. Despite his long history in bluegrass, Skaggs gets no slack from the music's fan base, he says.

"I think now I have to be very, very creative," he says. "I have to be much, much more creative than I did back then. Even though there was more competition in country music than in bluegrass, I had a niche. At that time, there was nobody that was doing that really traditional mix of bluegrass and country together. Randy Travis did come along after that and found great songs from Paul Overstreet and people like that. But I felt like I had a niche that was working."

In the much smaller world of bluegrass, with lower levels of record sales, Skaggs comes under a lot of scrutiny; what he's up to is a matter of considerable interest to industry and fans.

"It feels like everybody is watching," he says. "I feel like I have to be really creative and walk the line for the dyed-in-the-wool bluegrass fan who still swears up and down that Lester Flatt is the best bluegrass guitar player in the world and says, 'Cody Kilby? Who's he?' We drew them in with (the CDs) *Bluegrass Rules*, *Ancient Tones*, and *History Of The Future—Shady Grove* and things like that. We have really tried to

Through Fifty-Year-Old Eyes: Ricky Skaggs and The State of Bluegrass

keep up our allegiance to the really traditional bluegrass fan."

To meet both needs—satisfying the traditional fan and opening some new doors in bluegrass—Skaggs looked to Music Row and beyond to find CD material that would be new to most ears.

"There's a lot of folks that never heard Mr. Monroe do 'Sally Jo,'" Skaggs says of the Kershaw Brothers tune, recorded by Monroe in 1957. "That felt like a great opening." Out of the 13 songs on the CD, 11 are new ones. "It's brand new music, and it's really important to me to do that," Skaggs says. "I've had people from Peter Wernick on down say I'd love to hear you do a record of brand new stuff."

Even though he's not selling millions of records in mainstream country any more, Skaggs still gets the top-drawer songs that are often hard to come by for bluegrass acts. Not that the songwriters wouldn't all like a Tim McGraw cut, too, he concedes.

"There's something about getting a Skaggs record that means something to those writers downtown that grew up listening to you," says the singer, who operates his Skaggs Family empire out of offices in Hendersonville, Tenn., northeast of Nashville. At a party for the CD release, every writer that had had a song placed on the disc showed up to help celebrate, he notes.

Having been around the music business—on various levels—for 35 years means that Skaggs has a realistic idea of what works as far as promoting a record and what could well be a waste of time. For instance, he elected not to pursue a music video to promote "Brand New Strings," even though CMT expressed interest in seeing one.

"We were having a hard time seeing that CMT was actually adding to record sales, for someone who is my age, someone like myself," he says. "Nickel Creek, yes. The camera loves Alison Krauss, and that is a big help. Dolly (Parton) and Patty Loveless—promoting their bluegrass things, that really helped. But we started kind of seeing what radio would play. If they are not going to play the real traditional bluegrass stuff, then what will they play? For the comparatively small universe of bluegrass stations, Kentucky Thunder cuts such as 'Little Maggie' and 'Walls Of Time' were like money from home. Bluegrass stations were eating it up, but when it came to Americana and Triple A, we were getting things like 'Halfway Home Cafe' [from *History Of The Future*] played."

The 2003 Grammy season brought a whopping five nominations for Skaggs—three with Kentucky Thunder and two for his *The Three*

Thomas Goldsmith

Pickers collaboration with Doc Watson and Earl Scruggs. He emerged with one win, marking his ninth honor for popular music's most prestigious prize. For Skaggs, the attention, which was to become controversial from mainstream country execs who wanted awards for their own acts, meant that people were absolutely listening to what he and his talented band were doing.

"We started taking the kind of material that we selected a whole lot more seriously," he says. Three instrumentals on the disc were written for a Disney project that never materialized; Skaggs was able to get rights to them back. The pieces demonstrate something remarkable: that after decades of playing multiple instruments, he is still coming up with new techniques, new licks, and new enthusiasm. His mandolin playing on *Brand New Strings* is at least as strong as any he's ever done.

"Being away from it for a long time like I was, it's become an old acquaintance brought new again," Skaggs says of the mandolin. "That was one of the things that I loved about coming back to bluegrass, was that I was going to be playing mandolin full time."

So, has Skaggs actually been practicing? He laughs and says, "No, not really." His wife Sharon, herself a fine picker and singer, has him doing too much stuff around the house.

"I play a lot on stage, and riding down the road in the bus, I'll play," he says. "I have been working early in the morning with melodies that come to me. I was going through Crossville, Tenn., and this mandolin tune was in my head. I raised the curtains on the bus to see where we were and it was Crossville. So that became the name of that song."

Another focus involved finding songs that said something, which to Skaggs means, among other things, saying something positive. "I feel like the lyrical content of the songs has got something of substance to it. 'Spread A Little Love Around' and 'Enjoy The Ride,' those are powerful songs." Skaggs is a committed Christian and his faith is well known in the bluegrass community. It's a big deal, his Christianity—something that's widely discussed and sometimes criticized in bluegrass circles. But he doesn't bring the subject up until asked about it, even though several tunes on *Brand New Strings* make Christian references. His instrumental "First Corinthians 1:18" was inspired by his habit of regularly reading the Bible. The passage referred to reads, in the King James Version: *For the preaching of the*

Through Fifty-Year-Old Eyes: Ricky Skaggs and The State of Bluegrass

cross is to them that perish foolishness; but unto us which are saved it is the power of God.

"It just so happened I was reading First Corinthians that day," Skaggs recalls. "Just dwelling on that message, I just heard this melody in my head and got my little tape recorder out and put it down." Skaggs' beliefs are the core of his existence, he says, noting that controversy has sometimes come along with outspokenness on spiritual matters. "I just believe so strong in God and I really try to be a good disciple of the faith, to be an honest man in my business, in my everyday dealings with people," he says. "I want to be the same offstage as on. A man's religion is usually what he does when he's by himself. Someone asked me the other day, 'Do you think your faith has hurt you?' Yes, I'm sure it has. People that don't speak never get in any trouble."

In his days of big-time country stardom, Skaggs says, his record company used to call him on the carpet for speaking too openly about his Christianity. He still talks about his convictions at shows, but says he's learned not to hit people over the head with it. "Sometimes I'll talk about the songs I am going to do and relate it to my life or to an incident that's happened to me," he says. "Sometimes at churches, we'll talk to folks about salvation and what it's meant to me. I have learned over the years not to try to force-feed people. In the early days, there were times when I was like a kid with a butcher knife. I didn't use sound judgment like I should have."

However, he'll never stop talking about his Christian beliefs, Skaggs says. He refers to Matthew 10:32, in which Jesus says, "Whoever acknowledges me before men, I will also acknowledge him before my Father in heaven" (NIV). Enlarging on this, Skaggs says, "It's not just in the day of judgment that the Lord will acknowledge me. He acknowledges me every time I stand up and speak for the Lord. How much more would you want to talk about Jesus if you knew that every time you spoke His name He would acknowledge you before God?"

Skaggs returns to the question at hand: how can bluegrass keep reinventing itself, nearly sixty years after it first reached critical mass in the hands of Monroe, Flatt & Scruggs, and a small handful of other brilliant musicians? After all, other styles stopped growing and took on museum-piece identities (like traditional New Orleans jazz) or changed so much as to be unrecognizable (like Chicago's original elec-

Thomas Goldsmith

tric blues). Known, and even sometimes notorious, for his attention to detail, Skaggs says everything counts when keeping bluegrass current—from song choice to making sure that his records really pop out of the speakers.

"We are always trying to get more level on tape so that the records are louder, so people don't have to crank them up in their car, unless they want to," he says. On a recent car trip, he was elated to hear that the presence and power of a Kentucky Thunder recording stood up well to the highly-produced sound of classic pop music. "They had played an Elton John song and they played 'Little Maggie,' and it stomped," he says. "I thought that was so cool. 'Little Maggie' just stands up right with it and says, 'Give it to me on the chin, I can take it.'"

Skaggs' live sound, the one they fooled with at sound check until they got it right, also makes a difference, he says. "Every little detail is thought out and planned. Our stage show is so loud because we want young people to be able to feel the music."

Perhaps buoyed by his faith and his successes of recent years, Skaggs says things look great to him. "I am so encouraged at the future of bluegrass," he says. "One thing that really encourages me is the quality of songs that are coming to bluegrass. And seeing these young musicians that are coming along—Kilby and Andy Leftwich—they are the athletes of music. To me Cody and Andy are just as qualified as [Nickel Creek's] Chris Thile and the Watkins kids.

"I think the material we are getting and the quality of music we are getting is going to be the future of bluegrass. Seeing it through fifty-year-old eyes, I am able to see it a little differently."

Back at the suburban amphitheatre outside Raleigh, it's a little after 5 p.m. The autumn sun is beginning to fade and there's a chill nudging the air. But dozens of fans are already lined up at the entry gate, armed with chairs and spreads they can use to settle on the lawn in front of the stage. They're here to hear this decades-old music, this thriving bluegrass, as it meets the twenty-first century, in the hands of Ricky Skaggs.

HIS MICKEY MOUSE WAYS
An appreciation of Waylon Jennings

by Dave Hickey
From *Texas Monthly*

So how would you feel? It's 1958. You're 21 years old, spinning wax at a two-bit radio station in the middle of West Texas, just happy to be out of the cotton patch and not knowing nothing about nothing but Ernest Tubb, Pepsi-Colas, drive-in movies, and Moon Pies. That's you, and one day your good friend, who is also your mentor and role model, who also sees a lot more in you than you see in yourself, waltzes into the booth at the radio station, tosses you an electric bass guitar, and tells you to learn how to play it. He's taking you on a rock and roll tour, starting next month, January of 1959. A week later, your friend flies you to New York City and puts you up in his Greenwich Village apartment. You sleep on the couch, learn the bass, rehearse with the band, and explore Manhattan. The two of you have your picture made in a Grand Central photo booth. Then you climb on the bus, and in a wink, you're crisscrossing the frozen Midwest in the dead of winter with a bunch of one-hit wonders, playing rock and roll shows in high school auditoriums and basketball gyms.

By the end of January you've played twenty shows. Your friend has decided to take you to London as his opening act, which is nice, but that's a few weeks away, and right now it's forty below in Duluth and the heat on the bus is out. The tour moves from Duluth to Clear Lake, Iowa, and nobody has any more clean clothes. West Texas boys (on account of their dirty minds) require clean clothing, so your friend charters a plane from Clear Lake to Fargo so you can all find a laundromat before the next night's show. After the gig in Clear Lake, however, you and the guitar player get wangled out of your seats on the plane.

105

Dave Hickey

"You're not going with me tonight?" your friend asks. "Chicken out?"

You say no, that the Bopper wanted to fly.

"Well, I hope your damned bus freezes up again," your friend says.

"Well, I hope your ol' plane crashes," you say, and, of course, it does.

Your friend is dead, slammed into a frozen wheat field, and you are sitting in a Minnesota truck stop, staring out at the frozen morning, realizing that, just for a minute there, you were sort of about to feel free. Then you feel bad about even thinking that. You're nothing now in the middle of snowy nowhere, and the promoters don't want the band to go home. They offer to fly you to your friend's funeral, first-class. They offer you more money if you'll stay on the tour. What decides it, though, is that you are a West Texas boy, a bad-weather cowboy, and a man of your word. So, like a fool, you stay, but you get no tickets, first-class or coach. You get no money, and at the end of the tour, in a daze, you go home. You've got no friend and you've got no future. How do you feel?

Well, first, you're extremely angry, and second, you don't care anymore. About some things (like businessmen, lawyers, and bourgeois respectability), you will never care again. You've just been awarded a thirty-day doctorate in the music industry, so, from Jump Street, you trust no one except out of laziness and make few friends because, somehow, it seems, you kill your friends, and anyway, you are too far gone for any but the farthest out. From now on you will sit a long way back from the screen and see yourself acting out the roles that life requires of you—son, friend, lover, husband, music star, culture hero—but you will never take any of them very seriously.

You're plenty screwed up, in other words, and if you had a shrink, if anybody in West Texas had ever heard of a shrink, he would probably diagnose a permanent case of low-grade depression, dissociation, and survivor's guilt, along with a heavy dose of the old *And Suddenly* syndrome. He would probably prescribe the pills you're taking anyway, because at this point, you are morally certain that the better things get, the more likely they are to blow up in your face; that the brighter the sun, the softer the woman, the sweeter the song, the darker the oncoming storm. The future closes like a shutter in these moments, so you live in the music, which has its own time. You can strip it down, tighten it up, clean it off, and ride it like a rising wave.

His Mickey Mouse Ways

The music, in the moment of its making, sets you free, but it doesn't cure anything—and, really, it never will.

On February 13, 2002, in Chandler, Arizona, Waylon Jennings died in his sleep, at the age of 64, of having lived. Six months later, we gathered in Lubbock at the second annual Buddy Holly Music Festival and Symposium, to remember him together. Waylon's son, Buddy, was there, as were Richie Albright and Billy Ray Reynolds, his primal rhythm section. Billy Joe Shaver, who wrote the archetypal Waylon songs, showed up, and Lenny Kaye, who co-wrote *Waylon*, the autobiography, flew in from New York, on leave from his gig with Patti Smith. I flew in from Las Vegas to reminisce about my years as an embedded journalist in the outlaw music movement. We all sat at a long table in a white conference room, like a posse without the sheriff.

In ragtag fashion, we projected the man we knew back onto the things we had heard and, in doing so, imagined the narrative that opens this essay. It seems a plausible one to me, and all the more plausible since we had known Waylon Jennings at various times and in varying circumstances, and clearly, we knew the same man. We recognized his preternatural, ironic self-awareness, although we didn't all call it that. Billy Joe, in fact, looked at me funny when I used the phrase, but we all located the trick of his charm in his benign sense of his public persona as a crazy cartoon of himself. Somehow, he could throw bullshit at you with one hand and wipe it off with the other. In a world full of evil dudes pretending to be good guys, Waylon was a good guy pretending to be an evil dude and never quite succeeding.

You would see him driving around Music Row in some butterscotch, gold-trimmed, East L.A. pimpmobile, dressed up like the "third outlaw" in a spaghetti western, and you would smile, knowing that no one bore less malice in his heart. Onstage, he would step up to the mike, swinging that Telecaster from his hip, and glare out into the lights, projecting an aura of dark, unrepentant machismo with so much good-hearted irony that the aggression bore only the faintest hint of real menace. Out in the audience, you got the buzz of his sexual charisma, but you knew you were one of the gang, that Waylon was sincere in his insincerity. But it was not all a joke. Some things were taken very seriously indeed, and if you crossed the line, you quickly saw the glint, and things got a little, uh, gritty.

You had to violate the code for this to happen, and those who did

Dave Hickey

invariably thought that it was all a joke, that Waylon was totally inside the ongoing party. Eventually, you figured out that, onstage or off, Waylon Jennings loved the party, the performance, and the costumes. He loved the distance they put around him, but part of him was always standing outside, leaning against the proscenium, watching from the wings and keeping things in line. Proper distinctions had to be drawn, because Waylon had rules. He knew the difference between being a man and being an animal, between being crazy and being insane, between being bad and being mean, between being an outlaw musician, a thieving crook, or just a plain old scuzzball, predatory criminal. He never confused these modes of transgression, and although he lived by the Code of the West—as all West Texans must—Waylon never confused cowboys on the stage and cowboys on the range. He insisted, in his music and in his presence, that these distinctions be observed as a hedge against self-delusion.

Having said this, of course, I must concede that guarding oneself against self-delusion has never been a high priority among drug addicts of my acquaintance, myself included. Among this delusional legion, however, Waylon Jennings was by far the least deluded. I remember once, not long after I arrived in Nashville, asking Waylon why the locals took speed rather than smack and barbiturates, like us Manhattan sophisticates did. He said, "Hillbillies and hairdressers take speed because they're not comfortable, but they still have to work." That, I thought, just about said it, although it's clear to me now that Waylon's discomfort derived in large degree from the self-awareness that made him so appealing.

One night on the highway, in his new shiny bus, on the teetering brink of his pop success, I asked him how he liked his new audiences. "Well, it ain't exactly living in the love of the common people," he said dryly. He went on to explain that when you start performing, you play for people who are just like you, and that's not really performing. Then you perform for people who just like you, and that's really fun. Then, "if you're lucky," you end up performing for people who want to be you, and that's really not as much fun because these people who want to be you always hate you a little because they're not you. They secretly want you to fail so you can know how it feels to be them. "Actually," he said, "it's not that complicated. There's a lot of people in a room. One guy's got the microphone. Everybody else's got the beer. They're all having about the same amount of fun."

108

His Mickey Mouse Ways

I sat there and thought that knowing this much about yourself and your audience was probably not much of a benison for a performer. It does, however, account for some of Waylon's special virtues. In "Good Hearted Woman," for instance, there is a line that goes "She loves him in spite of his wicked ways she don't understand." Waylon never sang it that way onstage. He always sang "She loves him in spite of his Mickey Mouse ways that she don't understand." Because, I think, Waylon knew what wickedness was. He knew he wasn't it, and his comic vision of Mickey Mouse machismo let everyone in on the joke. He could characterize himself—in a phrase at once self-deprecating and deftly cosmopolitan—as "too dumb for New York City, too ugly for L.A.," and no other singer in Nashville would even dare.

He could stand in the wings, watching himself onstage, and write, "I've seen the world with a five-piece band looking at the backside of me." I can't imagine another country performer confident enough in his own masculinity to acknowledge that he knows the band is looking at his butt. And what other leather-clad, asphalt cowboy could walk up to a fellow who's bitching about somebody being "a g——m queer," drape his arm around the fellow's shoulder, snuggle up close to him, and say, sotto voce, "Aw, come on, Hoss. We all just grab onto something warm and worry 'bout the details later." If you were familiar with the pathological caginess of most Nashville singers, this cowboy hipster candor was scary at first. Then you realized how profoundly Waylon did not care, and ultimately, I think, the magic cloak of this not caring kept him alive for more than six decades. Because the truth was that if Waylon wasn't on the stage, in the studio, on the bus, or having dinner with his wife, Jessi, he was in trouble or about to be.

His gift to us, of course, had nothing to do with being in trouble, although it got him into some. He made strong music. He sang great songs that said things beautifully and spoke with some precision to the times for which they provided the soundtrack. More than that, of all the artists with whom he is associated, Waylon Jennings had the most passionate sense of how you put things together and what things you leave on the bus. He was an artist, in other words, and an artist of his time. At the exact moment that American painters and sculptors were cutting away the obfuscation and expressive nonsense that had accrued around American art during the post-war period, at the very instant that the kids at CBGB's were beginning to jettison the pretentious theater that was drowning rock and roll, Waylon was taking country

Dave Hickey

music back where it never had been.

He stripped away the decorative bric-a-brac that had plagued Nashville product for decades and created contemporary roots music in the minimalist tradition—a music that was not really simpler, just stronger, better organized, and more totally focused than anything that came before it. Dispensing with virtually everything but the rhythm track and the vocal, he changed the focus of the sound from the orchestral grandeur of the setting to the sinuous muscularity of the music's forward drive. Abandoning the pop-hillbilly flummery of contemporary country songs, he embraced the poetic license and compression of lyrics like Billy Joe Shaver's. In the end, he made a new music that, like the singer of Billy Joe's song, "left a long string of friends, some sheets in the wind, and some satisfied women behind."

The trick was in the bass and drums, and Waylon's producer, Jack Clement, helped with this. As Richie's drums got sharper and cleaner and the bass got louder, the tempo could get slower and the vocals softer, so everything fell into balance. The songs rode on the bong-bong of this "Cajun march" that Richie and Waylon invented—it sounded like an old four-four but bounced like a bluesy twelve-eight, with hidden triplets flowing through the drum track, accentuated by Waylon's Telecaster. To Nashville ears, it sounded like nothing or, even worse, like rock and roll, but it moved like a new wheel on an empty highway and still does, although there are no more empty highways and no more hipster cowboys at the Dairy Queen. Even so, history keeps a special place for artists like Waylon who scrape off the paint and carry out the trash, who bet their whole heart on the unadorned shape of the music. You have to be crazy to do it, of course. You know that soon enough the vehicle will be repainted, that stripes, chrome, and all manner of gewgaws will ultimately accrue, but what you have done doesn't go away. It survives at the heart of the music.

And Waylon survives as well, on his records, of course, but most profoundly in the memory of fading gypsies like those who gathered in Lubbock, who never saw bad done so well. This is the picture of Waylon that I carry with me today: We are milling around the crowded greenroom after a show in Atlanta. Waylon is flopped down in the middle of a leather couch, flanked by two exquisitely coiffed, extremely plump white ladies. The ladies are attired in pastel pantsuits, and the three of them make a nice tableau—the gaunt King of Darkness bracketed by two painted and powdered Easter eggs. Waylon sits

His Mickey Mouse Ways

forward with his elbows on his knees, grinning and soaked with sweat. His hair hangs in wet, greasy ropes, some of it plastered across his forehead. His shirt is stuck to his body, and his wristband is stained with dark blotches. He sinks heavily into the pillows of the couch while the fat ladies seem to float weightlessly. I am imagining the strain the ladies are putting on their knees, trying not to look heavy, when I realize that, at that moment, they are not heavy at all. They are in heaven.

I sit down on the arm of the couch and find the three of them in a deep discussion about the almost insurmountable difficulty of running a beauty salon in Atlanta, Georgia, what with taxes, zoning, sorry help, and the burgeoning complexities of interracial hairstyling. Waylon is contributing what he can, which is more than I would have expected. His limited experience of beauty salons, I surmise, has been considerably enhanced by his wide experience with beauticians. Also, Waylon is a small businessman himself. As he points out, he started off as a very small businessman, picking Texas cotton and getting paid by the pound. The ladies chatter away, giddy but perfectly at ease. They are telling this dangerous outlaw things they have never told anyone, but they are not complaining, as they are wont to do, because Waylon is not a complainer and he is contagious.

Whatever they expected as they tiptoed backstage, it was never this! They are having a conversation with Waylon Jennings! It's better than the sex they fantasized about and thought they wanted but didn't really. Waylon knows this. He knows that, as a culture, beauty-salon ladies are incurably romantic and less worldly than they like to pretend. They are not prudes, exactly. They will have sex with you if they must, but what they want is Scarlett and Ashley. They want the rituals of courtly flirtation, and Waylon, with his devil smile and attentive gaze, is giving them that. It occurs to me, as I blatantly eavesdrop, that Waylon is selling a hell of a lot of records with this little gesture. Then I feel bad for having thought it, because Waylon Jennings, in that moment, is clearly happy as hell to be chatting with the fat ladies, behaving like the perfect young cowboy, being thoughtful and curious and whimsically generous, living in the love of the common people.

112

RHONDA VINCENT: ENJOYING THE VIEW

By Ralph Berrier, Jr.
From *Bluegrass Unlimited*

"I prayed for you."

The little boy stood directly in front of Rhonda Vincent, right across the table of CDs and T-shirts. He said he kept her in his prayers, as many had done last December when Vincent underwent an emergency surgery on her pancreas. They prayed down in Jekyll Island, Ga., where she and her band, the Rage, had to cancel a gig. They prayed the following week when she endured two more surgeries, including one to remove her gall bladder.

She thanked the little boy, as she did all the others who stopped by her merchandise table that unseasonably hot May afternoon during the Doyle Lawson Music Festival in Denton, N.C. The surgeries had been painful, and they kept the bluegrass star off the stage and off the road for...well, about a whole week. That's as long as she could stand to be away from performing, singing, and meeting all those fans who love her and pray for her.

"I probably went back about a week too soon, but I'm a workaholic," Vincent said during an interview in her custom-designed Martha White tour bus. "I like to keep going. That was my way to get over my misery."

That kind of work ethic and fan-friendly attitude has made Vincent one of the shining stars in bluegrass today. She's a bona fide bluegrass triple-threat: great vocalist, outstanding musician, and dynamite live performer. And let's just say it-she's also easy on the eyes, which hasn't hurt in garnering a huge fan base since she quit flirting with Nashville's contemporary country scene in the 1990s and recommitted herself to bluegrass. Her three albums for Rounder (*Back Home*

Ralph Berrier, Jr.

Again, The Storm Still Rages, and last year's terrific *One Step Ahead*) have shipped more than 230,000 copies in four years, according to the label, and she has been named the IBMA's top female vocalist each of the past four years. She's a bundle of energy, prone to biting her fingernails down to the nub between performances. On stage, she leads her excellent band through a dynamic, lively show. With an eye toward fashion and eye appeal and an ear toward old-school bluegrass, Vincent has helped keep the music viable and fun in the 21st century.

All the while, she is a serious, tough-minded bandleader and businesswoman. She is unafraid to replace musicians in her award-winning group, even those who are rated among the best players in bluegrass. She worked hard to win the right to represent Martha White Flour, which re-established its relationship with bluegrass in 2001, and now she rides to festivals in style in the impossible-to-miss blue and white bus. After more than thirty years of performing (even though she only turns 42 on July 13th), she gained control of her career upon her return to bluegrass and knows exactly where she wants to go, how she wants to sound, and how she wants to look.

One need look no further than the cover of "One Step Ahead" to see how she's changing the hidebound image of bluegrass. There she is in the photo, standing in a rush-hour city setting, clutching a mandolin and wearing leather britches and a skimpy, belly-button-baring top. Shortly after the album's release, a friend called to say Vincent's picture was posted in the window of a New York City record store. "You're not going to believe this," the friend gushed, "but your poster is right next to Madonna's in downtown Manhattan!"

The Material Girl and the Mandolin Mama, side by side, neither one looking out of place. Yet, she's still as sweet and wholesome as a bluegrass diva should be (she doesn't drink, smoke or cuss, by the way), whether she's singing a gospel number in a white dress or picking a mandolin solo in a red halter top.

"You can be hip and cool and play acoustic music," she said. "That's the image I want to project."

But being hip and cool isn't what earned her those IBMA awards, including Entertainer Of The Year honors in 2001. It's not what elicited all those prayerful petitions when she was sick. Talent and hard work did that. While Vincent's look might be Vanity Fair, her sound is Flatt & Scruggs.

"She's a great talent, but one of the things that sets her apart is her

Rhonda Vincent: Enjoying the View

work ethic," said Ken Irwin, co-founder of Rounder. "She's always thinking, always working. On her days off from playing, she'll do radio interviews or press interviews. She's always looking for some way to promote her and her band's career. She has that drive, as well as a great voice, musicality, looks, and she's great at dealing with the fans."

Vincent has heard some folks describe her work ethic differently. To some, she's not just talented, driven, and dedicated, she's headstrong, demanding, and difficult. That may be true. That is, if you believe requiring a high level of musical expertise from her bandmembers makes her demanding, and charting her own professional and creative course makes her difficult. She can live with that.

"I'm just doing my thing," she said. "I've heard all the rumors out there—'She's hard to work for'—all of that. I'm very fair and I expect a high degree of expertise and conduct."

Vincent doesn't always use her bandmembers on her recordings, which has probably bruised a few musical egos. Instead, she brings in bluegrass big shots that have included Aubrey Haynie, Ron Stewart, Stuart Duncan, and Bryan Sutton, and guest vocalists that include Dolly Parton and Alison Krauss. While recording *The Storm Still Rages* three years ago, Vincent even replaced a couple of fiddler Michael Cleveland's breaks, just as Cleveland was on the verge of being named IBMA's Fiddle Player Of The Year. He eventually left the Rage in 2001 and began a successful solo career.

She makes these moves because she's not afraid to make the tough decisions that every great bandleader has to make. "Rhonda is strong in all her opinions, but she is very understanding and open to ideas," said Hunter Berry, Vincent's fiddler for the past two years. "She's the leader. Rhonda will do what she feels is right for her and the group, because nobody else will be making those decisions for her."

Her bandmembers know of her industry reputation and they make fun of it on stage. When they perform the Martha White theme, Berry instructs the audience how to holler the "uh-huh" and "yes ma'am" responses in the verses. "You keep practicing that 'uh-huh' and 'yes ma'am' and you can join the band," he says. "Because that's what we say all the time."

Certainly, Vincent has experienced her share of personnel changes since 2000. Fans know, however, that turnover among bands is as much a part of bluegrass as the three-finger roll. Bill Monroe cycled through dozens of Blue Grass Boys and his place in history is fairly

115

secure. Today's groups change lineups more often than the New York Yankees, yet hardly an unkind word or rumor is uttered about those bands at festivals or in internet chat rooms.

Could it be because none of those bands is led by a strong, opinionated woman? Perhaps.

"Sometimes people don't respect a woman in a man's world," said Herb Sandker, her manager, who also happens to be her husband of twenty years. "She's trying to change that. She's definitely not as hard to get along with as some people paint her to be. Her fans know her to be kind and giving. The industry might have a different perception. She's closer to what the fans think."

Vincent grew up playing bluegrass and country music. She starred in her family's band, the Sally Mountain Show, based in her hometown of Kirksville, Mo., where she still lives with Sandker and their daughters, Sally and Tensel.

Playing in that band with her parents Johnny and Carolyn and younger brothers Darrin and Brian, Vincent learned her licks and earned her chops. She made her performing debut at age three, played on TV at age five, and recorded a 45 rpm single of "Muleskinner Blues" at nine. At the grizzled age of twenty-three, she had recorded eight albums.

Even as a teenager, though, she wanted to explore music beyond her family's tried-and-true bluegrass.

"Musically, I wanted to expand," she said. "I used to cry when I was a teenager when we would play a show. I'd been singing 'Muleskinner Blues' since I was nine, and I had to sing it every night.

"I started going through a banjo phase at that time. I'd heard the Seldom Scene and decided, 'I want to do that.' I heard David Grisman and New Grass Revival. I learned every Sam Bush break [on mandolin] by slowing the record down to hear every note."

Finding a place for those influences in a Sally Mountain Show set wasn't easy.

"People would come to the house and we'd play 'Little Log Cabin In The Lane' and I'd try to throw in a Sam Bush break," she said. "That didn't go over too well."

She tried the contemporary country market in the mid-1980s and again in the '90s, recording two albums for Giant, *Written In The Stars* in 1993 and *Trouble Free* in '96. Giant promoted the albums without much fanfare and neither did very well on the country charts. Vincent

Rhonda Vincent: Enjoying the View

wasn't comfortable singing the '90s versions of drinkin' and cheatin' songs, either.

"I was like a Missouri hillbilly," she said.

Chastened by her final foray into mainstream country, Vincent once again returned home and put together her first version of the Rage. She met Rounder's Irwin and they discussed what kind of music she really wanted to perform and record.

"Ken and I agreed that there wasn't a female doing in-your-face, kick-butt bluegrass," she said. "There was a void."

She also brought a few of the tricks she learned from mainstream country, such as hair-styling, makeup, clothes, and videos.

"All the stuff I learned in country music helped," she said. "Then TV started to catch on in 2000. Where a brick wall used to be, now doors were opening."

She's a sought-after duet singer, who has sung with the likes of Alan Jackson, Pam Tillis, and Dolly Parton, and recently finished a session with Faith Hill. These are heady days for the lifelong perfomer and small-town girl from Missouri, evidenced by a recent trip she took a few months back with her daughters.

The girls had heard country hunk Keith Urban was to sing at the Grand Ole Opry and they begged their mother to take them to Nashville to meet him. At first, she balked, but then she rescheduled a planned trip, booked a flight to pick up her daughters and whisked them to Nashville, where they met Urban backstage at the Opry.

"We had to capture the moment," she said. "You don't have many moments like that and when you do, you have to make them last."

Spoken like an artist who has worked her way to the top and is thoroughly enjoying the view.

118

THE BIG SHOW
Music is business and business is good for Tim McGraw

By Edward Morris
From *The Journal of Country Music*

"It's a great time to be a superstar in country music," says talent manager Scott Siman. He should know. He manages Tim McGraw, one of the handful of country artists who can sell a million new albums the first few weeks out and fill arenas without the support of a gaggle of midlevel acts. Within a period of two days in November of 2002, McGraw released a new album, *Tim McGraw and the Dancehall Doctors*, and a lavishly illustrated coffee table book and starred in his own NBC-TV special. It was an image rollout as cunningly choreographed as a Rockettes' routine, and it underscored the mindset and industry muscle that the 35-year-old singer has developed over the past decade. Riding the wave of this media surge, McGraw is conducting a 50-plus city tour in 2003 titled "Tim McGraw And His Dancehall Doctors' One Band Show."

Increasingly, country music looks to its superstars to keep the business running. Comparatively few artists sell enough records to pay back the money it took to launch them. A debut album that sells half a million copies will still leave its label deep in the red. Thanks principally to releases by such superstars as McGraw, the Dixie Chicks, Shania Twain, Faith Hill and Kenny Chesney, country music sales in 2002 were up 12.2 percent from the year before. Every other format saw a decline in sales. According to Nielsen SoundScan, the company that monitors such figures, nearly 77 million country albums were purchased last year. But most country artists sold in modest numbers. Emerging acts didn't emerge very far.

"All you have to do is look how concentrated the sales are in the top 10 acts and then look at the drop off," observes Chuck Flood,

Edward Morris

whose firm, Flood, Bumstead, McCready & McCarthy, manages business and finance for such acts as Vince Gill, Patty Loveless and Lee Ann Womack. "Go back and get SoundScan [totals] from five or six years ago and look at how many units you had to sell for a week just to get on the charts. And look at it now. . . . Some weeks, you can be selling less than 1,000 copies and still get in the Top 75 on the country albums chart."

"It's really hard to be a new and developing artist right now," continues Siman, who also represents Jessica Andrews, Billy Gilman and Carolyn Dawn Johnson "It's hard to create critical mass and a break anymore. It's hard to make enough noise, to get enough penetration. Are there enough listeners at country radio? Are there enough press opportunities?"

Like all well-established performers, McGraw has a fairly wide range of income sources. The biggest one by far is concert ticket sales, which account for about 66% of his total take. Following it are record royalties (12%), merchandise sales (10%), sponsor revenue (5-7%) and royalties from producing records (5-7%). *Tim McGraw and the Dancehall Doctors: This Is Ours,* the book McGraw co-authored with Martin Huxley, made *The New York Times* bestseller list and has sold more than 200,000 copies. (An author's royalty rate is usually 10% to 15% of the book's cover price, a figure which would be split here.) McGraw denies himself one major source of money that other artists routinely tap into—songwriting royalties. More on this point later.

Tim McGraw first lifted his head from the primordial soup of country wannabes in a much more congenial time. His debut single came out in 1992, when country music still ruled the roost. "Welcome To The Club," his first charted single, topped out at a pale No. 47 in *Billboard.* The two singles that followed were even more anemic. McGraw's turnabout came in early 1994 with the release of "Indian Outlaw." While the song was cartoonish in its depiction of native Americans, it was so infectiously good-time and goofy that it caught on swiftly and rose to No. 8. Its followup, the thoroughly sentimental "Don't Take The Girl," gave the Start, Louisiana, native his first No. 1. It also demonstrated his penchant for recording songs of all themes and tempos, a trait that persists.

In the spring of 1996, McGraw and Faith Hill were paired for the CMT-sponsored "Spontaneous Combustion Tour." The spontaneity, it turned out, was not limited to the stage. The two young performers

The Big Show

fell in love and were married on October 6 of that year, thus becoming country music's first "royal couple" since the all-too-brief reign of Keith Whitley and Lorrie Morgan. If this was the expansive side of touring for McGraw, the deflating side came on June 3, 2000, in Buffalo, New York, when he was working as the top-billed opening act for George Strait. As almost everyone has read, fellow-opener Kenny Chesney took an allegedly unauthorized ride on the horse of a deputy sheriff who was assisting with backstage security. When the guards tried to pull Chesney off the horse, McGraw came to his friend's aid and was arrested for assault, a crime that carried the possibility of a prison sentence. After all manner of legal maneuvering on both sides, McGraw ultimately went to trial and was acquitted.

McGraw has had conflicts with his long-time label, Curb Records, too, albeit at a much lower profile. He has made it clear that he will not take any creative direction from the label. In his new book, he doesn't even deign to mention Curb by name, but he does say, "Ever since *Not A Moment Too Soon* [1994], we've kind of kept everything in-house when I make a record. My label never hears anything until we're done." In speaking of these run-ins, McGraw tends to be droll and understated in his criticism, seldom if ever invoking that "me against the Philistines" riff that became Waylon Jennings' stock in trade.

As Siman sees it, McGraw has grown so successful by now that he doesn't have to depend on Curb's good will to keep his momentum. "Maybe [his career] could be a little bit bigger if everybody worked totally, absolutely, completely together on everything. But they can't stop us. . . . In terms of touring and record sales and all that kind of stuff, no. We're going. We're rockin'."

Mike Curb, the legendary impresario who owns McGraw's label, denies there is any significant rift with the singer. "Record companies and artists—when they have a long relationship—will disagree every once in a while on a song or some small issue," he says. "But the 12-year relationship that we've had has been phenomenal. I can think of hundreds of things we've agreed on, and just very few things where we've ever disagreed." He acknowledges that McGraw wanted a new album out in 2000, while the label opted instead to release a greatest hits package. But he points out that both albums were released (with *Set This Circus Down* being pushed up into early 2001) and that both went No. 1.

Curb says there have also been minor disagreements about the

Edward Morris

choice and release of singles, brought on by radio's tendency to play album cuts rather than singles the label has designated. "We've had that happen a couple of times, like with 'My Next Thirty Years' and 'Something Like That,' when we've had other singles planned. So managing those types of things have never been easy. But if that's the biggest problem anybody has, that's good. There'll come a time in everyone's life when we're wishing that radio would just play us."

While McGraw has complained about his label, Curb notes that he has also praised it. It was the label, he says, that found and urged McGraw to record "It's Your Love," the duet with Faith Hill that won the CMA Vocal Event of the Year in 1997. McGraw thanked Curb publicly for bringing him the song. "He's been very fair to us when we deserved it. Now this is his record, and he deserves the credit. He doesn't need to thank us for this. We need to thank him for making such a great record. If we win album of the year, I'm going to thank Tim and say, 'This was all you.'"

An entertainment attorney who later became an executive for Sony Music in Nashville, Siman signed on as McGraw's manager in early 1997. "There were two major factors that convinced me to do something that I said I'd probably never do, which was be a manager," Siman recalls. "[First], I listened to some of the early music on *Everywhere*. They'd just started to record it. I went, 'Oh, my god! These songs are phenomenal.' I think I heard 'Everywhere,' 'It's Your Love' and, maybe, 'Where The Green Grass Grows.' I thought, 'Wow! This is not a good record, it's an amazing record.' Then I spent some time with Tim, and I saw a guy who was just totally focused on his career. He had just married, and he was going to have a family—I guess Faith was pregnant at the time. So he was like, 'I'm going to be a dad. I've got things I want to do here. I've got responsibilities, and I'm ready to go do whatever it takes.' I saw that focus, that purpose it always helps for an artist to have. He had it in spades. It was a great thing to watch."

Siman also appreciated McGraw's enthusiasm for traditional country music. "One thing I always enjoy about Tim is that we'll sit around, and he'll get a guitar and we'll all start singing Merle Haggard songs, Johnny Paycheck songs. He's a big Keith Whitley fan—I mean a *huge* Keith Whitley fan—and we'll start doing every song Keith Whitley ever recorded, just backstage with a guitar. All the time I've spent with him, I've always enjoyed his involvement with the history

The Big Show

and the tradition of country music and those great singers.... I think that's a big piece of who Tim is. People will say there's a big '70s rock influence to his music. Absolutely. And he'd be the first to tell you. It was cool he had a chance to open [the American Music Awards] with Elton John because he grew up listening to Elton John. But the reality is that it's a marriage of the Merle Haggard-, Keith Whitley-kind of music with '70s rock."

The fact that McGraw is headstrong and focused are qualities Siman says he relishes. "I've learned over time in the music industry that the artists are right most of the time and that we in the business are probably wrong most of the time. It's hard sometimes as a manager or record executive to let go of that control of your artist. But I've learned that to be an effective manager, I need to take the artist's vision and make it better, make it become a reality as opposed to trying to change his vision. I would rather work with an artist who had a vision and a plan and knew what they wanted to do and help them get there than to try to spend my day inventing a vision or direction."

Instead of micromanaging, Siman says, McGraw sketches in the outline of what he wants done and leaves the details to others. That process holds true whether he's designing a TV special or co-producing a record for one of the artists he admires. "A year ago, last December," Siman says, "we sat down and said, 'OK, if everything could be the way we wanted it, what would it be?' We said we wanted to do all these things we've done. The idea of doing a kind of coffee table book segued into 'What if we gave everyone up there [in the Allaire Studio in the Catskills] cameras and journals to take notes on the making of this record?' That's what led to the theory of the book. And then with the TV special, it was like, 'Well, where do you want to do it?' And he said, 'I want to go home. I want to go to Start, Louisiana. I want to do it in my hometown.' His hometown, of course, is a stoplight. There's a cotton gin right across the street from where he grew up, and he said he wanted to do it there. . . . I think one of the reasons this show was so successful was that it showed who he was. His vision for that cotton gin was this: What if it were a working gin in the daytime but in the night it was a nightclub?"

McGraw has his own memories of pulling the special together: "It was a lot of hard work. For the last couple of years we'd kicked around the idea of having a special and talked with some networks that wanted us to do it. But I never like to do anything unless I'm confident in

123

Edward Morris

what I'm doing. I don't know what people have told you, but I like to do it my way. Even in the studio, I don't think I can do things conventionally and go by conventional wisdom. I can't go in and just sing any song and produce it like everybody else and make my words sound smooth and sweet, like everybody else. That's not going to work for me. I'm not that kind of singer, and I don't think I'm that kind of artist, either. I've got a definite point of view of what works for me. So until I had it kind of confirmed to where I could go in and design the stage I wanted and the camera shots the way I wanted them and have the director I wanted for the show and be able to do it where I wanted to do it—to have complete control—I didn't want to do it. NBC gave us that control. . . . It was really cool to be doing it in my home town."

The TV special was a big expense for McGraw, at least initially. "In our particular case," Siman points out, "there was no label support whatsoever. Tim undertook it completely." McGraw and NBC-TV put up more than $1 million each to bring the show to the air. Still, Siman considers it a worthwhile investment: "I think it translates directly into additional records sales. You get to an audience outside of the format, and any time you have a chance to get your artist exposed outside the format, it's a very good thing. People can look at that and say, 'Hey, I like this,' and maybe they'll go buy the record, they'll go buy a ticket or maybe they'll tune into country radio to figure out what's going on there. So it's just is a real opportunity to get to a huge audience in a very short period of time." The week following the broadcast of the special, McGraw's new album sold 602,000 copies, about twice as many as any of his other albums had during their first week out.

"You can make some very good money and you can sell some records [with a network special]," Chuck Flood says. "But I think the real advantage is to let the world connect and see you. You're reaching so many people. And just the stature of having a network special makes people go, 'Wow!'" Adds his partner, Mary Ann McCready, "It gives you the chance to tweak and update your image and have an impact on the public emotionally. Hopefully, all this will result in increased record and ticket sales. It probably ramps up your merchandise numbers too."

Tim McGraw and the Dancehall Doctors is McGraw's most expensive album to date. It involved, among other niceties, renting, refurbishing and redecorating the Allaire recording studios in the Catskills

The Big Show

Mountains of New York and lodging his band, recording crew and support staff there for 10 days. In the end, the album cost more than $800,000 to make. His first album topped out at less than $125,000.

As unsettling as the media glare and legal hassles were, Siman considers the Buffalo brouhaha an "overall plus" for McGraw. "There's always that theory that there's no such thing as bad publicity. Certainly, the awareness level went up. But I think where he really shined in Buffalo was that he stood up for what was right. He didn't just go, 'Fine. Here's some money. Make it go away.' It really wasn't about him. It was about Kenny Chesney. Basically, Tim stood up for his friend. It's kind of that red badge of courage. When you're placed in that position, do you turn your head and walk away or do you help your friend? He helped his friend, and in the end it cost him a lot of money in legal fees and time in having to go up there and defend himself. Sure the publicity was big, but standing by your friend is part of what we do in country music."

Standing by friends is a favorite topic of conversation among those who work with McGraw. In a business where band members, managers, publicists and other satellite personnel are hired and fired on whim, friends and associate praise McGraw for his loyalty. The fact that his new book, album and tour all spotlight the name of his band, the Dancehall Doctors, testifies to this point. His newest bandsman has been with him since 1994. Mark Hurt, who co-manages with Siman, has been on staff for 13 years.

"You want to build a team around you that believes in what you're doing and feels like they're a part of it—a vital part of it," McGraw explains. "To me, it's about personalities as much as anything else. The band's been with me a long time. They worked for me when I couldn't pay them. In some of the early days, I borrowed money from these guys and used their equipment and their van. A lot of it's loyalty, but, you know, they've become my friends. And they've been my friends from the first year we started playing together. Mark Hurt, he sold T-shirts and was our road manager. We *are* my career."

"Tim is a very, very adamantly loyal guy," Hurt says. "A lot of people hire and fire based on the needs of the tour. It'll be this guitar player this year and another guitar player the next. Tim and I have always agreed that we should do enough business in any given year [to keep the band going]." McGraw did his 12-date mini-tour last year, Hurt says, to keep the band and crew paid and insured. Although he

Edward Morris

did not have attendance and ticket sale figures for all 12 shows, Bob Allen, who compiles the "Boxscore" concert grosses columns for *Billboard* and *Amusement Business*, says that 10 of the dates drew a combined attendance of 88,122 and grossed $4,078,624 in ticket sales. Extrapolating from these figures, the entire tour drew approximately 105,600 ticket buyers and grossed around $4,896,000.

Apart from his household staff, the artist has about 20 people on permanent payroll, including the eight-man band, tour manager, production manager, lighting director, front-of-house engineer, monitor engineer, stage manager, gear technicians, etc. "Everybody has a real job and gets a check," Hurt adds. "It's based on Tim's acumen that security is a very hard thing to find in this business."

Even if a recording artist has no songwriting skills at all, it is common practice for successful songwriters to "co-write" with the artist. It's a practice that financially benefits both parties. The legitimate songwriters are virtually guaranteed that the artist will record their joint compositions, thus gaining their songs commercial exposure. And the artist gets a share of the royalties these songs generate from airplay (performance royalties) and from record sales (mechanical royalties). Because McGraw sells so many records and gets so much airplay, there's probably not a songwriter in Nashville who wouldn't jump at the chance to "co-write" with him. But McGraw plays it straight and declines this easy money.

"First, I don't think I'm any good at songwriting," he says. "I'd love to be able to sit down and write a song, and maybe one of these days my focus will change. But producing is a real artistic outlet for me. It's a way to look at music and try to get things out of it that I can't necessarily get out of myself—to go at it at a different angle, to try to make music at a different angle from [that of] an artist. I'll hear something and say, 'Man, Jo Dee [Messina] could really tear this up. This is what I would do if I could do it. I can't, but I know Jo Dee can.'"

Siman says it doesn't bother him that McGraw has chosen not to deal himself in on what are essentially other people's compositions. "No. Not at all. He's dabbled in writing a little bit here and there. I think, in the end, there are two things that keep him from doing it. One is that he knows how good the Nashville songwriters are. He's totally in awe of what they're able to do. And, two, he doesn't have the time. . . . He's been more concerned about developing himself as a producer." As a producer, McGraw splits the 4% royalty paid on the

126

retail price of albums sold with his fellow producers.

This past year, McGraw showed up faithfully at the several No. 1 parties thrown for writers who had penned his hits. But he invariably stayed in the background and left the spotlight to them. He moved in for pictures only when asked. One party was for Craig Wiseman, Jeffrey Steele and Al Anderson, who co-wrote "The Cowboy In Me." "Craig kept my career going there for a while," McGraw told the celebrants. He said he met Wiseman at the Hall of Fame Inn Lounge on Music Row the day he moved into town in 1989. Wiseman had a band and McGraw asked him if he could sing a song. "You'd better be nice to people," Wiseman observed. "You never know where they'll end up."

Product endorsements yield big money for McGraw, both in direct financial support and in spurring ticket and record sales. "One of our huge endorsement partners has been Bud Light," says Siman. "When I first got involved, that was one of the things I was tasked with—to go out and look for endorsements and sponsorship opportunities for Tim. Early on, we were able to put together the Bud Light deal. One year, the deal was with Uniroyal Tires; but the second touring year I was with him, we were able to secure the deal with Bud Light. They've been wonderful. They've given him the opportunity to do national television commercials. Not only do they give us money to make our tours better and to promote and market our tours and do the national TV commercials, they've also been really good at looking for special opportunities. For example, last year they spent a million dollars to buy a spot on the Academy Awards show. This year they did the same on the Super Bowl. So it's not just been about what works for them; they're also doing things that work for us. They bought spots on the American Music Awards, the Country Music Association Awards and the Academy of Country Music Awards. They've put something back into our format as well." Currently, McGraw is in the middle of a multiyear agreement with Bud Light. Hurt declines to say how much the company has paid McGraw directly and in support of his records and tours.

To get a major sponsorship these days, Flood explains, "you've either got to be a superstar or a hot new act—I mean platinum, or close to it." But, he adds, such sponsorships can be "extremely lucrative because there's not much in the way of additional costs associated with creating that income stream. Except for commissions, it all flows

Edward Morris

to the artist's bottom line."

The 2003 One Band Show tour is particularly expensive and arduous, according to Hurt. "To make it all work from a financial perspective," he says. "I basically have to do four shows a week. So I can't go over 350 miles in any given night. These guys are loading trucks until 2 or 3 in the morning and five hours later they've got to start unloading. Under that scenario, it's a pretty tight schedule." He estimates it cost McGraw "in the neighborhood of $1 million" upfront to get the tour on the road.

For the tour, McGraw and his band work on an ultrawide stage that's bare of such common techno-clutter as instrument cases, mix consoles, racks, etc. The stage goes wall-to-wall, extending into the stands. "Tim is able to walk right up to the rail where that seat is that's right next to the stage," Hurt says, "the seats that normally suck because of the amp racks in front of them." Built beneath the center of the stage is a hospitality room for the band and VIPs. There is a 12-feet by 8-feet tunnel running under each side of the stage as an emergency exit. "It's very polished, very simple," Hurt adds. "Basically you've got a big black Darth Vader sitting at the end of the building, and you can see nothing but the stage itself. There are four levels: two stage left and stage right, a center performance area that's a third level and a rear riser that serves as a fourth."

McGraw's March 11 show in Nashville demonstrated the effectiveness of the staging. Massive though it was, the set had so many sides adjacent to the audience that McGraw was able to make eye and hand contact with many more fans than if they had been arrayed at the front of the stage. McGraw performed for well over two hours without taking a break Near the end of his set, as the crowd roared for an encore and watched images of his children on the giant TV screens on each side of the stage, McGraw appeared as if by magic on a platform by the sound board at the back of the arena, singing "Tiny Dancer." True to his tour's title, he spoke frequently of his band and spotlighted each of its members. While George Strait and Alan Jackson, who played the same arena earlier, may have drawn slightly larger crowds, McGraw's was unquestionably the loudest and most demonstrative. Whatever his shortcomings as a vocalist—a point he routinely brings up in interviews to the consternation of his managers—he was certainly a master at engaging his audience.

There are 65 to 70 in McGraw's road crew (including the band,

The Big Show

seven video camera operators and up to 16 follow-spot lighting technicians). The caravan includes 10 equipment trucks and seven to eight crew buses. Crew salaries range from $1,250 to $5,000 a week each. The buses rent for $15,000 a month, with the fuel, drivers, maintenance, cleanup and the use of satellite dishes and generators all costing extra.

"You may be selling 10, 15, 17, 18 or 20 thousand seats at an average ticket price of $40," Hurt says, "but you have to realize that it costs you half of that on a given day and in a given building [to do the show], and that does not include your trucks, buses, personnel, sounds, lights and videos. . . . On any given day, you'll leave up to a quarter of a million dollars in a [host] city—renting a building, hiring local manpower, advertising, all of the things that have to happen to put this show up. . . . In Chicago [for example], if I can do a show for $250,000, I'll be a shrewd man. I can go to Birmingham, Alabama, and if it costs me $100,000, I'm in trouble. It's that varying a number. Keep in mind, that's the local cost."

Hurt says that merchandise sales are not as profitable as one might think. "You have to figure that most major touring artists will average somewhere between $5 and $8 per person per day in attendance," he explains. "If you've got 10,000 people in the building, you're going to do between $50,000 and $80,000 in merchandise sales. But you're going to leave 25% of that on the table, after you pay the sales tax. Most businesses will tell you if they can keep 25% or 30% of their cash flow, they're knocking it out of the park." Some arenas demand up to a 40% of the merchandise sales, Hurt says, but artists who draw well can usually negotiate that cut downward. "If they've got a stone-cold winner coming to town, they'll make exceptions." In the years McGraw is on tour, about 90% of his merchandising income is from items sold on the road. The remainder is from Internet sales. The merchandise offerings online are different, Hurt says, from those available in concert venues. Only a few McGraw items, notably a calendar and the book, are sold in regular retail stores.

For the first time, McGraw is selling a fixed number of advance tickets to his fan club members through his website—and at a smaller surcharge than Ticketmaster tacks on. "We didn't strike a deal directly with Ticketmaster," Hurt says. "We struck a deal with Music Today, which is a company owned by Coran Capshaw, who manages the Dave Matthews Band." Capshaw created the company, Hurt

Edward Morris

explains, to give a special break to die-hard fans who travel from concert to concert, taping the Matthews shows and exchanging them online. "Capshaw basically went to war with Ticketmaster for a while over their exclusivity with the buildings and what have you. . . . The end result is [that his company now has] an agreement with Ticketmaster that allows for a percentage of the tickets to be made available to fan clubs through the Internet." Hurt calculates that McGraw's online ticket prices "are typically 30% to 50% less than what you would pay if you called [into Ticketmaster] with a credit card, requested that the ticket be mailed to you and took all the options Ticketmaster gives you."

"The Internet has been a significant part of Tim's career," Siman observes. "Reba [McEntire] and Tim were the two [country music] people who [first] said, 'Hey, let's do something with our website and try to make something happen.' . . . He was the first artist to debut a video on his website. We've done webcams at concerts. He was the guy who ended up charting a record—'Things Change'—off the CMA Awards. We were able to get a track [from the awards show] out there on the Internet. Everybody downloaded it, and some of the stations wanted to play it. It was kind of cool that that happened." McGraw pays for the design and maintenance of his website, drawing on funds generated from fan club dues.

Complex as his current life may be, McGraw says he has no nostalgia for his simpler days of struggle. "Being in my late teens and 20s and playing music on the road was a lot of fun. But the stress mentally of thinking about what you're going to do with your life to be successful and wanting a family—all that stuff far outweighs the pressures, to me, anyway, of being a successful artist and maintaining it. That's opened up a lot of doors and given me a lot of freedom, artistically and personally."

He wants to record with Faith again and wishes radio's gatekeepers were more open to her latest music. "I'm a little disappointed with radio right now, especially where Faith is concerned, because I think there's a lot of prejudice out there about what they think she's doing. I don't think it's necessarily that they think she's left the format. They're just kind of pissed that other [formats] can play her music . . . . There are a couple of guys who think they're more important than the artist."

As for himself, McGraw says he's still hungry. "I'm hungry about

The Big Show

making better music. I like going out and doing my shows and knowing that they're selling well. Playing's not as much fun if you go out there and see empty seats. It's a lot of fun when they're packed. Forty thousand people in an arena create a lot of energy. You can't ever get tired of that."

132

DWIGHT YOAKAM: HILLBILLY REDUX

By Bill DeMain
From *Performing Songwriter*

"I'm a honky tonk man and I can't seem to stop," Dwight Yoakam sang on his first hit, back in 1986. Fifteen albums, twenty years and twenty-three million sales later, Yoakam has been good to his word, sticking close to his barroom-meets-Bakersfield sound and earning himself a place in the California country club alongside the trinity of Buck, Merle and Gram.

While many achy-breaky, boot-scootin', redneck trends have come and gone in country music over the last two decades, they haven't affected Yoakam's sound or vision in the least (oddly, in the past few years, his music has been deemed "too country for country radio"). If anything, Dwight has dug the heels of his scuffed-up Dagos in further.

Not to say he's been stagnant. On standout albums such as *Gone* (1995), *Tomorrow's Sounds Today* (2000) and his latest, *Blame The Vain*, he's let his hillbilly twang mingle with decidedly non-country textures, such as Tijuana Brass-style horns, Beatlesque string quartets and Jimmy Webb kitchen sink arrangements. The result of these hybrids is as fresh and startling in its way as anything Beck and the Dust Brothers have cooked up.

Of these nods to classic music of the past, be it rock or country, Yoakam says, " It's meant to reaffirm the validity of that music. Quality is timeless. It will clearly define itself. And so I make reference to and acknowledge things that I feel have been dismissed, trying to restate those musical and cultural elements clearly and vehemently."

In case you didn't already know, Dwight Yoakam is a very bright guy.

He was born October 23, 1956 in Pikeville, Kentucky and raised in Columbus, Ohio. He started playing guitar when he was nine years

Bill DeMain

old and wrote his first song shortly after. In high school, Dwight excelled in music and drama, taking the lead role in plays such as *Flowers for Algernon*. He also did comedy and impressions, including a mean Richard Nixon.

After a year of college, he dropped out and began the trek that would take him from Nashville to Los Angeles. As he discusses in the following interview, he came to country music stardom through the unlikely door of the LA punk scene of the early '80s (and it was that scene that influenced Dwight's trademark look of spider-tight jeans and a cowboy hat with a shadowy tilt). Along the way, he hooked up with guitarist/producer Pete Anderson, who became his musical director and helped him earn twenty-one Grammy nominations (he's won two). Of Yoakam, Anderson has said, "Dwight has, still has and has had the potential to be the most important country artist of his time."

Unfortunately, the creative partnership is now in limbo. In 2004, Anderson sued Yoakam for damages and revenue lost after the singer backed out of a national tour in 2002. Whether the two will mend fences and work together again is uncertain. In the meantime, Yoakam has ably self-produced *Blame The Vain*, enlisting players such as Keith Gattis and Mitch Marine from the neo honky-tonk scene that's been flourishing in LA clubs like King King and Molly Malone's over the past few years.

Yoakam also has a healthy side career as an actor. Since his convincingly scary turn as the abusive stepdad in *Sling Blade*, he's costarred in *Panic Room* and *The Newton Boys*. In 2005, you can see him in three pictures - the Tommy Lee Jones-directed *The 3 Burials of Melquiades Estrada*, *Banditas* (starring Salma Hayek and Penelope Cruz), and *The Wedding Crashers*. And in the time-honored tradition of country artists, he's also recently entered the world of food endorsement, with Dwight's Bakersfield Biscuits.

We caught up with Dwight Yoakam on the phone as he was preparing to shoot a video for "Blame The Vain," the first single from his new album.

Do you see any parallels between this recent honky tonk movement and the LA "cowpunk" scene of the early 1980s when you were coming up?

Oh yeah, a lot. It's cyclic in most cities that have a musical legacy. It ebbs and flows. Here, it goes all the way back to 1966, when Clarence White was playing up in El Monte at the Nashville West

Dwight Yoakam: Hillbilly Redux

club and Chris Hillman took everybody up there to see him, including Gram Parsons, who had recently arrived from the east. And that begat the Byrds' *Sweetheart of the Rodeo* album, which begat country rock in LA. Then that moment ebbed. I arrived out here in 1977, but it wasn't until about 1981 that things blossomed again with the whole scene with the Blasters and the neo-country rock of cowpunk. It was myself and Lone Justice and all those other acts. It led to me having my career, and now it's kind of come back around again.

Both the new album and Population: Me *include players and writers such as Keith Gattis and Mike Stinson, who've come out of this scene. It sounds like it's been a source of inspiration to you.*

Yeah, since late 2002, when I got off tour and kind of wandered into Molly Malone's. The first Wednesday of every month, they were having what they called the "Sweethearts of the Rodeo" night. It became the "Sin City All-Stars" night. I saw Mike Stinson there. Keith Gattis and I met there, then I sat in with him at the King King Club on Hollywood Boulevard. That was a night called "Eastbound and Down." It was Bryson Jones, Wayland Payne, Keith Gattis and Mitch Marine. I sat in with them. The outgrowth of that was conversations that led to Keith and I hanging out and playing music together at my house, and at Billy Bob Thornton's, with Warren Zevon one night, when we were doing a track for Warren's last album. Then Keith and I did a benefit concert together, an acoustic show. I'd been doing the big band for a long time, and I found a new sense of inspiration doing something that was very stripped-down and austere. It turned into a forty-two city tour, and that led to me wanting to expand on the thought in the studio.

During the cowpunk movement, was there a sense of rebelling against the country music establishment?

Yeah, we knew we were bucking the odds, but also, there was a great legacy of country acts being signed on the west coast. Buck Owens, Merle Haggard, Tommy Collins. The whole California country sound, which is what the Bakersfield Sound was.

Before you moved to LA, you tried Nashville. Did you have a romanticized notion of the city?

Yes, and it's not what you anticipate it to be (laughs). It's not a

Bill DeMain

bunch of honky-tonks and neon signs. It's a very sophisticated and beautiful city. Architecturally - the Belle Meade area, the replica of the Parthenon, Vanderbilt, all of it. And it's a very subtle city, in a lot of ways. Music Row was pretty subtle, especially when I was there in '77. It was sleepy, almost like an adjacent college area. There was no sign that pointed towards the entrance (laughs), for lack of a better way to describe it. And that was bewildering and confusing for me, I think. There wasn't really a live music scene at the time that was club-oriented. It's not like it is now on lower Broadway, where you can play.

It was around the time of Urban Cowboy, *which for someone who liked real country music, must've seemed like the ultimate in artifice.*

It was the transition from the Outlaw movement to the beginning stages of that Urban Cowboy movement. And that music just went beyond the apex of the curve and off the road (laughs). It just didn't interest me. If there was anything that was raucous on that soundtrack that was interesting, it was maybe the Eagles' "All Night Long," with Joe Walsh. That had more to do with honky-tonk in some weird way than some of the other things. But everything is cyclical. All things expand and contract in their own time and place. I'm sure I was more viscerally oppositional to it at the time. But retrospectively, it was just the nature of how things evolve. And then devolve (laughs).

Did you do the usual thing of meeting with a lot of publishers in Nashville and pitching your stuff?

I wasn't in Nashville that long. Maybe two months. Later I went back, and I'd spend some time with my dad in Louisville, then drive down for a couple of days at a time and hang out. That was in 1981. I tried to pitch songs. I had a few more contacts, vis-a-vis some folks I'd met in LA by that time. Some demos I'd made at the time ended up on my box set. So I had some people to see. But that still was not the moment there for me, and it wasn't going to happen. So I came back out to LA and put my shoulder to the grindstone and continued to play the clubs. I quit playing the country bars and started playing the showcase clubs and just played my own material. I made less money, but in the long run, had an opportunity to make a living doing it.

A lot of your early songs like "Bury Me" and "South of Cincinnati" have a strong sense of place. There's a famous Hemingway quote where he said he

Dwight Yoakam: Hillbilly Redux

wasn't able to write about where he grew up, in Michigan, with any clarity, until he moved to Paris. Was is that way for you when you hit LA in the late 70s?

Absolutely. I feel that in the extreme. I was born in Kentucky, raised in Ohio and grew up in California. I was twenty years old when I landed here in the west, and I became an adult here. I read that about Dickens too. He didn't write a lot of the great stories he wrote about London in the dead of winter until he moved to the Tuscan area of Italy. He was living in Italy writing about early nineteenth century London. So yes, vantage point is everything. That's probably what allowed me to write about my home and family.

Judging from an early song like "You're The One," which was written in 1979, it sounds like your songwriting voice was already strongly in place by then.

I got here in '77 and it was a couple of years of finding myself. It was evolving to the place of being able to write stuff that wasn't overly burdened with triteness. But I'd written and made up songs since I was young. I just hadn't been able to have it coalesce in a cohesive kind of fashion, where it flowed with any strength, until my early adult years. And that's when things like Merle Haggard's writing, Buck Owens's writing, John Prine's writing really started having a major impact in my life, and became inspirational to me. You hear something like "Holding Things Together," [Haggard song from 1974] you start to hear deeper, clearer meaning.

Did you do a lot of dissecting of their songs?

No. I don't come to music that way as much. Pete (Anderson) and I used to work in a way where as a producer, he would analyze more. I tend to finger-paint a little more, I guess. I'm feeling it on an intuitive level when I listen to their songs. Then I would just find myself emulating mood and tone. I mean that in an almost visual sense. As in, what I see in my mind as I close my eyes. Tone in a shaded sense. In terms of light. That's a strange way of talking about it, but I visualize musical moments. I have a visual experience. It's almost like chanting.

Do you mean chanting, as in meditation or putting yourself into an altered state?

Yeah, that's what it is for me. I don't sit down and say, "Now I'm

Bill DeMain

going to write a drinking song." It's like, "No, dude" (laughs). My earliest memory with a guitar, when it was too big for me to even try to play, once I was able to master a few chords - and I haven't much outdistanced that mastering yet - I would sit, almost in a catatonic way, then go away with that sound, whatever the chord was, whatever the riff was. I still write with that approach as a basis. For me, it's music first. It's usually vowel sounds. It's intoning on top of that melodic progression. Some sort of vowel sounds that have an emotional articulation. Then from there, I've kept little scrap papers and journals of song thesis lines. Lines come to me in a moment. Often times, if I jot down a line, I'll think of a melodic way to express it. One begs the other immediately to follow. When it starts with the music first, it doesn't necessarily give way to an immediate coherent thesis of verbal articulation. But it gives way to some kind of vowel-consonant intoning of emotional articulation, in terms of color. Something wants to come out. I know this sounds really nuts, but it's almost as if a song wants to come from somewhere. From the other side somehow, it's trying to press its way into this plane of existence, vis a vis my skull (laughs).

I've heard Keith Richards interviewed and he also talks about that whole idea of writing to vowel sounds: "ah-ee-ooh" and so forth.
If you think about ah-ee-ooh, that's one of the way we articulate emotion. It's like moaning. Sadness. "Oh." Pleasure. "Aahh." As human beings, we articulate emotions through these sounds. There's a whole theory about the power of letters and words and names. If you do anagrams of almost any word, like "evil" is "vile." Why is that? Certain words contain letters, almost like a code. I once saw Clint Eastwood's name as an anagram, and it was "old west action" (laughs).

Have you done an anagram of your name?
Eh, well . . .

I'm looking at your name and I see "mighty oak" in there.
Well, you take whatever you can get. If I can get an acorn, I'll take that (laughs).

You were describing this book.
It has to do with words and letters and how we use certain letters

Dwight Yoakam: Hillbilly Redux

to articulate emotion. Linguists have done in-depth studies, but in this particular case, they were talking about how it's not anything supernatural. It's probably more prosaic, in how prose formed. In almost every language on earth, the word to describe mother has an "M" in it. Vowel sounds, and consonants too, are important to my writing. They shade things in different ways. But it's interesting, what Keith Richards was talking about. From the time we're infants to the time we pass on, even our most visceral primal place is to make those vowel sounds. Even dogs do it (laughs). They howl. That's a vowel sound.

How has your approach to songwriting changed over the years?
I've learned to write very much in the moment, and not be worried about completing any given thought or song thought, lyric thought. Just capture everything I was feeling in that moment on these little Sony handheld cassette recorders. It was the most freeing thing I've ever stumbled on in my whole journey as a songwriter. I was doing The Newton Boys for about four months in 1997, and I realized that I wasn't going to be able to come home and set aside time to stare at the wall and write these songs. I had these fractured moments of inspiration, and I realized that I'm thinking all day long of musical thoughts. I thought I should start keeping these cassettes everywhere. I brought the tapes home with me, and it progressed from there. I've not stopped it since. It allows me to almost co-write with myself. It allows me to go in and cut the tracks, because I have the structure done, even if the lyric isn't finished. I allow myself the wonderful freedom of cutting that track, living with that, and then letting that direct me further into how I'm going to write the lyric. It lets it find its place. It lets the universe take care of the job for you. If you don't meddle with it too much, it'll happen like it's supposed to.

Let's talk about the new album. I like the way it starts, with one note of feedback.
Kind of an anemic homage to "I Feel Fine" by the Beatles. Recently, I was reading George Martin's notes on that particular session. It's interesting, in one of the books on the Beatles, he was talking about the tracks. McCartney thought maybe he had done the feedback. And Lennon had claimed to do it. George Martin said, "No, it was John." But contrary to what John said, the moment was planned. But the interesting thing was, it was with an acoustic guitar. It wasn't

Bill DeMain

an electric guitar. The top on his note, it starts to rattle and vibrate like only an acoustic guitar does.

I think it may have been the Beatle Gear book that you're talking about. Do you have a side of you that goes in for the nerdy fan kind of stuff?

I'm certainly curious about what went on and why, about what they were using, how those sounds were arrived at. But it was just an afterthought, that feedback. A gentle homage to John Lennon and "I Feel Fine."

When you make a gentle homage, as in that song or the Glen Campbell-ish arrangement of "The Last Heart in Line", do you have any intention beyond just honoring a style that you like?

No. In the case of the feedback, once it happened as an accident, then we focused on, "If we're going to do that, let's get it to sound in that way, let the top rattle like John's did." I had to play with it and find a sweet spot for the feedback. But the other stuff kind of happens on its own. There's a bit of a Jimmy Webb moment in "The Last Heart in Line" that led to us crafting the arrangement that way, towards a Glen Campbell-esque style. There's no forethought about things being done as an homage. It's really something that's born out of an organic moment.

It's an energetic, young-sounding record.

Thanks. It really was a journey of joy making this record, a journey into the unknown. It was a moment in my life and career that I'll cherish always.

Having said that, you've been in the business a long time and have had your share of ups and downs. How do you avoid the creeping cynicism that can affect your work?

Constantly look and seek inspiration outside yourself. That has inspired me. For instance, going out in 2002 and hanging at Molly Malone's on a Wednesday night and watching Sweethearts of the Rodeo. And allowing yourself to continue to find inspiration by not becoming methodical, not succumbing to rote method. Saying "There are no rules," and "I'm going to express myself in a way that excites me and inspires me and makes me feel like I'm sixteen years old again, in a gold lamé suit with a reckless joy about it all." The abandon might

Dwight Yoakam: Hillbilly Redux

put you out through the fence and into the dirt a little bit, but if you can get it back up over and onto the track, you've still had a lot of fun (laughs). The song that is really the thesis for the new album in some ways, is "I Wanna Love Again." [Sings] "I wanna love again, feel young again, the way we did when it was true." That was really the thesis for the spirit of this whole album.

What do I need to know about Bakersfield Biscuits?

(Laughs) Look on the website and there's a story about the biscuit boy that you can read and you can learn everything you need to know. Buck Owens teased me into doing something special for his restaurant opening two years ago. I was going up to play, and he said, "No, you've got to do something special." So I had some biscuits done by a baker down here and sent them up there as "Dwight's Bakersfield Biscuits." They put them on the menu and people liked them, and it led to this insane kind of journey off into the food business that I started, then stopped, then started again, and now it's kind of running on its own inertia (laughs).

It's a tradition for country music singers to lend their name to restaurants and food products.

Exactly. From Martha White sponsoring the Grand Ole Opry to Minnie Pearl's fried chicken to now. Bakersfield Biscuits are gonna take me down the road (laughs).

Last thing, if you were teaching a class on songwriting, what would you tell your students?

Listen to your inner voice. That sounds cliched and trite, but it's the hardest thing in the world to actually accomplish. Try to be still enough to hear what's there to listen to. Find the peace, in time and place — literally and figuratively — to be still enough to hear all the beautiful music that's there to hear.

142

VOICE OF AMERICA
Mark O'Connor's distinctive style and music incorporate many influences, but they could only come from his homeland as Nick Shave finds out.

By Nick Shave
From *The Strad* (London)

Mark O'Connor is used to feeling like an outsider. As a teenager growing up in Seattle he absorbed the Texan fiddling styles of his tutor Benny Thomasson only to be cast out by his contemporaries who played bluegrass or Canadian fiddle music. A prodigious talent, he went on to win the National Old-Time Fiddlers' Contest so often that he was asked to step aside and refrain from entering. Since then he has continued to cultivate his own style of playing, not only mixing up regional country styles but also skipping between musical genres to record albums that have topped both classical and jazz charts. He's neither classical virtuoso nor jazz cat, but a fiddler of diverse talents—and that's the way he likes it. "When you're a kid you don't want to be different, but I've probably got more eccentric as the years go by," reveals O'Connor. "I find comfort in that."

As a folk fiddler and composer O'Connor is central to keeping national traditions alive in American music. Whether paying tribute o jazz violinist Stephane Grappelli on his latest *Hot Swing Trio* disc, In *Full Swing*, or arranging bluesy tunes for the likes of Yo-Yo Ma and Edgar Meyer on *Appalachia Waltz*, O'Connor's is a distinctly American sound. You need look no further than the titles of his best-selling orchestral works, ranging from *Liberty!* and *Fanfare for the Volunteer* to *The American Seasons*, to sense that he is composing in the Copland

143

Nick Shave

tradition, drawing upon his national heritage to create a sound that is both unique and reminiscent of his country's past. And with his recent release, entitled *Mark O'Connor: 30-Year Retrospective*, you can expect the underlying sounds of the American south to unit the diverse range of regional styles that he plays with, from bluegrass to jazz.

At a time when White House policy is at its most controversial, the notion of American patriotism in music is a sensitive issue, one that O'Connor tentatively picks over during our interview at London's Landmark Hotel. It's not that he feels his music lacks nationalistic sentiments — on the contrary, he agrees it's patriotic — but more that he's anxious not to associate his promotion of America's musical roots with contemporary trends in politics. Though he has performed his *Appalachia Waltz* at the White House, written the a cappella "Folk Mass" in memory of the victims of September 11 and performed in America's celebration of Israel's 50th birthday televised by CBS, O'Connor is keen to distance himself from any current political agendas. "I think my music reflects American history and roots and that's very rare in classical circles," he asserts. "Music and art should lift spirits rather than bring them down; though my music might be representative of a great country, it's supposed to indicate the better side of things, not accentuate the worse."

O'Connor's musical roots lie in Seattle, where he grew up with his mother's passion for classical music and took lessons in classical guitar. After an early foray into flamenco, his teacher encouraged him to enter the classical guitar competition at the University of Washington. He won in both the youth division and across all age categories, despite being just ten years old. Not content with proving his prodigious talent on just one instrument, however, O'Connor picked up the violin a year later and, on taking lessons with Thomasson, excelled at the fiddle too. By the age of 14 he had learned to play around 250 Texan folk tunes. "The guitar seemed more staid and classical in construction than violin," recalls O'Connor: "I used the violin to find my own voice."

Could he not find his voice through playing, say, Vivaldi? "Expression is more direct in folk," he explains. "Partly due to improvisation, but with fiddle music there's so much scope to interpret the music – to play the same notes, but approach them differently. In my lessons, Benny would teach me by playing incredible variations and would challenge me to come back the next week and play them differ-

Voice of America

ently. He challenged me to find my own voice. He didn't do that with all his students, but I was heading down that creative avenue."

O'Connor's creative avenue took him from lessons with Thomasson to gigging with Grappelli. At first he toured with Grappelli's jazz ensemble, playing on guitar. In turn, Grappelli gave him lessons in jazz violin, nurturing his natural rhythmic sensitivity and picking up from where Thomasson had left off. "I would say that between them Benny and Stephane had everything I ever wanted to learn. Their phrasing was key to their great success. Benny was a better bower, but Sephane had the greatest left hand of anybody around. So I feel I'm lucky to have learnt with two people who were the best in the field, who came out and changed the way people thought of their instruments."

On graduating from high school in 1979 O'Connor had already recorded four traditional fiddle albums on Rounder Records. Taken with the idea of studio work, he parted with Grappelli's ensemble and headed south to Nashville in hope of finding work as a session musician. An outsider, he found his acceptance on the country circuit was slow. "I was very different to the other players," he recalls. "I wasn't the typical country music buff. The rap on me was that I was too classical, too rock, too jazz and too bluegrass to be a country musician." He laughs. "What you gonna do with that?" In response to the criticism, O'Connor changed nothing about his playing. Local record producers grew accustomed to his style and he was soon voted Nashville's (CMA) Musician of the Year—not once, but six years running.

To meet him, you wouldn't guess that O'Connor is the sparky virtuoso fiddler that wows audiences around the world with displays of knuckle-breaking pyrotechnics. His speech is languid, with thoughts ordered carefully yet uneasily into line. Dressed in beige from head to toe, it's only his slight Southern drawl that suggests his lifelong affinity with the Deep South. That, and the fact that his voice takes on a new level of seriousness when he talks about the culture there. "There's this kind of wild, crazy aspect of the South that has produced lots of novels, movies and music; it's a hotbed for people to just reach into their soul and figure out humanity," he explains. "The South has been so representative of the arts, like rock 'n' roll, blues, country – all the regional folk styles. The further north you go, the more the music sounds of Canada and Europe."

When it comes to composing, O'Connor assimilates the sounds of

Nick Shave

the South into his own style. Most of the folk tunes within his orchestral and chamber works — unless otherwise credited — are his own, born out of his musical upbringing. Take his most recent work, *Violin Concerto No.6*. Commissioned for this year's Proms in London, the piece was inspired by O'Connor's visit to the Frank Lloyd Wright Auldbrass Plantation in South Carolina. O'Connor uses the structural layout of the building as a guiding principle for the work, its hexagonal geometry inspiring six major themes and a six-part fugue in the final movement. His folk idiom, with its reliance upon fourths and fifths and toiling rhythms, evokes the place's atmosphere and geographical setting; through this language he relays his impressions of the building and the wide-open spaces of rural America.

"I make quite a departure from most of the European folk composers who actually went into the field to capture melodies of the folk and brought them back," he says. "I never had to do that because I was sort of born out of those traditions. I guess most people would associate my music with Copland, Gershwin and Bernstein, all of whom have influenced me. But what I have steered away from is this real European classical model of music making."

O'Connor's desire to draw folk material into the classical arena first found it's public expression in 1990 when, jaded by the treadmill of country music recording dates, he abandoned his career as a session musician and turned his hand to composition instead. It was a natural transition, occurring at a point when he was looking to free himself from the restricting rhythm sections of his session ensembles and perform, quite literally, at his own tempo. "It was an unusual time because I do get a lot of ideas and I forget them, but these ideas wouldn't leave my head for six months," he recalls. "I had 20 minutes of my *Fiddle Concerto* written in my head, as it turned out. I just had to figure out — from books on orchestration and talking to copyists — how to write it down." In 1993 he premiered the concerto with the Santa Fe Symphony; he has since performed it more than 150 times.

Tellingly, the *Fiddle Concerto* was first released on the Warner Bros. pop label to which O'Connor was signed at the time. With his next release – the second concerto, *Fanfare for the Volunteer* – O'Connor moved to the Sony Classical label. Teaming up with Sony Classical artists Yo-Yo Ma and Edgar Meyer to perform *Appalachia Waltz*, O'Connor entered the classical market. A medley of original and newly composed folk tunes, *Appalachia* Waltz blurred the boundaries

Voice of America

between Texas-style country fiddling, classical trio writing, jazz, Celtic, and American 'roots' music. It became a classical hit and was even in demand at the White House. "There I was, playing my *Appalachia Waltz*, with the great Yo-Yo Ma, for a state dinner in front of President Clinton," reels O'Connor. "I could have actually stuck out my hand and touched the top of the president's head if I had wanted to. It turned out he has a photographic memory and had memorized the entire contents of our liner notes." Though the trio was invited on first name terms, O'Connor would never call Clinton anything other than "Mr. President."

Appalachia Waltz signified O'Connor's rise towards classical status, but he denies he went through any crossover process in order to move into the classical arena. At a time when Sony Classical was seeking to diversify into new musical territories and redefine classical music, O'Connor provided a fresh and accessible sound. The crossing over, he says, was more a marketing stunt dictated by Sony's music moguls than any stylistic transition he went through. "They're grasping at straws sometimes when they're marketing this stuff," admits O'Connor. "But there's no doubt that they have to market it some way, because people just gotta hear about it. If you listen to my music closely, you'll realize that I'm not crossing over to anything, but just extending what I do on my instrument through what I grew up listening to."

Not that O'Connor will turn down the opportunity to draw comparisons between himself and the great performers and composers of the past. Writing in the inlay notes to his solo release, *Midnight on the Water*, he compares himself to Paganini. Both studied the mandolin and guitar in addition to the fiddle and began (performing) at an early age. He dedicates his *Six Caprices* to the Italian master and it's the technical challenges of O'Connor's works that pay tribute to Paganini's own writing. The pieces flash through breakneck tempos and polyphonic writing, all the while asking for a rhythm that dances and a tone that sings. "One of the biggest challenges of my caprices is their rhythmic intensity," says O'Connor. "You have to keep up this rhythmic drive throughout the passages as well as tackling virtuosic finger work. They're a great vehicle for classical violinists who want to open their minds to new repertoire."

Though O'Connor has made the transition from writing "fiddle concertos" to writing "violin concertos" over the years, there's no mis-

Nick Shave

taking his self-taught technique. When he plays, you can see he's a fiddler by the bend of his knees, the hunch of his shoulders, his incredibly loose bow arm and the way in which he beats time with the heel of his left foot. His sense of rhythm — high-lighted by his use of vibrato and glissandos — is second to none. "The interesting thing about folk music culture is that a lot of this stuff is just happening and you pick it up," he explains. "But to develop a smooth bow arm I used to practice by holding the violin under my neck, reaching [under the violin] with my left hand and grabbing the wrist of my right hand, while trying to get as much out of the bow as possible. I did that every day for a while and when I went back to normal playing it had really trained the muscles in my wrist to be able to play flowingly back and forth."

Away from the concert platform O'Connor's self-motivated teaching techniques have come into their own. Every year he gathers together a renowned clutch of folk and jazz musicians for conferences in San Diego — where he now lives — and Tennessee. Students stay on campus, spending the first two days taking classes in many genres of music, including jazz, Latin, classical and rock, specializing in chosen genres towards the end of their five-day course. "I feel like I am helping to instigate an American school for strong playing," enthuses O'Connor. "We cater to every ability and to all ages, levels and styles of playing. I'm there for the entire week and it's like a big, long party; every minute I'm not there is like missing out."

Scottish fiddler Carol Cook first collaborated with O'Connor two years ago, playing principal viola with the Metamorphosen Chamber Orchestra in O'Connor's performance of *The American Seasons*. She has since taught Scottish fiddle at O'Connor's camp. "His strength is that what he's doing is so unique," she says. "I guess with all great artists, like Grappelli and Heifetz, you hear them on the radio and you know who you're listening to. It's the same with Mark because his music couldn't be played by anybody else. But at the same time he'll never play the same phrase in the same way twice, but will always do something different, play with a slightly different sound or mix it up in improvisation. That's a great trait for people to learn from."

Though O'Connor has followed his own path from fiddling competitions to the classical field, he's finding his eccentricities are now paying off. To start the coming season he plays *The American Seasons* with the Los Angeles Philharmonic Orchestra, his *Double Concerto* with the Delaware, Colorado and Portland Symphony orchestras. At

Voice of America

the same time he's looking forward to working on a commission for a double concerto from the San Diego Symphony. In less than a year he will have written six concertos that he can play in concert halls around the world. That's no small achievement. "I have made incredible strides," agrees O'Connor. "It's like if you have a good idea and you know it in your heart, you know there's nothing else you can do. You're so inside your ideas that you just stay with them and people will notice you eventually. That's just what happens."

150

O BROTHER, WHAT NEXT? MAKING SENSE OF THE FOLK FAD

By Benjamin Filene
From *Southern Cultures* (University of North Carolina)

After *O Brother, Where Art Thou?* spurred a surge of interest in all things folk, I got calls from friends coast to coast. Since I wrote a book about folk revivalism, they assumed I'd be thrilled to see that the film and soundtrack had once again sparked interest in traditional music. I watched the movie; I listened to the soundtrack album; I read the breathless testimonials from the new folk fans. But the whole thing left me grumpy. Recently, I've been trying to figure out why.

I'm not a purist: I'm not griping about the fact that the performers benefiting from the revival are longtime commercial popularizers like Emmylou Harris or a Californian neo-billy like Gillian Welch, both prominent on the *O Brother* soundtrack. I'm not a protector: I'm not so much worried that the more traditional rural voices getting swept up in the revival—performers like Ralph Stanley—will get burned or somehow shorn of their edge as they get Hollywoodized. I'm not a hoarder: I don't have that feeling of remorse that comes as something that used to be private and precious and one's own—something that perhaps was personally transformative in one's coming-of-age period—gets commodified and spread casually across the globe.

Such tinges of regret are to some extent built in to any folk revival; they are inherent in the concept of trying to bring mass popularity to a cultural form beloved for its isolation from mass popularity. Indeed, it wouldn't surprise me if the *O Brother* phenomenon made some longtime public folklorists, revivalists, and preservationists uncomfortable.

Benjamin Filene

There is always some shock and regret when you get what you asked for—in this case when the music that one has been protecting and pitching, praying and proselytizing for all these years suddenly, seemingly with hardly any effort at all, is all over the airwaves and in everyone's living room. But I'm not a longtime public folklorist, revivalist, or preservationist. And yet, as a cultural historian, I find that today's folk chic bugs me, too.

The *O Brother* revival—and my reaction to it—has deep roots. It's no coincidence that director Joel Coen, and his brother, producer Ethan Coen, chose the 1930s, sepia-toned in their filmic memory, as the backdrop for their romp through American folk culture. Of course, efforts to preserve and popularize so-called "folk" materials go much further back than the thirties, but an array of efforts to embrace vernacular American culture did coalesce powerfully during the Depression. We're still dealing with the legacy of that intense burst of revivalism—directly in the sense that you can trace a lineage back from today's revival artists and cultural brokers to the thirties and indirectly in that thirties revivalists shaped our assumptions about what a revival is, who gets revived, and how. As influential as the revival of the fifties and sixties was and is, it was a wave that emerged from currents set into motion in the thirties by a group of ambitious cultural brokers who set out with missionary zeal to change how Americans saw their musical heritage.

Today's revival is in many ways the fruit of this group's work—people like John Lomax and, especially, his son Alan, Ben (B. A.) Botkin, Charles Seeger, and his son Pete. What, then, has nearly three quarters of a century of "cultural brokerism" brought us? Is the *O Brother* revival what the advocates of the thirties had in mind?

To some extent, the answer is yes. Let's think about what the cultural brokers of the thirties were trying to do. First, as driving forces behind the revivalist movement, the Lomaxes, Botkin, and the Seegers urged that folk culture be recognized as a distinctively American form of culture. For over a century before, American artists and intellectuals had been struggling to create "high art" that measured up to European elite-culture standards; for two generations folklorists had been collecting remnants of British ballads, in effect treating American folk songs as diluted versions of British ones. The thirties folk advocates rejected such Eurocentric approaches. America doesn't need to ape European arts, they said; we have our own forms of

O Brother, What Next? Making Sense of the Folk Fad

cultural expression, vibrant and worthy in their own right. In their 1941 songbook *Our Singing Country*, John and Alan Lomax wrote that American musicians "have created and preserved for America a heritage of folk songs and folk music equal to any in the world."[1]

Today this American-centric cultural argument has taken hold so completely that it is hard even to recognize it as an issue. In a world economy dominated by a single superpower, American popular culture is our main export. Doubt about our cultural distinctiveness feels like an issue from another era. The confidence with which this issue is handled, though, illustrates how thoroughly ingrained the cultural outlook of the thirties revivalists has become, indeed, the idea of studying and redeploying America's musical heritage is at the core of the current revival. In a dynamic that the older revivalists would well recognize, the current vogue for traditional music is reinforcing for a new generation the idea that the building blocks of today's global pop culture lie back in seemingly forgotten corners of American culture—the local, the rural, the long ago. Pop vocalist Natalie Merchant, for example, formerly the lead singer for 10,000 Maniacs, recently decided that she needed to reinvigorate her pop sound and rededicate herself to her craft. Her answer? She listened to field recordings by Alan Lomax, pored through books of folk song, and took courses on American folk music at Bard College.[2] The technopop star Moby took a more literal approach to his apprenticeship. On his 1999 album, *Play*, he quotes audio samples from Alan Lomax's 1959 *Sounds of the South* field recordings. Most pop performers, of course, don't quote Mississippi folk songs, but the idea of returning to American roots—so central to the thirties revivalists' mission—is again a legitimating rite of passage for younger artists and a way for older artists to reinvigorate themselves.

For the revivalists of the thirties, though, a second fundamental tenet was that American folk music was not just in the past. Inspired by functionalist anthropology, they saw folk songs not as isolated relics but as vital parts of living social systems. Traditions survived because they served functions for their adherents, and there was no reason to think that folk forms would stop filling these needs for people anytime soon. Folklore was not dying but was present everywhere, and everywhere transforming and revitalizing itself. "Folklore," B. A. Botkin wrote, "is not something far away and long ago, but real and living among us." "A piece of folklore," echoed Alan Lomax in *Our Singing*

Benjamin Filene

Country, "is a living, changing thing."[3]

This more robust conception of folk culture led the thirties revivalists to challenge the older assumption that folklorists must focus their studies on the isolated backwaters to search for regions free of modern technologies. "The tendency," Botkin said, "has been to restrict the folk to the backward, ignorant, and illiterate members of society and to emphasize the anachronistic and static, the useless and so meaningless aspects of folklore to the neglect of its living and dynamic phases." Rejecting this emphasis on the vestigial, the functionalists embraced the whole world of culture around them as fair game for "folklore." Under Botkin, for example, the Federal Writers Project began collecting urban folklore, gathering the songs and stories of New York Jewish needleworkers, Pennsylvania steelworkers, and Connecticut clockmakers. It was this wide-open attitude, in fact, that led the young functionalists to embrace hillbilly music, which, as a contemporary genre intended for commercial audiences, would have been anathema to more purist collectors. Charles Seeger called hillbilly music a "super-hybrid form of some genuine folk elements which have intruded into the mechanism of popular music." Botkin concurred that "'hillbilly' has its place in the hierarchy of American folk styles," emphasizing that folk music as a whole "is not a pure but a hybrid activity."[4]

As any comparative literature major today can tell you, the thirties folklorists were ahead of their time in embracing "hybridity," a fact apparent not only in postmodern academia but also in pop culture, including today's folk revival.

The contemporary folk boom seemingly encompasses everything from bluegrass to blues, Celtic reels to Cuban rumbas, Afro-Beat to zydeco. Sometimes an acoustic guitar alone can be enough to draw the label "folk." The soundtrack to *O Brother, Where Art Thou?* ranges from African American hymns to work songs to a Jimmie Rodgers pop song to a putative hobo ballad. Contemporary bluegrass queen Alison Krauss appears side by side with the gospel group the Fairfield Four and a prison field recording. To the album's producer, T Bone Burnett, like Alan Lomax or Ben Botkin before him, the American folk tradition is elastic enough to encompass all of these genres and artists, and he freely sprinkles them across the soundtrack.

When the 1930s functionalists argued for the adaptability and vitality of folk song, though, it was not an idle demonstration of hip

O Brother, What Next? Making Sense of the Folk Fad

open-mindedness. A third core belief, emerging and in some ways enveloping the previous two in importance, was that folk culture should be seen as an alternate source of strength in a time of crisis in America—as a counterculture, really. During the Great Depression, as the country's economic system crumbled, there was a growing sense of despair about American society—not only about its economic and political viability but about the very culture and character of its citizens. Who or what was to blame for the catastrophe the country faced? The Depression drove many middle-class Americans to reevaluate what forces in society were good, powerful, and sustaining. Many concluded that the blame lay not with ordinary Americans but with the mainstream institutions that were supposed to have been serving them. People were drawn to those who seemed to exist outside the modern industrial world, able to survive independent of its inhumane economy and not lulled by its superficial luxuries—the outcast, the folk, the impoverished and dispossessed. Think of novels such as Steinbeck's *Grapes of Wrath*, the photojournalism of *Life* and *Look* magazines, or the "I've-seen-America" books of Margaret Bourke-White and Erskine Caldwell, and James Agee and Walker Evans, with downtrodden men and women standing bedraggled but proud before the camera. Outsiders appealed to Americans as symbols of how they wanted to see themselves during the Depression: independent, proud in the face of hardship, straightforward, beholden to no special interests.[5]

The folk revivalists of the thirties were building on this same cultural impulse. When John and Alan Lomax embarked on their famous field recording trips in the 1930s, they sought traditional folk music in the "eddies of human society," self-contained homogeneous communities cut off from the corrupting influences of popular culture. They wanted to record people who had not been contaminated by radio—not so much to document a tradition before it faded away but to demonstrate that there were still cultural forms not contaminated by radio.

The notion of people making their own music from scratch, often with handmade instruments, drawing on traditions free from commercial manipulation, suggested an independent, self-sustaining culture that could endure any crisis—an alternative, more vital American culture. The thirties revivalists, in other words, documented folk cultures in hopes of turning contemporary culture upside down. That's what

Benjamin Filene

Ben Botkin meant when he said folklore should be "germinal rather than vestigial"; what Charles Seeger meant when he said the question should not be "'is it good music' but 'what is the music good for?'" Folk music was to be an agent of change that carried Americans through the Depression *and beyond*, the bedrock for a new, more grounded, more vibrant, more democratic future. Folklore, as Botkin stressed, should be "not only 'Back where I come from,' but also "Where do we go from here?'"[6]

Does the contemporary revival share this countercultural aspect, this forward-looking vision? In some respects, certainly, it does offer an alternative to mainstream musical fare. At the 2002 Grammy Awards, the *O Brother, Where Art Thou?* artists were strikingly incongruous next to their fellow album-of-the-year nominees, the Irish rockers U2, rappers OutKast, and pop-soul singer India.Arie. (Whether or not they were incongruous with the last nominee, Bob Dylan, is a debate unto itself.) In a Britney Spears bubblegum-pop landscape, the Stanley Brothers, not to mention the Carter Family or Lead Belly, do stand out. Indeed, part of what has fueled this folk revival is a restless dissatisfaction with contemporary mainstream culture. Many people, having been actively consuming pop culture since their preteen years, find that it leaves them empty. A common lament is that today's pop music sounds prepackaged, driven by MTV and product tie-ins more than artistic expression. The music on corporate-owned radio, on quick-cut videos, and in mega-mall CD stores feels like so much junk food, more detritus in the disposable culture of our age. Many feel nostalgic for a time they never knew but that they intuitively feel must have existed—when culture, when emotion for that matter, came unmediated, when there was substance that transcended the packaging.

Both this feeling of emptiness and the corresponding yearning for something more substantial are legitimate and potentially powerful. And for many people, *O Brother, Where Art Thou?* did bring to light music they had never heard before that became personally meaningful and enriched their understanding of American traditions. I fear, though, that this new understanding is not as deep and will not be as long-lasting or transformative as folk advocates—or even the new audiences themselves—would wish. The reasons lie embedded within the *O Brother* revival itself and in its historical antecedents.

What I think rankles me about the *O Brother* phenomenon is that

156

O Brother, What Next? Making Sense of the Folk Fad

even as the artists it features gain a degree of fame and fortune and a passel of awards, the revival in several key respects holds them and the music itself at a remove, depicting both as relics from another world and time. Remember B. A. Botkin's words: "Folklore is not something far away and long ago, but real and living among us"; or Alan Lomax, folklore is "a living, changing thing."

At every turn, the appeal of this music today seems to be its isolation from contemporary reality. Most directly the film and soundtrack strive for a geographic marginalization. *O Brother* depends on the songs of some wonderful commercial artists who have built careers in Nashville, Los Angeles, and New York by singing about issues with deep personal relevance in the here and now.

Yet *Down from the Mountain* is the title of the live concert album that followed the soundtrack, implying that the mainstream commercial artists on the album had just trekked out of the hills down to Nashville's Ryman Auditorium. The liner notes to the soundtrack itself play into the same myth of a foreign world: "There is another Nashville, with a kind of music so distant from what the city's commercial center cranks out as to be from a different planet. It thrives in the community's nooks and crannies like a cluster of quietly smiling mountain wildflowers."[7]

Beyond being geographically isolated, the music in *O Brother* is frozen in time. The movie itself, set in 1937, has the look of a faded memory, like stepping back into the pages of a dusty old copy of *Let Us Now Praise Famous Men*. The Coens told director of photography Roger Deakins that they wanted the film to look "brown and dirty and golden, like a period picture book of the Depression." Deakins pointed out that the movie was being shot in lushly green Mississippi, but the Coens were undeterred. To get the right look, Deakins digitized the whole film and removed the green. "We gave it an ochre feel," Deakins recalls. "I kept having to say to them, 'Just imagine it'll be all yellow'."[8]

The soundtrack album evokes the same mood of a bygone era. In graphic design, the liner notes have masterfully attained the look of a tattered scrapbook carried around for too long in someone's banjo case. The graphics feature fragments of pages torn, perhaps, from a *Farmer's Almanac*, FDR campaign buttons stuck through faded newspaper clippings, and photos that look to be affixed with electrical tape.

The text of the liner notes builds on this mood by depicting the

Benjamin Filene

music as childlike and pure. The author of the notes, Robert K. Oermann, describes the album as a celebration of "this gentle music" and offers Joel Coen's wistful assessment that the film was "a Valentine to the music." Oermann then constructs a historically awkward narrative of the despoiling of this delicate homegrown bloom. "The original country sound," he declares, "first flowered during the Depression." But Oermann goes on to say that the "innocence of this rustic, acoustic kind of country" was "drown[ed] out" by other genres, including "the razzmatazz of western swing" and "the cream crooning of singing cowboys."[9] But western swing and singing cowboys themselves took hold in the late twenties and thirties, during Oermann's supposed Golden Age. In Oermann's nostalgic formulation, in other words, the pure sound was so delicate and innocent that it was dead practically before it started.

Yet if this music is so gentle, so innocent, so pure, so delicate, why is it so violent and disturbing? Both the film and soundtrack open with an Alan Lomax field recording from 1959 of a prison chain gang singing about a prisoner getting shot by the sheriff. Other songs deal with the pain of adultery, abandoned children, hard times on the slaughterhouse killing floor, and being grabbed by the ice-cold hands of death. Even the bouncy hit "I Am a Man of Constant Sorrow" is hardly light fare upon closer inspection, with the words "For six long years I've been in trouble/... I never expect to see you again / For I'm bound to ride that northern railroad / Perhaps I'll die upon this train."

The film itself only ratchets up the pain and pathos, featuring hooded Klansmen; one-eyed Bible-selling con men; heart-of-gold, yellow-teethed gopher-eating dullards; and sold-my-soul-at-the-crossroads bluesmen. In interviews and press releases, the Coens have turned to Greek myth to account for the over-the-top aspects of the film, as if to suggest an archetypal element to the story. But stereotypes are archetypes without the timelessness. The links to *The Odyssey* strike me as superficial compared to the resonances with old-style Hollywood caricatures of the South. I suspect the Coens turn to Homer to shield themselves from the charges of having created a string of cardboard cutout depictions of the Old South. Southern actress Holly Hunter, Penny Wharvey in the movie, says that the Coens' South "is not the one I grew up in. But ... [w]hat are you going to do? It's based on *The Odyssey*."[10]

More than classicism, though, the Coen brothers' most powerful

O Brother, What Next? Making Sense of the Folk Fad

shield from such P.C. criticism is ironic detachment. For all the chaos in *O Brother*, pain and pathos are *not* the mood. This is a comedy, right? Violence, disfigurement, poverty, racism are not sources of sorrow or recoil but amusement. These are just a set of literary tales, the film's zany quality suggests. Like *Pulp Fiction*, the violence is cartoonish and is served up with a heavy dose of irony. The CD disc itself has a convict stripe on it, but we know this is a wry joke, nothing to take any more seriously than the fact that the disc is made to look like a phonograph record.

Cartoonish eccentricity is prime Coen brothers territory. From *Raising Arizona* to *Fargo* they have gloried in lampooning the misfits, the marginalized, the skewed and the skewered. It makes for enjoyable, playful movies that sit well with our postmodern sensibility, our feeling that we're watching a series of plot elements clang against each other, not the stories of real people and their lives.

Anyone who knows anything about folk music traditions knows that gothic and gruesome images are standard fare, not something the Coen brothers dreamed up. This is the "Old, Weird America" that critic Greil Marcus has identified as a longstanding component of folk music and, indeed, folk revivals. Marcus coined the phrase to describe the alternately chilling and outlandish world that musicologist Harry Smith created out of commercial hillbilly and blues songs in his 1952 multivolume *Anthology of American Folk Music*. Marcus surveys the murderers, talking birds, train wrecks, drug addicts, drowning victims, stabbing victims, and suicides in the *Anthology* and writes, "The whole bizarre package made the familiar strange, the never known into the forgotten, and the forgotten into a collective memory that teased any single listener's conscious mind." Marcus finds this alternate America to be a bracing contrast to McCarthyism and the consumption-obsessed culture of the 1950s, which prioritized sugary conformity. To Marcus and so many other listeners who encountered the Anthology in the fifties and sixties and in the decades since, the performers on the compilation sounded "like visitors from another world." Sixties revival performers Jim Rooney and Eric von Schmidt recalled that when they first heard the collection they assumed that "all those guys on that Harry Smith *Anthology* were dead. *Had* to be."[11]

Yet the *Anthology* is not really as much a world apart as Marcus and others would have it. As Marcus himself notes, when the collection came out in 1952, the artists it featured were only twenty to twenty-

Benjamin Filene

five years past their commercial primes, and most were still very much alive in the South. Jeff Place, archivist at the Smithsonian's Center for Folklife Programs, has pointed out that Smith's "rediscovery" mission would be chronologically akin to someone today unearthing a crop of songs from New Wave punk bands from circa 1980—"Look!" they might say, "Adam Ant! Blondie!"[12] But it's not only chronologically that Harry Smith's folk have been artificially pushed back into the past. As historian J. M. Mancini observes, the very performers that Marcus et al. have idealized as the avatars of marginalized old, weird America were actually very much *in step* with the Jazz Age consumer culture of the 1920s—listening to the radio, buying goods on credit (including factory-made instruments), migrating to cities, and taking advantage of an emerging, racially hybrid regional culture. As Mancini says, these artists "represent not a dying past of homemade banjos, isolated rural communities, and weird murder ballads, but the integration of Appalachia into a nationalizing market and consumer culture."[13]

The "reality" of the folk performer's world, though, is not at the core of the current revival, just as it wasn't for the revival of the fifties and sixties. The idea of folk culture as geographically isolated, chronologically removed, and socially deviant remains instrumental to the current folk vogue. People are drawn to the notion of the "old, weird America." How can we reconcile this fascination with aberrance and deviance with the contemporary revival's nostalgic romancing of folk culture as pure and innocent? I see them as two sides of the same distancing phenomenon. What we today are looking back on with fascination and even envy is these songs' seeming capacity to express intense, unvarnished feeling. Our daily reality has been so co-opted by media—in everything from staged "reality TV" shows to a made-for-TV war—that we experience even the most catastrophic events as mediated. The more on-the-spot and graphic the depiction of daily reality becomes, the more it all seems like a movie of someone else's life. So we look back on both the innocence *and* the violence of these folk songs with the intrigued, somewhat bemused air of world-weary anthropologists—or, more accurately, of world-weary consumers of other people's experiences. Isn't it *fascinating* that people felt the kind of pain expressed in "Killing Floor Blues" or "Po' Lazarus" or "House Carpenter's Daughter"? Isn't it *fascinating* that people could sing of lemonade springs and bluebirds singing and candy mountains without a smirk? Isn't it *fascinating* that people were confined in all-black pris-

O Brother, What Next? Making Sense of the Folk Fad

ons and that they worked with their legs bound by manacles? Both the idealism and the exoticism of this imagery seem from another world, and we watch them with the detached fascination we might give a carnival sideshow.

This cultural dynamic has helped spur an undeniably vigorous folk chic, but I fear that detachment of this sort is not a healthy foundation for a sustained revival. The danger is that folk culture, since it has been appropriated at such a distance, becomes just one in a series of fashion products that savvy consumers of global culture try on and discard—like hip-hop jeans, rain-forest body lotion, and Indonesian sarongs. Does anyone remember the swing-jazz revival? That was so mid-1990s, right? Roots becomes another brand, "authenticity" another accessory. Moreover, since its cachet depends on its marginality, as soon as mainstream culture "discovers" an example of true folk grit, its appeal is already compromised. Like vacationers looking for the next "unspoiled" vacation paradise, folk consumers are continually forced to push on toward the next outpost. The folk fad, then, becomes an ephemeral *flavor du jour*, not a deep, sustaining current in American culture.

How did we get into this situation where music that so many people feel so deeply about is held at such a remove and consumed so casually? Ironically, the roots of this dynamic lie in contradictions embedded in the same thirties revival that begat today's folk surge. Even as functionalists like Alan Lomax or the Seegers urged Americans to embrace contemporary folk cultures and argued that they could revitalize a compromised society, they, too, held the folk at a distance. They remained deeply ambivalent about where the folk belonged: past or present, urban centers or hinterlands, pop culture or subculture, middle-class mainstream or outcast deviance.

For example, even as the thirties revivalists urged that folk song be recognized as a vital, ever-adapting force and pushed to collect urban folklore, there was a strong countervailing sense in their work that folk song *can't* exist in the present and that true folk artists emerge, pristine, from nowhere. This view goes back to John Lomax, who in the Lomaxes' 1934 book *American Ballads and Folk Songs* wrote, "A life of isolation, without books or newspapers or telephone or radio, breeds songs and ballads."[14] Thirty years later the revivalists were still deeply ambivalent about the notion of an elastic, contemporary folk repertoire. Think of the tale of Bob Dylan going electric at the 1965

Benjamin Filene

Newport Folk Festival and an enraged Alan Lomax trying to pin Dylan's manager to the ground while Pete Seeger hunted for an ax to cut the cables.[15]

Likewise, even as revivalists urged that folk performers be treated as artists and exemplars of American cultural achievement, they marginalized them as exotic, untutored outsiders. As early as 1925, folklorist Archie Green has found, hillbilly songs were being hyped as old-timey expressions of the untutored folk. The Victor catalogue for that year praised the songs as produced by "unlettered and never self-conscious chroniclers."[16] Often, assumptions about the folk were touched with an edgy frisson of violence. Why, for example, was Alan Lomax *looking* for all-black prison chain-gang songs like "Po' Lazarus" in 1959? Surely he couldn't claim any longer, twenty-five years after his first trips south, that these men were isolated from radio? No doubt he felt some illicit thrill, a thrill I think audiences still feel today, in the pent-up force of these prisoners working against their will.

You can see all these contradictory expectations bound up in the story of Lead Belly.[17] "Discovered" by John and Alan Lomax in a Louisiana prison in 1933, Lead Belly came with the Lomaxes to New York City after his release in 1935, eager to earn a living through his music. There the Lomaxes promoted him as a violent, animalistic force. In a letter previewing his coming attraction to the local newspapers, John Lomax wrote, "Leadbelly is a nigger to the core of his being. In addition he is a killer. He tells the truth only accidentally.... He is as sensual as a goat, and when he sings to me my spine tingles and sometimes tears come. Penitentiary wardens all tell me that I set no value on my life in using him as a traveling companion. I am thinking of bringing him to New York in January."

The *New York Herald-Tribune* grasped the idea: "Sweet Singer from the Swamplands Here to Do a Few Tunes between Homicides" read its headline about Lead Belly's arrival. This image brought Lead Belly attention, but it also constrained his ability to reach broad audiences. His cachet within the revival depended on having a raw, emotive sound, but he needed to smooth out some of this rawness if he hoped to garner mass appeal. He was a fan of pop songs, including singing cowboy Gene Autry, but the Lomaxes discouraged him from singing such material. And if Lead Belly did tone down his performances, he was seen as compromising what made him an "authentic" performer in the first place. Caught in this trap, Lead Belly never

O Brother, What Next? Making Sense of the Folk Fad

achieved commercial success in his lifetime. Only when he was safely in the past, dead in 1949 at age sixty, could he be "rediscovered" and elevated into a primal folk archetype.

These contradictory sets of expectations that Lead Belly faced constitute what I have called a "cult of authenticity." that the thirties revivalists erected. The folk musician was expected to be a master craftsman but raw, a powerful showman but unself-conscious and devoid of commercial attributes, an exemplar of American character but untrammeled by societal norms. As Lead Belly's example shows, these contradictory assumptions can trap performers. It's a dilemma that continues to this day. Jeff Tweedy was formerly the darling of the alt-country crowd during his days with the pioneering band Uncle Tupelo, but he says he felt he had to lose his alt-country "baggage" and break free from traditionalists' rigid expectations before he could take his current band, Wilco, in new directions. Likewise, the garage-rock band the White Stripes, Jack and Meg White from Detroit, feels a strong connection to American roots traditions, but the group fears becoming caught in the web that snared Tweedy. The band dedicated an album to bluesman Blind Willie McTell and covered Son House's classic "Death Letter" blues, but the two live in fear of having their authenticity evaluated. Says singer Jack White, "We're white people who play the blues, and our problem was how do we do that and not be fake." Likewise, the Whites feel stymied as to how to translate folk music into political change. "The blues could be very political," White says. "You know—Lead Belly sang about Hitler. But I shy away from doing anything like that because I'm scared of novelty. I'm scared of having nowhere to go with it."[18] Inadvertently, then, the thirties revivalists spawned an emphasis on authenticity that undercuts two of their main tenets: that folk music is a flexible, vital contemporary form and that it can be a powerful force for political change.

The cult of authenticity not only stymies performers; it tangles up listeners as well. I see some of its paralyzing effects in my own reactions to contemporary music. It helps to account, I think, for the grouchy response I have to some of today's popular folk material. If a performer is too rough-hewn, it often strikes me as scam primitivism. Come on, I feel like saying, no twenty-first-century musician can legitimately pose as an isolated, raw mouthpiece of tradition. Your music is a practiced art and should be portrayed that way. On the other hand, I find that if revival performers seem *too* polished, their folk alle-

163

Benjamin Filene

giances start to seem like calculated put-ons, and I question their legitimacy as traditional practitioners. I admit that this double whammy is
unfair, yet the revival's long preoccupation with "the real thing" invites
constant reevaluation and repositioning of performers and audiences
alike on an authenticity scale.

I'm not sure it had to be this way. Historian Kyle Barnett points
out that we don't ask for the same degree of anticommercial authenticity from films or television (or, I would add, theater and literature).[19] Moreover, while questions of "keeping it real" do to some
extent dog punk and hip-hop musicians, no genre seems quite as beset
by them as folk. Even jazz, romanticized and racialized by music critics for a century, seems to allow musicians more room to grow and be
respectable individual artists—lionized but necessarily animalized.

Is there a way out of these dilemmas? How might folk music claim
not just short-term popularity on the charts but the broader role that
the thirties revivalists imagined, becoming a fluid, flexible contemporary form and an agent for societal change? In trying to tease out an
answer, my thoughts turn to Pete Seeger, whom I heard live for the
first time in the fall of 2002 in a memorable concert. Seeger has been
performing for over sixty years, and I found it interesting to note what
parts of his persona and his performance have had the most staying
power. One thing seems clear: in an age of irony, earnestness is not the
answer. Seeger's aw-shucks radicalism seems like a relic from another
era, to the point that its oppositionality hardly registers. Once black-
listed and called before the House Un-American Activities Committee
(he nobly refused to testify), Seeger hardly seems a threat to the gov-
ernment now. President Clinton awarded him a National Medal for
the Arts and a Kennedy Center Honors award for lifetime achievement in the arts. A straightforwardly political statement from the stage
nowadays seems more like a period piece than a call to action—just the
sort of novelty that Jack White of the White Stripes so fears.

Indeed, the earnestness of the sixties folk revival is fodder for parody in the latest "mockumentary" written and directed by Christopher
Guest, *A Mighty Wind*. In the tradition of *Waiting for Guffman*, *This Is
Spinal Tap*, and *Best in Show*, the film skewers the sixties revival for its
preachiness. Guest and his ensemble cast found the musical movement
to be an easy target: "There is a kind of pomposity and a little bit of
an arrogance about folk music and folk artists," reflects actor Eugene
Levy. "You find there's not a lot of people with a great sense of humor

O Brother, What Next? Making Sense of the Folk Fad

about themselves and about their work. They're just too intense; they're trying to get out the message."[20]

Surely this is a sad commentary that "trying to get out the message" sets you up for parody. Yet there is another side to the folk revival—other than message music—that Christopher Guest and crew wouldn't think to ridicule.

Some contemporary revival practitioners have managed to sidestep the strictures of authenticity and ally themselves not with a certain canon or a particular sound but to the folk process itself—the process of digging for vernacular roots, creatively combining them into new forms, and giving them fresh life through personally meaningful art. I think of Bob Dylan—nearly four decades after supposedly spurning the folk revival—still busily brewing up his own idiosyncratic blend of blues, hillbilly, gospel, Tin Pan Alley, and rock 'n' roll. I think of Jeff Tweedy's Wilco getting together with British political rocker Billy Bragg to write melodies for newly discovered Woody Guthrie lyrics. I think again of the White Stripes with their pounding blues rock or of bluegrass fiddler Mark O'Connor collaborating with Itzhak Perlman and Wynton Marsalis.

And I return to Pete Seeger and the remarkable performance I witnessed. Seeger is not and never was authentic. Even in his jeans and holding his banjo, he looks more like a town selectman than a hillbilly. Performing at the City University of New York's Graduate Center, he didn't pretend the auditorium was a juke joint or a barn dance. It was the here and now that mattered to him, and that's what moved me to tears that night. Seeger's own voice is so tattered he can only generate a warbly whisper, but through gesture and sheer will he led a crowd of four hundred in spirited song. *This* is the side of Seeger that has staying power—his sheer joy at the process of building, sharing, tweaking and twanging the elements of vernacular song. This approach, which once seemed so different from Dylan's, now looks very much the same, and it's their greatest legacy. Whatever form this music takes, Seeger seemed to be demonstrating, it just has to be part of the world we're making.

I believe Pete Seeger would tell the Coens not to treat the folk as spooks to be pulled from the crypt, not to create mental maps that relegate them to the backwaters of time or geography, but rather to treat folk traditions as part of a powerful stream that is endlessly folding in new currents, breaking off into fresh new rivulets, and washing over

Benjamin Filene

new terrain. These have to be living, swirling traditions. For all my criticisms of the Coens, I did get a glimmer in *O Brother, Where Art Thou?* that perhaps they do have some instinct for this more free-flowing vision. At the end of the film, the TVA floods the valley—symbolizing the rush of popular culture that would soon threaten to drown out southern distinctiveness. The destructive power of the torrent at first seems overwhelming, but in the depths, seemingly from nowhere, a banjo and a phonograph float by. Are the Coens saying that these old-timey elements are being washed away forever or, as I like to think, that they are about to surface and float along with the current? This, I would argue, should be the Coens'—and our—beginning point for a sequel to *O Brother, Where Art Thou?* and the musical revival it spawned, a story that starts when the sepia tones wash away and folk traditions bob up into the clear light of day.

Notes

[1] John A. Lomax and Alan Lomax, eds., *Our Singing Country: A Second Volume of American Ballads and Folk Songs* (Macmillan, 1941), xi.

[2] Jon Pareles, "Natalie Merchant, No Strings Attached," *New York Times*, 13 March 2003, E, 1.

[3] B. A. Botkin, in *Fighting Words*, ed. Donald Ogden Stewart (Harcourt, Brace and Co., 1940), II; Lomax and Lomax, eds., *Our Singing Country*, xiv.

[4] B. A. Botkin, "The Folkness of the Folk," *English Journal* (College Edition) 26 (June 1937): 464; Federal Writers Project described in B. A. Botkin, *A Treasury of American Folklore: Stories, Ballads, and Traditions of the People* (Crown Publishers, 1944), xxii, 9-10; Charles Seeger in "Conference on the Character and State of Studies in Folklore [Proceedings of April 11-12, 1942 conference]," *Journal of American Folklore* 100 (October-December 1946): 512; Botkin, *Treasury of American Folklore*, 819.

[5] I discuss thirties populism in similar terms in *Romancing the Folk: Public Memory and American Roots Music* (University of North Carolina Press, 2000), 64-65. The phrase "I've-seen-America" is Joe Klein's, from his *Woody Guthrie: A Life* (Alfred A. Knopf, 1980), 146.

[6] B. A. Botkin, "WPA and Folklore Research: 'Bread and Song',"

Southern Folklore Quarterly 3 (March 1939): 14; Charles Seeger, General Considerations for Music Directors in Leading Community Programs, 1937 (unpublished), in Ann M. Pescatello, *Charles Seeger: A Life in American Music* (University of Pittsburgh Press, 1992), 142; Botkin, *A Treasury of American Folklore*, xxii.

[7] Robert K. Oermann, "'Old-Time Music Is Very Much Alive' But You Won't Hear It on 'Country' Radio," liner notes to *O Brother, Where Art Thou?* soundtrack, 088 170-069-2 DG02, UMG Recordings, 2000.

[8] Ronald Bergan, "On the Run with Joel and Ethan," *The Guardian*, 15 August 2000, http://www.guardian.co.uk/arts /story/0,3604,353916,00.html.

[9] Oermann, "Old-Time Music."

[10] "Down the Road Apiece: *O Brother Where Art Thou*," *Preview* 45 (May-June 2000), preview-online.com/may_june00/feature_articles/obrother/index.html.

[11] Greil Marcus, *Invisible Republic: Bob Dylan's Basement Tapes* (Henry Holt Co., 1997), 95, 94.

[12] Jeff Place in National Public Radio interview, "America's Folk Music Anthology: 50 Years Later, Harry Smith's Music Collection Still Rings True," 17 July 2002.

[13] J. M. Mancini, "Reviving the Folk Revival," *Common-place* 3 (October 2002): 3.

[14] John A. Lomax and Alan Lomax, eds., *American Ballads and Folk Songs* (Macmillan, 1934), xxvi, xxvii.

[15] What Seeger and Lomax actually did that evening in Newport remains the subject of much debate (see *Romancing the Folk*, 183-84). Regardless, their rage at Dylan's performance was real.

[16] Archie Green, *Torching the Fink Books and Other Essays on Vernacular Culture* (University of North Carolina Press, 2001), 30.

[17] I discuss Lead Belly's case at greater length in *Romancing the Folk*, 47-75, from which the material cited here is drawn.

[18] Joshua Green, "Been There: Wilco's Jeff Tweedy Talks about Losing His Alt-Country Baggage," Salon, 17 March 1999, http://archive.salon.com/ent/music/int/1999/03/17int.html; Hugo Lindgren, "Questions for the White Stripes: Rock 'n' Rules," *New York Times Magazine*, 9 March 2003, 17.

[19] Kyle Barnett, "The Lomaxes at the Gates of Culture: Authenticity and the Creation of 'Folk Music'," paper delivered at American

Benjamin Filene

Studies Association annual meeting, 16 November 2002.

[20] In Greg Dean Schmitz, "*A Mighty Wind.* Greg's Preview," Yahoo Movies, 19 June 2002, http://movies.yahoo.com/ shop?d=hp&cf=prev&id=1808412293, 2.

LOST NOTES AND MYRIAD BLESSINGS

John Prine's first album of new material in nearly a decade takes up cancer, kids and true love

By Michael McCall
From *The Nashville Scene*

Leave it to John Prine to find a silver lining amid life-changing adversity. Having a section of your neck and throat cut out during surgery for cancer would be traumatic for anyone. For it to happen to Prine, one of the most celebrated singer-songwriters of the post-Dylan era, was earth-shattering. Because he also makes his living performing around the world, and because he'd finally found marital and domestic bliss, it could have been the stuff of Greek tragedy.

Just as Prine's songs consider the reprehensible and the glorious as inevitable aspects of life, he's come to see the humor and humanity in what he's endured. "I'm singing in a lower key than before," he says. "I really didn't realize it until recently, but this is a good thing. When I sing, it's so much easier and more natural, I can't believe I didn't figure this out until the surgery sort of forced me to do it. I feel like this is the voice I should've always had. To me, it sounds more like the way I talk."

Then he laughs, letting out a raspy, staccato chuckle. "Of course, I don't sound so good when I talk, either," he cracks.

Like many singer-songwriters in the wake of Bob Dylan, John Prine emerged in the 1970s with sharply observed songs and a quirky voice. Like the best of them, Prine's craggy intonation added to the

169

Michael McCall

charms of his material. His calling card has always been writing about everyday characters with wisdom, insight and humor, and his wry phrasing and hoarse, husky tone brought a warmth to his folksy sagacity and wit. Like many great songwriters—Dylan, Townes Van Zandt, Tom Waits, Guy Clark—Prine's peculiar voice suits what he has to say. "I guess if you keep making the same mistake long enough, it becomes your style," he says.

Being who he is, Prine can't help but finding funny stories in his brush with mortality. He likes to tell of the Houston radiologist, who professed that he was a fan and said he could shield Prine's vocal cords during the six weeks of radiation treatments the singer underwent following his radical neck dissection. "I asked him, 'You've heard me sing, right?'" Prine recalls with another laugh. "I told him not to worry about my voice because I never really have. I told him I'd rather make sure we got all the cancerous cells out of there."

As a cancer survivor, Prine didn't at first notice how his voice changed; he was just glad to be able to sing again. "You know, the other great thing is that all my old songs seem new to me again, because I sing them differently," he says. "They're fresh because they sound different, and I do think they sound better now. It was kind of a gift; after singing them for 20 or 30 years, it's like I get to rediscover them."

Prine's lower, more relaxed tone brings to life *Fair & Square*, his first album of new material in nine years. As whimsical as ever, his new work reflects other changes in his life, too. There are more love songs, and his observant takes of the quotidian seem less sardonic and at times more deeply blue. He can still get across his anger. While he's always woven social commentary into his work—he even was tagged a protest singer early in his career—the album's anti-Bush tirade "Some Humans Ain't Human" is his most pointed political blast since 1972's "Your Flag Decal Won't Get You Into Heaven Anymore."

"I felt like I had to write something about how I feel about the way things are in this country right now," Prine says of the song, a harangue aimed at callous individuals and calculated, lying leaders. "Some Humans Ain't Human" compares heartless people to a neglected home freezer full of old frozen pizzas, to "ice cubes with hair" in them and to "a broken Popsicle." The song further asserts that jealousy and stupidity don't equal harmony.

But the zinger that's creating controversy, and causing some to

Lost Notes and Myriad Blessings

walk out at his shows, comes in the last stanza. "Have you ever noticed / When you're feeling really good / There's always a pigeon / That'll come shit on your hood," Prine asks, speaking rather than singing at this point. "Or [when] you're feeling your freedom / And the world's off your back / Some cowboy from Texas / Starts his own war in Iraq."

"What bothers me the most is the way this administration is toward people who are dissenting, the way they're coming down on people," Prine says. "They act as if you're not supporting the troops if you have anything negative to say about Bush or any of his people. That seems totally un-American to me. It's the total flipside of what this country is supposed to be about."

Prine acknowledges that his commentary usually comes from character sketches or story songs. "Some Humans Ain't Human" has its humorous side, especially its carnival-sideshow arrangement, but the songwriter wanted to make his sentiments clear.

"I just got to a point where I didn't want to be silent about it," he goes on. "I thought if I didn't say anything, then people might take it that I was supporting what is going on. If I went out and got hit by a car tomorrow, I wouldn't want anyone to think I was a Republican."

Prine is seated behind the desk of Al Bunetta, his manager of several decades, and the physical changes wrought by his surgery are evident. His neck is disproportionately smaller than it was before he contracted cancer, and the changes in his jaw have caused his lower bite to recede. Yet he's not self-conscious about the changes, which marks another way he departs from most artists. Never vain, Prine has always accepted his disheveled appearance, looking like the everyman who could have lived on the same block as the offbeat characters who populate his songs.

Prine and Bunetta founded Oh Boy Records in 1984, four years after John moved to Nashville. The label has maintained a quiet presence on Music Row over the years, issuing recent albums by Todd Snider, Janis Ian, Kris Kristofferson and Shawn Camp while reissuing vintage country recordings and tending Prine's weighty catalog, as well as that of his old friend, the late Steve Goodman.

As he sits, Prine's hands frequently move along the desk, as if looking for something to do. A chain-smoker since his teens, Prine nearly always had a cigarette between his fingers until he was diagnosed with cancer in 1998. Most of his publicity photos dating back to the '70s even include a partially smoked cigarette. Seven years on, he's still not

Michael McCall

sure what to do with his fingers.

At age 58, Prine, who grew up in Maywood, Ill., talks about how nearly everything in his life has turned upside down in the last decade—and how he's just fine with that. "You know, I don't really sit and think about it a whole lot, but my life is completely different from what it once was," he says. "I don't want to say it's one thing. Certainly, being a dad is a big part of it. Having the cancer, that made some things change, too. They weren't really subtle changes. Some things had to change real fast."

For one, he's given up his nightlife, which was legendary among his close-knit friends but little known beyond that. Through the first 25 years of his career, Prine maintained such a humorous, approachable quality that only those close to him knew how much he liked to party. A friendly imbiber, he didn't burn destructively like his peer Townes Van Zandt or recklessly like Steve Earle, but he'd hold court well into the night and into the morning, spinning stories and playing music with small groups of friends.

"All of a sudden, and for the first time ever, I'm leading a normal life," Prine says. "Especially now that my boys are in school, I'm up at 6:30, and I'm in bed by 11. It's a total flip-flop."

Prine married his third wife, Fiona, in 1990; their oldest son, Jack, is 10 years old, and his brother Tommy is a year younger. Fiona's 23-year-old son Jody lives at the family's home in Green Hills as well. Despite his health scare, Prine figures having children late in life was just right for him.

"If I'd had children earlier in my life, I think I would have had a tendency to see what my limits were, and that wouldn't have been good," he says. "I didn't realize it, but I was all ready for children to come into my life at the time they did. I didn't know I was looking for anything, but it sure came along at the right time."

Prine now attends the boys' sporting events and often is home when they come in from school, which makes him more of a hands-on father than most of the lawyers and businessmen in his neighborhood. "I've got a good home life," he says. "It's about as steady of a home life as I've ever had. I'm there with the boys a lot, and Fiona is just a really good person. I'm lucky to have her. She's brought order to my life, which is a good thing, because if she hadn't, I probably wouldn't be here. I guess the magic of that comes out in the music."

Indeed, *Fair & Square* features more love songs than Prine has ever put on an album. He started in that direction shortly after marrying Fiona. "You Got Gold" and "I Want to Be With You Always" were standout tracks on 1991's *The Missing Years*. The new "Glory of True Love," with its chiming melody and unabashed celebration of just how precious it is to find someone to share your life with, comes across like a follow-up to "You Got Gold" written a decade after the joy has settled in and deepened.

Similarly, the new "She Is My Everything" brims with playful toasts to the woman he adores, while "Long Monday," written with Prine's friend Keith Sykes, bemoans the fact that, after a weekend of making love and music together, it's time to go back to work. As he drives off, he's still high on love, humming, "You and me / Sittin' in the back of my memory / Like a honeybee / Buzzin' 'round a glass of sweet Chablis."

Oddly enough, Prine's best work often follows periods when he's considered retiring from making records. *Bruised Orange* came after he left Atlantic Records, where he made his first four albums, three of them with producer Arif Mardin. (Mardin now works with Norah Jones, who recently covered "That's the Way That the World Goes 'Round," a song from *Bruised Orange*.)

Prine left Atlantic in 1976 as the commercial crest of the singer-songwriter movement waned. Jerry Wexler, the famed talent scout who had brought Ray Charles, Aretha Franklin and Wilson Pickett to Atlantic, had given Prine his first record deal as well. But Wexler had left the company, and Ahmet Ertegun had recently signed Led Zeppelin and the Rolling Stones to lucrative deals. The record industry had evolved, focusing on hard rock, dance music, funk and the emerging punk movement. The acoustic singer-songwriters who had risen in the early '70s no longer received the airplay or the record company promotion they once had.

"Atlantic had become part of Warner Bros. and moved into Rockefeller Center," Prine told the *Scene* in a 1995 interview. "I remember when I first went into the old Atlantic, and it had all these gold records by these great R&B and jazz artists. It was a friendly place. It didn't seem like a big corporation. But by time Jerry left, that wasn't the case anymore."

The pop music industry was evolving from underground clubs, music halls and offbeat record stores to arenas, strong-arm promoters and chain stores. Prine no longer felt connected to it. He nearly left

Michael McCall

the business, considering becoming a fisherman, among other things. He traveled to Nashville because he'd met Cowboy Jack Clement, and he hung out at Clement's famed Cowboy Arms Hotel and Recording Spa, writing songs and recording stray tracks.

The recordings eventually were scrapped, but Prine seemed creatively renewed. He signed with David Geffen's Asylum Records, which still held out some hope for the commercial possibilities of acoustic music. He then set up shop with his old buddy Steve Goodman in a Chicago recording studio. Even though the sessions were marked with heated arguments between the two friends, the result, *Bruised Orange*, featured several of Prine's most enduring songs, including "Fish and Whistle," "There She Goes," "If You Don't Want My Love," "Crooked Piece of Time" and the one-of-a-kind "Sabu Visits the Twin Cities Alone."

After *Bruised Orange*, Prine wanted to experiment with his sound, perhaps wanting to punch it up in the way Neil Young or Joni Mitchell altered their work as times and trends changed. Proud of the rocking band he'd been touring with, he huddled in Memphis' Sun Studio with Knox and Jerry Phillips, the sons of Sun founder Sam Phillips, who also lent his wild-eyed advice to the proceedings. The album that resulted, *Pink Cadillac*, updated its rockabilly fervor with the raw, noisy spirit of punk.

But Asylum didn't understand the album and hardly promoted it. Frustrated again with his record company, Prine went into Muscle Shoals and created *Storm Windows*, another rock-combo album whose slicker sound had the strengths of albums by Tom Petty or Bob Seger. It, too, was ignored. Prine is a better rocker than he's given credit for, and his raucous version of The Carter Family's "Bear Creek Blues" on *Fair & Square* nicely recalls that era.

For the last time, Prine severed his ties to a major label and again considered quitting. He could earn enough money touring to keep alive, he reasoned. But Bunetta, his longtime manager, brought up the idea of starting their own label. Bunetta had successfully run a mail-order label, Red Pajamas, which marketed the music of Steve Goodman, whom he also managed. Prine agreed to give it a try, and so they founded Oh Boy Records, named for the exclamation in one Buddy Holly's most famous songs.

"I don't think I would've continued doing this if I had to jump from label to label," Prine says. "There was something missing. I'm

Lost Notes and Myriad Blessings

not a control freak or anything close, but what they do and what I do is two different things. They're trying to market music the same way you sell blue jeans and cars. My music's not really made for that."

Still, he never envisioned a label that would be thriving 20 years later—and that would serve as a role model for a growing movement of artist-owned indies. "I'm completely amazed we're still here," he says, crediting Bunetta's hard work and industry expertise for keeping the label afloat despite the fact that Prine's released just six studio albums in its 21 years of existence. "I think he does it with mirrors and smoke sometimes, but thank God he has. It gives us something to talk about."

Having his own label gives Prine the freedom to operate in ways that other artists can't. He's put out two live albums and a live DVD, as well as re-recorded an album of his best-known songs (*Souvenirs*) and released another of cover songs of male-female duets (*In Spite of Ourselves*). Owning Oh Boy also encourages him to write and keep recording rather than just to rely on his income from concert touring, which is considerable.

This time around, though, between family obligations and health considerations, he had to change the manner of his writing. "I'd always just kind of wait for songs to come," he says. "They'd arrive in batches, two or three at a time. I could let it happen most any time of day. A lot of the time that would happen to be about 3 o'clock in the morning, or whatever, because I was sleeping until noon anyway."

With fatherhood, all of that changed. "When the songs weren't coming every couple months or so, I realized, 'Oh, I get it, I have to start making appointments to do this stuff,' " he says. "I have to say, 'OK, next Wednesday I'm going to write.' With the kids and the family, I have to schedule time to do other things. Otherwise, I'll just hang out with them."

Because the writing was taking longer, Prine started making demos on his own to show his songs to a potential producer. But he liked the sound of the demos, and eventually decided to record the album himself. He recruited Gary Paczosa as co-producer because he liked the sounds Paczosa got on albums by Alison Krauss and Mindy Smith.

Prine had been credited as a co-producer on *Aimless Love* and *German Afternoons*, the first two albums that he made for Oh Boy with producer Jim Rooney. This time, however, he assumed a much larger role in overseeing production than he did back then.

Michael McCall

"I'm going to have to write a letter of apology to Jim," he says. "Apparently, he was doing the whole darn thing, and I was just tagging along for the show. Now that I've really done it, I know the difference. It's definitely the first time I've taken a hold of the reins and ridden the thing all the way down to the end of the rodeo."

Even so, Prine's new album may be the most fitting production of his career. There's a warm, natural groove to each song, and the prominence of rhythm guitar and the gentle additions of accordion and steel guitar fit perfectly with his rolling style. *Fair & Square* also reflects the full sound Prine creates onstage with just his acoustic guitar and the bass of Dave Jacques and electric guitar of Jason Wilbur, who've served as his touring unit for several years.

"It's just a really good sound for what I do," Prine says. "I love it musically, and it's a comfortable situation. I never get wore out by it; I'm always excited about doing the shows. When I had the rock bands, it always seemed like we had the acoustic segments and the band segments. But now it all flows together, and we don't have to jump from one kind of music to another."

So, after all he's been through, here Prine is, traveling the world playing his songs and getting ready to release another batch of new songs. "It's like I have a whole new romance going on with life," he says, shrugging as he smiles, as if he's as mystified as anyone with the way things turned out. "It's like there's a new shine on things. I'm feeling like I'm dug in pretty good."

THEY'RE BACK: RODNEY & DOUGLAS DILLARD

By Nancy Cardwell
From *Bluegrass Unlimited*

Some musicians are born to play music together. The world's musical landscape world be a different place if it were not for vocal and instrumental combinations like Bill & Charlie Monroe, Monroe with Jimmy Martin, Jimmy Martin with Paul Williams & J.D. Crowe, Bobby & Sonny Osborne, Jim & Jesse, Ralph & Carter Stanley, Ira & Charlie Louvin, Lester Flatt & Earl Scruggs, Don Reno & Red Smiley, John Lennon & Paul McCartney, Buck Owens & Don Rich, John Moore & Dennis Caplinger, Alan Munde & Roland White, Tony Rice & Ricky Skaggs, Ricky Skaggs & Paul Brewster, Rhonda & Darrin Vincent, Jeff Hanna & Jimmy Ibbotson, Tim O'Brien & Nick Forster (OK, the entire Hot Rize band), Herb Pedersen & Chris Hillman, Wayne Taylor & Shawn Lane, Russell Moore & Doyle Lawson, Alison Krauss & Ron Block, Sam Bush & John Cowan, David Parmley with Larry Stephenson, Bela Fleck & Victor Wooten, Kate Wolfe & Nina Gerber, Dudley Connell & David McLaughlin, Chris Thile with Sara & Sean Watkins, Rickey Wasson & Dwight McCall, Sara & Maybelle Carter, Jim Hurst & Missy Raines, Laurie Lewis & Tom Rozum…. The list could go on for each of us, depending on the range of our personal tastes.

Faithful watchers of *The Andy Griffith Show* television re-runs and long-time fans of The Dillards, one of bluegrass music's most influential groups in the 1960s-70s, got a little more excited than usual after scanning festival fliers and ads in *Bluegrass Unlimited* for the 2004 and 2005 seasons. For the first time since 1968, brothers Rodney and Douglas Dillard are back performing together on a regular basis. Although they both went on to do ground-breaking and

Nancy Cardwell

wonderful projects on their own during the past 30 years, there's just something about Doug's banjo roll against Rodney's rhythm guitar and his emotional, plaintive at times, tenor-range lead vocals that nobody else can touch.

In an interview for *Bluegrass Unlimited* last summer, Rodney Dillard took some time off from touring in North Carolina to update us on what's new with him and his older brother, banjo stylist Douglas Flint Dillard.

"Doug and I have started back in, doing it again," he says matter-of-factly. "We just played a concert at Morehead City, N.C. that was great, and we played up in Oakboro where we sold out one show and did a second show, and we did a Mayberry reunion in the Midwest, in Newcastle, Indiana. Huck Finn's Jubilee in Victorville, California was a lot of fun. We got Byron Berline up to play with us, and Earl Scruggs was there. We had a blast. "

"We've got an agent," Rodney continues, "and we've seriously decided to go back and do select dates. We don't want to go out and hit it six to eight weeks at a time like we used to; it's not in me, nor Douglas. I think we've reached the point to where if we want to go out and have fun with the music and feel good about it; that's what we're doing," he grins across the telephone wire.

"I've had an eclectic career, doing all kinds of stuff—but it's always been connected with the business, whether it's been writing for people, writing shows, producing records, writing commercials or whatever. This going back and playing the music we started out doing is something like—maybe it's like those salmon that swim back upstream. We'll swim upstream, lay our eggs and die," he laughs. "When you get our age you need to keep active, and it beats mowing the lawn and puttering in the garden."

The original Dillards still get together occasionally for Mayberry reunions, to appear as their bluegrass-picking hillbilly characters in *The Andy Griffith Show*, the Darlin family. Mandolinist Dean Webb lives in Reeds Spring, Mo. and stays busy in the Branson area playing riverboat and lake cruises, along with other local music venues. Bass player/emcee extraordinaire Mitch Jayne has retired from playing music due to a genetic hearing illness, but he continues to write a newspaper column and does some songwriting out of his home in Eminence, Mo. He's also a much-in-demand speaker on Ozarks culture and humor, for groups across the country. The foursome's last

They're Back: Rodney & Douglas Dillard

music gig together was July 15, 2002 at Carnegie Hall, where they appeared with Arlo Guthrie and Pete Seeger.

"We all went back and wore our buckskins like we did when we started out," Mitch says, "and it was almost 40 years to the day when we played Carnegie Hall. Believe me, I came immediately home and said, 'That's the time to quit!'"

In addition to Rodney and Doug, the new combination of The Dillards includes a firebrand Branson theater veteran originally from Texas, George Giddens, on fiddle, mandolin and tenor vocals. "I've always liked George," Rodney says. "I've always liked how he played fiddle and how he went at it. He reminds me of how Paul Warren played. If (the bow) were a saw, (his fiddle) would be cut in two."

The fourth member is another multi-instrumentalist known chiefly for his fiddle playing, too: Buddy Griffin on bass. A former member of Jim & Jesse and the Virginia Boys, Griffin also heads up the bluegrass department at Glenville State College in Glenville, West Virginia. "I've known Buddy forever," Rodney says. "He's got a good sense of humor and he's intelligent and gets along with all of us. We've also started doing some twin fiddling in the show."

"Douglas and I have always been the groove (in the Dillards) because we're brothers, and blood's thicker than anything else," Rodney explains. "Doug and I will always be that groove because that's who we are. We were that groove when Dean and Mitch came into the band, and we're that groove now."

Their considerable contributions as songwriters, instrumentalists, innovative humorists and the role they played as co-founders of a new sub-genre of music (country rock) aside, The Dillards have proven to be one of the most immediately recognizable bluegrass bands in American pop culture simply because of the six shows they filmed for *The Andy Griffith Show*, beginning in 1964. There are more Mayberry fans now than ever because the show has never gone off the air, syndicated in constant re-runs on cable television.

Rodney hints at philosophical and spiritual reasons for the show's continued popularity—in addition to obvious things like endearing characters and good acting. "The fact that 22 million people watched the last CBS (Mayberry Reunion) special gives you a little insight into what the country is gravitating toward, maybe," he says, "because in these dangerous times people always want something that's safe. The values that show portrays are real important to people now."

Nancy Cardwell

Fans still feel very connected to *The Andy Griffith Show* and to the characters on it—even after all these years, Rodney says. "All the people who are left, we get together and it's become like a family reunion," he says. "Everyone's become very close over the years. They didn't drift apart."

Rodney has lived in the Branson, Mo. area for several years, managing Caravell Recording Studio in addition to writing, television production and performance work with comedian Jim Stafford and at Silver Dollar City, among other venues. "Caravell Studios has been purchased by a friend of mine, and we're gearing up to concentrate a lot on the gospel market, as well as the acoustic end of things," he reports. "We're talking about starting a label. Our duplication business has increased 400% in the last year, and we're constantly upgrading the studio. That's where I've been cutting all my stuff, and we've also done a lot of IMAX projects—for the Ontario Speedway and the Children's Museum in Indianapolis, most recently. We've also done some Disney stuff for the Tokyo park. And we serve the local folks, too; they're just as important to us as Disney.... For the retro people, we've got all the tube mic's, along with a lot of new mic's—C212A's. We're able to keep that warm, live sound even though we've also got digital (equipment)." Dillard will be a partner in the new version of Caravell Studios, which will be re-named Lynwood Studios.

In addition to touring with his brother in The Dillards and running a recording studio, Rodney also does speaking tours at churches across the country with his wife, clawhammer banjo player/dancer Beverly Cotton Dillard, who is usually also accompanied by their 13-year-old daughter, Rachel.

"I'm real excited about this; it's one of my passions now," Rodney says. "Our ministry is called 'Mayberry Values in Today's World.' I'll take an episode, and draw the parallels between Bible teachings and how Andy dealt with people in different situations. We talk about the fruits of the spirit and how Andy demonstrated those. We talk about how he raised his child and made him responsible for his actions—like in the episode when Opie killed the mother bird with his slingshot and Andy made him raise the baby birds.... We talk about how words can kill... Andy was always real careful of the words he used, even to the criminals in his jail. He treated everybody with respect. We go and we sing, and we talk and we give our testimony." They are booked through Johnny Cook in Wilmington, N.C., a preacher who used to

They're Back: Rodney & Douglas Dillard

occasionally appear on *Hee Haw*.

Rodney says he "always felt that we could use the popularity that we gained by being a small part of that show—which turned out to be bigger than I ever imagined—that would give me the opportunity to go into places where people would know me and I could talk about (spiritual) things.... I feel like I'm not a stranger anywhere I go. Once they put the face with the television show, they'll listen to me. It's a phenomenon that still amazes me."

Rodney says his Christian faith is something that has become more important to him over the years. Without going into a lot of detail, he says, "about 21 years ago there were some life-changing things that happened to me that took me off the path I was on, and put me on this one....I thank God that I left Hollywood and came back to Missouri to raise my son, because I raised him in church and he is now a lieutenant in the sheriff's department in a huge county in Tennessee that covers Johnson City and Kingsport. His name is Brian Dillard; he's been with the force five years. He made lieutenant and graduated at the top of his class...and I'm very proud of the fact because it took 28 hours a day to raise that child," he smiles. "But it *does*," he stresses, "if you're going to be a good parent in this day and age."

Rachel takes ballet classes and she has a mandolin, but she's most interested these days in becoming a veterinarian, Rodney says.

Even though he didn't end up staying there, in retrospect Rodney says he is glad the band went to Hollywood instead of Nashville in the '60s. "I think we would have gotten lost in the shuffle," he says. "Bluegrass at that time in Nashville was the unwanted stepchild of country music."

So what possessed four young guys from Salem, Missouri to pack up their instruments in 1962 and head to California to seek fortune and fame in the music business? And what did their parents think?

"They were very encouraging," Rodney grins. "The story is this: when we left finally and went to California we walked into this place which was like a petrie dish of political folk music where all the biggies hung out, like Joan Baez. It's now a comedy store, which I think is kind of funny because it was a pretty funny place anyway," he chuckles. "We walked into the lobby, pulled out our instruments and started playing. There were two people who heard us. One was the owner of Elektra Records. He saw us play, and that's how we got our record deal. The producer was there who produced and managed the Byrds,

Nancy Cardwell

and later was instrumental in getting The Eagles together, and he wanted to produce us. So we did that first album. They put a little blurb in *Variety* magazine, and Andy Griffith's people saw it and called us to come over and audition for them. So that's what happened. We were there not very long before we were working and had a record deal and were on a national television show in the top ten. As I look back on it, it amazes me," Rodney admits, noting how sometimes kids will go and do something because they don't know they can't.

Getting to California wasn't as easy, however. The band had a grand total of $9.50 when they left Salem, Mo. Rodney was 19 years old. "We got as far as Oklahoma City and ran out of gas, and slept in oil fields in this old '55 Cadillac," he recalls. "We checked in at the Y, ran up a huge bill there, and we coat-hangered the beds together so we could all sleep in two beds—so they wouldn't slide apart and somebody would fall through the cracks. I took the last dollar and a quarter—which was what a hair cut cost at that time—got a haircut and went downtown and got everybody odd jobs in town. Like Douglas says, we got so hungry we decided we would go down and give blood, but they wouldn't take our blood because we were from out of state! We earned enough money to survive—I mean, we were fighting over crackers in the waste can. This fellow named Pop Brainerd who owned a pop club in Oklahoma City gave us a job and paid us $300 a week. We worked one or two weekends and we got enough money to get us the rest of the way to LA."

From the beginning, The Dillards felt they were in the business of entertaining people as well as playing music. "Mitch and I developed this whole comedy act we had for a long time," Rodney says. "Of course in any kind of comedy act, you have the guy who plays the foil…. It was very similar to what the Smothers Brothers were doing at the time, but of course we'd never seen them and they were just sort of getting started, too. The humor enabled us to work urban clubs and go to New York and go places where Bill Cosby would open for us— I remember he opened for us once in Cleveland. We were working an entirely different circuit than the country music people were, and that's what saved us—going to LA. and developing a more sophisticated way of presenting our music. It was more than 'A great big howdy and a couple of doodies to you,'" Rodney smiles. "That's what got us into going to colleges; we had a different approach. We get a little— well, not political, but they knew we weren't dummies…. We realized

They're Back: Rodney & Douglas Dillard

that if you stood onstage and played your instruments like a juke box, that it wasn't going to have the same impact that it would if you could get (the audience) to enjoy your humor. Then the music just sort of sold itself."

The comedy developed along with the music. "Mitch and I argued a lot about what was what," Rodney says. "What you do is try stuff, throw out stuff that doesn't work and keep the stuff that does…. We had a great opportunity to present it to a wide spectrum of audiences. We worked with everybody from Elton John to Lily Tomlin. (Humor) helped bring our music to a whole different demographic and fans we've kept over the years."

The Dillards were a hot item on college tours in 1963-64, as well as at clubs like The Hungry I and The Bottom Line in New York. The band co-hosted a television show with Tennessee Ernie Ford for a week and played *American Bandstand* a number of times. "The Dillards did five television pilots," Rodney recalls. "One for Dick Clark, one for CBS, one for MGM with Linda Ronstadt and Hank Williams Jr., and one for Gene Autry at Melody Ranch…. None of them ever sold, but there was enough interest that they wanted us to do pilots."

Rodney says he occasionally writes songs now, but that most of the classic Dillards songs were written during the *Andy Griffith Show* era so they would have original material to perform—songs like Mitch and Dean's "Old Home Place," along with "I Guess I'll Never See My Home Again," "Dooley," "Old Man at the Mill," "The Whole World Round," "There is a Time," and "Doug's Tune," among others. (Doug had written "Banjo in the Holler" years before.)

The original material helped The Dillards get ahead, Rodney says. "The bands who really stand out are the ones who develop their own music. Nickel Creek is a fine example, and of course there are other bands, too. If you do all Monroe songs, or all Flatt & Scruggs songs— if you just want to play for your own amusement and enjoyment, that's great. But if you really want to say something in the music, you've got to say it the way *you* say it. Otherwise, you're just going to be a pastel of the original."

There was a lot of waiting around on *The Andy Griffith Show* set between scenes, because it was shot like a movie with one camera. "Sometimes we'd go out on location during the first part of the morning and then come back in the afternoon and shoot indoors. It was in Culver City and Hollywood—I think it's all condos now," he says.

Nancy Cardwell

How did the Dillards kill time between scenes? "Well, sometimes we slept in the jail. That was the most comfortable place to sleep," Rodney grins, "and hopefully nobody else would be in there already, like Denver. We'd sit around and talk and just have fun, and play music. We'd sit around with Andy sometimes and pick."

What was it like to be at ground zero, at the birth of the new hybrid that would become country rock music?

"It's a strange thing," Rodney muses. "After our third album on Elektra, the critics in New York said, 'These guys are not authentic because they have echoes on their records.' And I thought to myself, 'When is the last time they sat in some holler and played a banjo?' If they sat in our house, they would've heard it. We had one more album to do, so we did this very esoteric album with Byron Berline, *Pickin' and Fiddlin'.* It was a scholarly album; all the notes were written by Ralph Rinzler. We thought that would make the academics who wanted to keep the music the same, happy. But I'd reached the point to where I wanted to do something else. I always like R&B and I liked rhythm, so I added a rhythm section. On *Wheatstraw Suite* I started adding orchestration. Even before that when we were on Capitol with Douglas, we were cutting with drums and bass and doing different things. We were still utilizing the same three-part bluegrass harmonies, but adding an R&B or rock feel."

"I had an offer to go with a group who had a pop hit record and they were very hot at the time," Rodney continues. "I had a couple offers to go and do a series on television—some acting stuff. But I thought, 'I'm going to do this one album that I have in my heart,' and that's when I brought Herb Pedersen in. He was very instrumental and supportive because he thought like me. He wanted to broaden our horizons. So I worked in my back room on a tape recorder and put this whole concept together in my mind, and with Herb's harmony help I finally got to do something I really wanted to do, which was this 25 piece chamber orchestra with drums, banjo, mandolin and guitar—and it was called *Wheatstraw Suite*. And pedal steel, too. There was nothing much like that going on at the time. A friend of mine who was producing the Monkees got really interested in what we were doing. He got Douglas to record some with The Monkees and started adding some pedal steel. People started listening to what we were doing…. If you talk to Don Henley and ask him who his influences are, he'll tell you The Dillards. The European press has given us more credit than

They're Back: Rodney & Douglas Dillard

the American press has, for being the fathers of country rock. Of course now it's the grandfathers," he laughs. "It wasn't anything pre-determined or planned out. It just happened. *Wheatstraw Suite* was going to be my last album. I felt like I wanted to do more, and I felt claustrophobic musically. But it went on from there. *Copperfields* was after that, and the next album was *Roots and Branches*, which was a little more far out."

The country rock music scene blossomed in California and spread throughout the world, with artists like The Dillards, The Byrds, The Flying Burrito Brothers, The Nitty Gritty Dirt Band, Country Gazette, Gram Parsons with Emmylou Harris and The Eagles, among others, leading the way—crossing musical boundaries and trading band members back and forth. It was an exciting time. "I liked all the music that was happening at the time," Rodney says. "I think pop music hit the doldrums in the '80s and I lost interest in it."

Rodney and Doug met John Hartford in St. Louis, when they were still living in Salem. "Back then if you found another bluegrass picker within 100 miles, you considered yourself fortunate," Rodney smiles. "My mother and dad were working in St. Louis and owned a house in East St. Louis. Doug and I and John would get together, and as kids we would sit and play all night long. We finally got a voice/music tape recorder and stared experimenting with recording and made all kinds of real silly recordings. Douglas was in his early 20s and I was 16. I'd drive all the way up to St. Louis on the weekends after school and play music. In the summer time I'd come up there and we'd play in bars. Finally we had a band together. Douglas and John and I grew up together musically, and as a result of that over the years we picked together a lot and made albums. We talked about doing another one together, but we never did," Rodney says, falling silent for a moment.

"My dad played the fiddle and my mother played the guitar, and all my uncles played," Rodney says. "I grew up with music and grew up in it. Used to, when the guys in New York would write all this bad stuff about us changing the music, I thought, 'You have no idea what I grew up with.'"

The Dillard brothers cut their first record in 1959 on K-Ark Records in St. Louis. Rodney was 16, and he played bass. Doug was 21. The songs were "Banjo in the Hollow" b/w "My Only True Love." Their next project was a part of a gospel package advertised on KSBN,

185

Nancy Cardwell

a local 50,000 watt country radio station. They cut a total of eight singles, including "You're on My Mind," "Highway of Sorrow," "Mama Don't Allow" and a few others.

Rodney, who ranked in the upper 3% of his class academically in high school, remembers being called into the superintendent's office one day after one of their records was played on the Salem radio station. Rodney says, "He told me, 'You know what? You've got to quit this music because you're not going to get anywhere playing music. I know because I played saxophone in the Navy.' And I thought, 'Why are you telling me this? I'm going to show you something!' And you know what? The first time we did *The Andy Griffith Show*, they let out the National Guard in Salem so they could watch it on television that night. And I thought, 'There you go, Mr. Superintendent of Schools.'"

From the perspective of 42 years, here's what Rodney Dillard sees in the future for bluegrass music: "In some places it will go in circles, and in some places it will be concentric circles that spiral—with something added to it. But folks will always bring it back. There are some people who want to keep it pure, and I respect that. There are some people who want to add to it and change a little here and there, and I respect that. I do not respect people who have become musical bigots, who say, 'There's only one kind of music, and that's all there is.' That gives me a little insight into how they think about other things. If you're that close-minded about the rest of life, it scares me. I love traditional music, and I'm talking about the Stanley Brothers. I'm talking about Flatt & Scruggs, who were at the time a very commercial act. I don't have much use for people who put other people down for changing the music…. Bluegrass music will always be. I have noticed a change rhythmically, though, within its structure. You take something like The Stanley Brothers or Jimmy Martin—he was the bluegrass rock & roll rhythm player of the time. He flogged it," Rodney says with great admiration in his voice. "The music got to the point to where it jumped. It got kind of dog-legged and almost jug band-like. It didn't dig down into the meat of the rhythm. The music just got that way, with more of an emphasis on the back swing beat. That's how it's changed—I'm not saying for the good or the bad. Then you have groups like IIIrd Tyme Out that rock it like it used to be. The Johnson Mountain Boys; they brought it back around. When you get away form the original players of a style, it becomes revivalist music. I really like Dave Peterson & 1946. I like Nickel Creek's first album. But

They're Back: Rodney & Douglas Dillard

the computer way of recording now, with pitch correction, has changed the music a lot. That's why bluegrass festivals are great, because you get it raw—what you see is what you get. What you hear on records is not always what you get."

The first generation artists, who recorded without overdubs or Pro Tools "did it good," Rodney says. "The Stanley Brothers may have not always been right on, but there was something in the heart of it, and it didn't matter if it wasn't in tune. It's the heart of the music that's important in any kind of music. There's a lot of heart in Bruce Springsteen's music. There's a lot of heart in Mozart. I wonder what Mozart would've done with a keyboard and a MIDI?" Rodney laughs.

But then again, sometimes artists run out of things to say, Rodney points out. He's had a studio at his fingertips but hasn't recorded an album in several years. "I felt like I said what I had to say with *Wheatstraw, Copperfields* and *Roots & Branches,*" he says. "The reason I'm going out now is to do the old tunes. It's strictly acoustic, even to the acoustic bass. I went back into traditional bluegrass because I'm enjoying it," he says. "The new album that's coming out (with Doug) will be called *New Vinyl.*"

Rodney's son, Brian plays keyboards and drums. He has perfect pitch and his voice is strikingly similar to Rodney's. He plays "kind of new age, tangerine dream music," his dad says, smiling. "He's re-discovered The Dillards' music, and now he wants to do his arrangements in his own way."

If he has one message to convey to bluegrass fans, Rodney says it is that "Doug and I—the original guys who started this out—will finish it out. For whatever our time is, Douglas and I are going to continue to perform, continue to make records and continue to enjoy life—in a more moderate way," he smiles. "And I'm going to continue my ministry speaking at churches and the philosophy that goes with it. If you don't live it, it's worthless."

188

FAME FROM THE TIPS OF HIS FINGERS

Bill Anderson's bumpy career proves that nice guys can finish first

By Bob Allen
From *The Journal of Country Music*

Bill Anderson's career was in trouble. It was 1978, and the man who had dominated the country singles charts in the 1960s with hits like "City Lights," "Still," and "The Tips of My Fingers" was worried. It had been 1975 since he'd topped the charts, and, although he'd had a few records that hit the Top Ten in those years, he'd also had a couple of releases that struggled to get into the Top Twenty. So "Whisperin'" Bill Anderson decided to go disco.

"I was up in Buddy's [Killen's] office one day, and the disco thing was really hot everywhere back then and I kinda liked it," explains Anderson with a grin. "I said, 'Buddy, why couldn't you take just a plain, old country melody and put a disco beat to it?' Buddy said, 'I dunno, why couldn't you?'

"I'd been carrying this song ["I Can't Wait Any Longer"] around, which if you sang it straight, was almost like a bluegrass song," Anderson adds as he softly sings the hook line in nasal, high-lonesome style. "Buddy went over to the piano and started doodling around with it, and said, 'Why don't we make a disco record?' I said, 'Hey, I'm willing, if you are!' I've never been afraid of trying new stuff, and that was new all right," he laughs with glee.

"I Can't Wait Any Longer," a gushy country-disco record that stayed on *Billboard's* Hot Country Singles charts for 57 weeks, peaking at #4, raised the hackles of both purists and hardliners. The most char-

189

Bob Allen

itable saw the record as an exercise in sheer contrivance or as harmless, good-natured chart fodder. Others saw a dreadful example of Nashville's "pop crossover" movement — in which Anderson had fared well with " Still," his 1963 country chart topper that also went to #8 in the *Billboard* pop charts — taken to its most absurd and outlandish extreme. Even Anderson's hardcore fans were sharply divided over whether their musical hero had taken an artistic leap forward into the contemporary music market or an awkward misstep backward toward irrelevance.

As things turned out, the controversy didn't matter. Although "I Can't Wait Any Longer" was a hit, it would be Anderson's last hit as a recording artist. In fact, it was the very last time that one of Anderson's singles would reach higher than #20. Today, Anderson seems bemused rather than bitter when he recalls the circumstances that led to his left-field plunge into the disco craze.

"It became a real love-hate record in my career," Anderson concedes. "My long-time fans that liked songs like 'Mama Sang A Song' and 'Five Little Fingers' and 'Golden Guitar' didn't like it at all. But I found myself reaching new fans that had never paid much attention to me before, and they loved that whole *Ladies Choice* album. My regret now, looking back on it, is that I wish I'd tried to ride the horse a little farther. I really would have liked to, but the people at my record label [MCA] talked me into getting off. I really don't have many regrets in the music business, and I don't dwell on things like that, but if I had it to do over I'd have done more stuff like 'I Can't Wait Any Longer.' Even today I get more e-mail from people wanting to know where they can find a copy of the *Ladies Choice* album. There's hardly a day goes by somebody doesn't ask me that."

This comment says a lot about Anderson, who has often held the countervailing impulses of creativity and opportunism in awkward abeyance; occasionally, some would argue, he has lost the uneasy balance between the two forces. On the one hand, he is a country music icon: a member of the Grand Ole Opry since 1961, elected to the Country Music Hall of Fame in 2001, and winner of the CMA's Vocal Event of the Year in the same year, and he has won more than 50 BMI Airplay Awards. Yet for all his accomplishments, Anderson has never been an iconoclast, a stark stylist, or major innovator. No one has yet proposed a granite likeness of him on country music's mythical Mt. Rushmore which, if it existed, would no doubt include likenesses of

Fame from the Tips of His Fingers

contemporaries such as Willie Nelson, Merle Haggard, the late Johnny Cash, and Waylon Jennings. Granite is not Anderson's medium.

"I know I'm not technically a great singer; I realize my limitations as a singer," he offers candidly.

A twice-divorced grandfather of four, Anderson has never cultivated the sort of dark, antiheroic persona that many music fans find so appealing. Nor has he accumulated the boxcars of emotional baggage that are the stuff of which music legends are made. Aside from the occasional embarrassing domestic dispute, Anderson has always been a Dudley Do-Right, the perennial insider who plays by the rules. He is a mild-mannered, unassuming musical diplomat who is more apt to flash an aw-shucks grin than a menacing glower. And he's honest enough to admit that when originality has let him down, he's been quite willing to ride the wave of a musical trend when he sees a good one coming.

In person, Anderson is polite, considerate, and soft-spoken. Surprisingly tall and lean, he has the laid-back demeanor of a semi-retired businessman. At times, he's needed that gentlemanly sensibility. Just as his low-key, "whispering" vocal style translated into a respectable string of chart-topping hits in earlier decades, it has also inspired more than a few jokes and disparaging one-liners over the years. Anderson wrote his way into the business, then sang his way out of it, is one of the oft-repeated bits of comic exaggeration that circulated back when Anderson's recording career ran out of steam and he found career refuge as a TV host on the ABC Network's *The Better Sex*, and later, The Nashville Network's hokey but popular game show, *Fandango*.

Anderson himself has no doubt heard all these one-liners. But rather than take umbrage, he seems almost to delight in them. "Waylon [Jennings] did an interview with the local newspaper, in the early 1980s, and they asked what he thought of this new thing called The Nashville Network," Anderson laughs. "Waylon had watched Fandango, a game show I was doing on TNN at the time, and he said, 'What in the world is Bill Anderson doing on a game show? He has enough trouble trying to sing!' They put that in the paper! So I wrote Waylon a letter and said, 'Quit talking about my singing, or I'm gonna start talkin' about your movies.' And Waylon framed my letter and had it hanging on the wall of his office. He got a big kick out of that and we kidded each other a lot over the years. I was a very big fan of him

Bob Allen

and his writing and of him as a person."

Far from getting his back up over such barbs, Whispering Bill embraces such prickly disparagements and incorporates them, in his own self-effacing yet clever manner, into his deferential, crowd-pleasing persona.

In *I Hope You're Living As High On The Hog As the Pig You Turned Out to Be*, his chatty, anecdotal 1994 memoir, Anderson recalls a scene that transpired back 1967 when Johnny Cash and the Carter Family dropped by the set of a syndicated TV show Anderson was hosting. It was just before show time and the visitors asked if there was room for them in the evening's lineup. Anderson swiftly accommodated Cash and the Carters with a full half hour of air time. At one point during the taping, as Cash and Anderson bantered between songs, Cash made an off-handed crack about Anderson's vocal style. Deeply embarrassed, Cash immediately apologized and begged his host to edit his disparaging remark out of the taped broadcast.

"[But] I wouldn't have asked the editor to stop that tape for anything," Anderson recalled. "It wasn't that I was out to embarrass Johnny Cash, but I thought those few moments revealed a very human side to a legend, a side not many people had ever seen. It was a slip, and everybody in the world slips up. I knew he hadn't meant anything ugly by what he had said …. The show aired just the way it was taped, and there was no negative reaction at all."

James William Anderson III was born in 1937, in Columbia, South Carolina. He remembers that even as a child, he had an impulse to write—to write anything and everything.

"I worked during high school as the sports editor of the little weekly newspaper in the town where I grew up. I even did some stringer work for the Atlanta Constitution. I covered my school football and basketball for the *Atlanta Constitution* for a couple years when I was still in high school. I've always loved to write. If I got an assignment in school to write three pages, I always felt like, 'Oh boy, I want to write ten!'"

Like many successful artists, Anderson can also recall the one single moment in his early life involving one particular musical hero that set him on his future career trajectory.

"The first eight years of my life I lived in Columbia, South Carolina, and there was a fellow over there that had a band and did

Fame from the Tips of His Fingers

three local radio shows every day named Byron Parker," Anderson recalls, a tone of reverence and affection creeping into his voice as he remembers the musician who traveled with the Monroe Brothers as their announcer in the 1930s and later joined the WIS hillbillies. "Parker called himself 'The Old Hired Hand.' He also broadcast in Charlotte and Greenville during his career, and he made a few very obscure records on RCA [Bluebird], some of which have been reissued on [the] Bear Family [label]. Later, he was affiliated with Bill Monroe in some capacity. He had a hillbilly band—it wasn't even a country music band, but a forerunner of a bluegrass or country band. He was very, very popular in the Carolinas and he was my hero and I was his biggest fan. When I was five, six, seven years old, my next-door-neighbor got a job working at the radio station, WIS, in Columbia, where Byron broadcast, and she knew what a big fan I was. So, one morning she took me down to the station to see his show—that was live radio back then. To this day, I can visualize the whole scene; it's just indelibly stamped in my brain. I watched him do his show, sitting in this folding chair over in the corner, and afterwards he came over and shook my hand and called my name on the radio. I thought I'd died and gone to heaven!

"Everything I've read about Byron Parker talks about what a great communicator he was, what a great emcee. I realize my limitations as a singer. But I kind of believe that somewhere along the way I must have picked up some of the showmanship stuff, or some of the bull, from Byron Parker," he chuckles. "Because I've just had too many people tell me that."

When Anderson was eight, the family moved to the then small town of Decatur, Georgia, which has since been swallowed up into Atlanta's suburban sprawl. Anderson's father, who, like his mother, was a Georgia native, opened an insurance agency in Decatur. The business afforded the family a comfortable life, including at least one summer vacation in Nashville, where Anderson's father used his pull in the insurance business to get tickets and backstage access to the Grand Ole Opry. When the Andersons returned home to Georgia, young Bill's appetite for the music biz was whetted all that much more.

"When I was in the tenth grade in high school in Decatur I formed a band with three of my classmates and we entered a high school talent show," he recalls. "I sang a song that I wrote called 'What Good Would It Do to Pretend'." He pauses and softly sings the chorus of the

193

Bob Allen

song. "I sang that, and my fiddle player played the 'Orange Blossom Special,' and we won the talent show. People applauded and I thought, Hey man, this is kind of cool."

Soon, Anderson and his band were playing wherever and whenever they could around Atlanta. Eventually he landed his own afternoon show on a local radio station, and later earned a spot on Channel 36, an early Atlanta UHF-TV station with a mud-puddle reception area. "My senior year in high school, I was on television live every night from 7:05 to 7:30. But nobody could pick it up," he laughs.

Anderson went on to earn a degree in journalism from the University of Georgia, working his way through college as a sports writer. But it was another side job, as a country DJ at WJJC in Commerce, Georgia, that proved the springboard to his career as a country writer and entertainer. One night, while sitting on the rooftop of a hotel in the then-tiny crossroads town of Commerce, he wrote "City Lights."

"I recorded 'City Lights' in a little studio in Athens, Georgia," Anderson remembers with a tone of amazement. "I used to sit around the radio station at night, where we had access to all these books with lists of publishers and record companies. Shoot, I'd sit there at night after we went off the air and I'd write about 20 letters a night to any record company or publishing company I could find. Bob Tanner, at TNT Music in San Antonio, was the only person who ever wrote me back."

Anderson has particularly fond and enduring memories of another local music business wanna-be with whom he often crossed paths in and around Atlanta during the late 1950s:

"Roger [Miller] was in the Army then and was stationed at Ft. McPherson, which is right in Atlanta. I was working on the radio, about 50 or 60 miles from Atlanta. They used to bring shows into the Tower Theater, down on Peachtree Street, usually on Sunday afternoons and Sunday nights. I don't remember the first time I actually met Roger, but we were the local kids who would always worm our way backstage and try to 'germ' the stars," he recalls with a grin. "We just wanted to be there and soak it all up.

"I remember one Sunday Wanda Jackson was on the show, and we asked her if we could borrow her guitar. We took her guitar and stood over in the corner of the backstage area, and he'd sing me a song he'd written and I'd sing him a song I'd written, and we'd both talk about,

Fame from the Tips of His Fingers

'My God, wouldn't it be wonderful to be able to do what Wanda Jackson and all these people do!'

"I remember another Sunday, we were standing there and Ray Price walked by in one of those fancy Nudie suits he used to wear, with the Indian feathers and the whole thing. I remember Roger standing there, saying, 'God, what I would give to someday be able to wear that and just walk out there.' And in less than a year's time Roger was the tenor singer in Ray Price's band."

Because of the song, "City Lights," Anderson was soon hot on his friend Miller's heels. TNT Records in San Antonio released his version of 'City Lights' to modest airplay in 1957. "I sent a review copy to Charlie Lamb, who used to have *The Music Reporter*, a little trade paper in Nashville. Actually I was pushing the other side of the record, a little rockabilly song I wrote called 'I've Got No Song to Sing' — you gotta remember that country music was kinda dead in 1957. But Charlie Lamb bothered to turn the record over and see what was on the other side. He was so impressed with 'City Lights' that he took it to Chet [Atkins] at RCA. Chet recorded it on an artist named Dave Rich, and it got into the bottom of the charts. Ray Price heard the Dave Rich record on the radio."

Price, of course, covered "City Lights" and had a #1 hit with it in 1958. Shortly thereafter, Anderson signed with Decca Records in Nashville and embarked on his own major label recording career. His first "career" record came in early 1963, with "Still," a sentimental ballad that became a crossover hit a few years later and is still his signature song.

As Anderson recalls in *I Hope You're Living as High on the Hog as the Pig You Turned Out to Be*, he arrived in Nashville at a crucial time in country music's development.

"The city's prejudices and her idiosyncrasies notwithstanding, I've always figured I arrived in Nashville at just the right time," he wrote. "A new era was dawning in country music, but the old era still had a foot in the door. On any given day there was a marvelous mixture of yesterday and tomorrow stirring the pot.

"The first generation of country music superstars was still at the top of its game: Roy Acuff, Eddy Arnold, Ernest Tubb, Red Foley, Lefty Frizzell, Little Jimmy Dickens, Webb Pierce, Carl Smith, Hank Snow, Kitty Wells, Ray Price, Faron Young, Jim Reeves, Johnny Cash,

Bob Allen

Marty Robbins, Ferlin Husky and all the rest.

"But new names were beginning to crop up: Roger Miller, Mel Tillis, Loretta Lynn, Don Gibson, Harlan Howard, Tom T. Hall, Hank Cochran, Willie Nelson, John D. Loudermilk, Marijohn Wilkin and a guy named Bill Anderson—people who wrote their own songs and then went out on stage and sang them. In his autobiography, TV host Ralph Emery wrote that '... country music got its greatest infusion of talent in the 1960s.' The entire industry was on the verge of a transfusion of new blood, new creative sources and new energy."

Today, Anderson looks back at the 1960s as a golden era, in which he flourished as a writer-recording artist and was accepted as a member in good standing of an elite hillbilly community he'd long admired from afar. He toured with Patsy Cline and still feels lingering sadness at the loss of friends like Cline, Jim Reeves, Cowboy Copas, and Stringbean [David Akeman]. He fondly recalls some of the good, and bad, times he shared with these historic figures in his autobiography, where the perennial fan that has always lurked within him finds fond expression.

"I got to Nashville at a real good time," he adds. "We were still traveling in the cars, and it wasn't like everybody had their own bus or their own dressing room backstage. Shoot, we'd go into these buildings and there'd be one dressing room, and Jean Shepherd would want to change her clothes. She'd say, 'Boys, turn your heads!' So there was a little bit more closeness there, I think, than today, when people get on their separate buses and never even see each other.

"Some of the artists that had been here for a while and really were my heroes and idols, some of them became good friends," he adds. "George Morgan became a very good friend. He'd invite me over to his house for dinner, and we worked a lot of stuff together out on the road. Faron Young and I were also good friends. Faron loved to pick on me, and I didn't care. I think I took it in the spirit I should have taken it in. We became neighbors later on out on Old Hickory Lake and spent a lot of time together.

"George Hamilton IV and I got here about the same time, and he and I also had a lot in common," Anderson continues. "He'd gone to college over in North Carolina. My daughter always swore she was gonna grow up and marry his son!" he laughs. "We did a lot of family stuff together back in the early days."

Fame from the Tips of His Fingers

Just as Anderson recalls the 1960s as an exciting high point in his career, he recalls the 1980s as a nadir in both his personal life and his music career. In an era when the so-called New Traditionalists were capturing the lion's share of attention and antiheroes of the '70s Outlaw movement like Waylon Jennings and Willie Nelson had risen to superstardom alongside middle-of-the-road warblers like Kenny Rogers, Anderson's low key "countrypolitan" style fell out of fashion and seemed almost passé. Added to that were some serious reversals of personal fortune.

"The years around when my [second] wife had her car accident, in 1984, that was a very difficult time," Anderson recalls. "She had head injuries and she almost died. We had a six-year-old son that I had to become kind of mother and father to for a long period of time. At the time of the accident we were already separated, but the accident changed everything. It changed both of us to the point where we didn't know who each other was.

"Right about that same time I had gotten involved with the Po' Folks Restaurant chain. I was the national spokesman for them, a stockholder and a franchisee. We opened restaurants too fast and we got ourselves in trouble. It really began to unravel about 1986. I lost a lot of money on that. So did Conway Twitty, Buddy Killen, and several other people in town.

"I had a lot rougher time than a lot of people knew."

After his long, dry spell as a songwriter and nearly two decades without a hit of his own, Anderson says he grappled with sincere self-doubt and more than a little anxiety when he tentatively began his comeback as a songwriter in a mid-1990s music scene that bore scant resemblance to one he first stumbled onto when he arrived in Nashville in the late 1950s.

"The players had all changed, I didn't know the writers, I didn't know the producers, I didn't know a lot of the artists," he recalls. "[But] when Steve Wariner brought back 'Tip Of My Fingers' and it was a #1 record. I thought, 'Now, wait a minute, I wrote that song 32 years ago. If I wrote a song 32 years ago that can be a hit today, why can't I write some today that can be a hit today?'"

Anderson made his re-entry in a role that he'd seldom played in the past: that of the co-writer. In earlier years, he had co-written a few tunes here and there with Roger Miller, Buddy Killen, or Jerry Crutchfield. But deep down, he believed songwriting was meant to be

197

Bob Allen

an almost sacrosanct, solitary pursuit.

"My approach to writing in the old days was, get miserable as you can," he explains with a gust of laughter. "You know, you start getting miserable around ten o'clock, and by three o'clock you peak! I was stuck mentally in the notion that you pulled down the shades at three in the morning, or you wrote under the steering wheel of a car when you're on the road. I used to laugh and say, You can't write a song by appointment!

"I also used to really wonder if you could go into a room with another writer and really bare your soul. Because when you write, you're writing honestly and emotionally, and maybe somebody else isn't going to understand the way you feel about something. But I've found out you really can do that, if you've got the right idea and the right person."

The crucible for Anderson came the first time he sat down, by invitation, to co-write with Vince Gill. "I was a nervous little puppy walking into Vince's office that day," he guffaws. "Here Vince was, on top of his game, and here I was — I wrote some hit songs 100 years ago! I'm thinking, Can I do it again? …. I really didn't know."

But when Gill took "Which Bridge to Cross, (Which Bridge To Burn)," one of two songs he and Anderson co-wrote in that first session, to the Top Five in 1995, Anderson found himself on the A-list of co-writers. "That kind of gave me some legitimacy up and down the street. It just kind of grew from there," he recalled.

"I've really had to pinch myself a couple of times since then," he shrugs. "This has all far exceeded my expectations. I just wanted to get back into it and see if I could still write a couple of songs."

With his second coming as a songwriter, Anderson has regained the sort of currency along Music Row that eluded him during the mid-1970s and most of the 1980s. one of the crowing victories of this second coming is the song, "Whiskey Lullaby." The song, which he cowrote with Jon Randall and which was recorded as a duet by Brad Paisley and Alison Krauss for Paisley's million-selling, 2003 *Mud On The Tires* album. Released as a single, "Lullaby" topped the chart and has since been dominated for three 2004 Country Music Association Awards: Single of the Year, Music Video of the Year and Musical Event of the Year. Not surprisingly, now that he's in his mid-sixties, he occasionally muses about how his place in the greater musical scheme of things will be tallied, once his last song has been written and his last note sung.

"Well, I hope I'll have a box set one of these days," he offers with a shrug. "They had a policy at MCA, where I recorded for 23 years. They only put box sets out on people who either died or got elected to the Hall of Fame.

"Well," he adds with a chuckle, "I wasn't willing to do the one, but the other finally happened . . . So . . ." he laughs softly, "you never know."

200

A TRIBUTE TO TEXAS SONGWRITERS

By Ron Wynn
From *American Songwriter*

The state of Texas is known for wide-open spaces, maniac football fans, outrageous and entertaining politicians and a remarkable musical heritage that includes everything from shuffle blues and engaging troubadours to dashing western swing orchestras, colorful Tex-Mex and Norteno ensembles and cutting-edge jazz musicians. But above all else, Texas is known for its incredibly gifted singer/songwriters. No matter what type of tale you prefer, be it romantic, historical, allegorical or just plain entertaining, there's someone from the Lone Star State able to satisfy your urges.

We recently spoke with six master Texas singer/songwriters at various times over a five-week period and were consistently informed, surprised and delighted by their responses. As expected, there were more areas of consensus than disagreement from Billy Joe Shaver, Jerry Jeff Walker, James McMurtry, Nanci Griffith, Guy Clark and Pat Green when talking about songwriting. They all eschewed any notions about formulaic tendencies or procedural steps in composing, and none of them spent much time discussing record company or radio politics. In addition, they are all familiar with each other's music and often cited their fondness for particular artists, despite the fact none of the interviews were conducted simultaneously, and no one was ever told who else was being profiled. Finally, they consider themselves songwriters first and foremost, without concern for whether they should be deemed country, folk, pop, rock or Americana.

For Billy Joe Shaver, who grew up in Corsicana, Tex. and relocated to Nashville in the late '60s, songwriting has always been both a hobby and a means of self-expression. "I've never really thought about

Ron Wynn

why I became a songwriter from the standpoint of calling it a profession," Shaver says. "It has always been just the best way for me to really talk about the things that I've seen and experienced. There's no particular time that I like to write, and now it has gotten tougher at times for me to sit down and write, but as long as my memory holds up, I'll keep on writing."

Though at 63, Shaver remains among the most beloved singer/songwriters alive, he's never enjoyed commercial success to equal the critical acclaim or the adoration of numerous musicians. But the list of people who've covered his tunes includes Bob Dylan, Johnny Cash, Willie Nelson and Patty Loveless, and he wrote most of the material on one of Waylon Jennings' greatest releases, the landmark 1973, *Honky Tonk Heroes*.

When asked if anyone has ever done a song differently from how he conceived it, Shaver laughs and says, "I'm just happy anyone even cares enough to record them at all. I never worried about whether someone changed a line or dropped a verse. It was just an honor that they even covered it." Shaver's an emphatic, very dynamic vocalist, and his singing often recalls the intimacy and directness of both great Delta blues performers and classic country crooners. Among his triumphs are "Drinking Back To You," a tune he crafted while separated from his late wife and childhood sweetheart (whom he married three times), as well as "Day By Day," a number about loss that is both extremely personal and remarkably universal. "I still love singing, and there are times when the ideas come and I sit down and do it," Shaver says. "The best songs to me are the simple ones. They tell the truth and don't take too long to get to the point."

Shaver's 2003 release *Freedom's Child* mixed autobiographical fare with patriotic pieces that were actually done before 9/11, but still were extremely relevant in an era where fears of terrorism were never too far away from many people's thoughts. Though he's not exactly a hot commodity in terms of the marketplace, Shaver's music is still highly special to numerous fans that have suffered with him through the loss of both his wife and mother within a month of each other in 1999, and the death of his son a year later. They've also closely monitored his ongoing recovery from a massive heart attack, and will be thrilled to know that Shaver continues writing and making sporadic appearances.

Shaver credits the state's size and diverse communities with being the primary reason why so many great songwriters have either been

A Tribute to Texas Songwriters

born there or eventually traveled there. "I think because things are so wide-open here, it really is a challenge to any songwriter to use their imagination and challenge themselves. There are so many great story-tellers here, and that has always influenced the music. I think all of us at heart want to tell great stories, and everyone that I admire has that ability."

Shaver cites Jennings, Jerry Jeff Walker, Willie Nelson and Kris Kristofferson among his personal favorites, while also mentioning Nanci Griffith and James McMurtry as contemporaries whom he admires. The feeling is quite mutual for Texas artists to immediately cite Shaver as a primary influence.

Jerry Jeff Walker's life without question qualifies him as a modern-day troubadour. While others may arbitrarily insert lines about hitch-hiking or happenings on the road, Walker lived it. He once departed his upstate New York hometown and set out for Key West. One of his best and most widely known tunes, "Railroad Lady" (co-written with Jimmy Buffett), was written in a boxcar on the final run of the Panama Limited between New Orleans and Nashville. Their sole compan-ion—one bottle of Wild Turkey. The result was a classic that's been covered by Willie Nelson, Merle Haggard, and Lefty Frizzell, among others. Walker's been a street singer in New Orleans, a folkie in Greenwich Village, and part of the emerging country/rock movement that exploded out of Texas in the early '70s, though he had been there since the '60s.

Now he's a highly respected icon and star. But for Walker, writing a good song still thrills him after all these years, and he says there's always one key ingredient in every top tune. "Honesty is it for me," Walker says. "It isn't so much that you have to live everything that you sing about, or that every song has to be about a direct experience, but you have to be able to make what you are singing about believable. If it doesn't sound believable to you, it surely won't be for an audience, and they can tell when someone isn't being honest with them. For me, anyone who loves music and songwriting must respect it enough not to cheat the audience or the music."

"Sometimes I get the idea first, then build the music around it, and other times they just sort of come together," Walker adds when asked whether he constructs the melodies or lyrics first. "It really is different every time. There have been instances where I just got a lick and then

Ron Wynn

kind of built things off of it, and other times when it seemed that the lyrics were already written and it was easy to build a melody around them. I wish I did have some sort of routine, but it has never worked that way for me."

Walker calls Austin "America's greatest musical city for songwriters," and he's aided several emerging players like Todd Snider, whom he calls "a great, great talent," as well as Robert Earl Keen, Jack Ingram and Garth Brooks. Before that generation emerged, Walker worked, toured and collaborated with fellow singer/songwriters such as Guy Clark and Townes Van Zandt, both of whom he refers to as "all-time greats." Walker was also in the forefront of musicians taking control over their own destiny, founding his Tried & True Music label in 1986, after previously enjoying a good run on Elektra and MCA. He also credits Texas' unique geography for inspiring so many wonderful singer/songwriters, but feels that the diverse populations are just as important. "It seems that everyone in the state has a special story to tell, and if you go around and just listen, you get a lot of inspiration and ideas," Walker says. "I've had so many great things passed down to me and heard so much that I don't think it would be possible to ever run out of songs."

Interestingly, it was Walker's recordings of Guy Clark's "L.A. Freeway" and "Desperados Waiting For A Train" that helped make Clark an in-demand songwriter. Clark now resides in Nashville, and has lately achieved almost as much fame for building elaborate guitars as he did in past decades for his memorable compositions. Along with Walker and Townes Van Zandt, this threesome used to exchange ideas and polish their songwriting abilities while working in Austin.

While Clark immediately defers to Van Zandt when discussing that period, saying, "He was the most amazing and literate individual I've ever met," Clark soon developed his own reputation for compelling lyrics, cliché-free song situations, colorful, gripping language and descriptive stories. "There are days when it seems like nothing is working, but I have to write when I'm at home," Clark says. "I've found that you just can't do it on the road anymore, because you are always dealing with something, from sound checks to problems at the site or the hotel, or catching up with what's happening back home. So what I do is almost like going into isolation. You just have to put everything else completely out of your mind, sit there and sometimes just look out the window. But then other times, you sit down and it just

A Tribute to Texas Songwriters

seems to flow. Maybe other people can do a lot of other things while they're writing, or they can conduct conversations and write, but I have to shut out everything else when I'm writing."

Like his other comrades, Clark has been very encouraging and supportive to those coming behind him. Vince Gill, Rodney Crowell, Steve Wariner and Ricky Skaggs are among current Nashville acts that have cut Clark tunes, but he's also had plenty done by legends like Walker and Johnny Cash. Clark is still making first-rate music, with his most recent releases (*Cold Dog Soup* and *The Dark*) showing that he's able to make fresh-sounding music without abandoning his classic writing style. *The Dark* includes a tribute piece to Arizona Star, a '70s Music City character, plus a powerful cover of Van Zandt's "Rex's Blues," as well as two outstanding pieces co-written with Shawn Camp, "Magnolia Wind" and "Soldier's Joy." The disc shows Clark's ability to smoothly team with others, as he penned various works in tandem with Ray Stevenson, Steve Nelson, Buddy Mondlock and Rich Alves.

Although he no longer lives in Texas, Clark has fond memories of his time there, and echoes the words of his comrades regarding its impact. "There are many great writers in Nashville and this is certainly a wonderful area for songwriters, but there are qualities that are unique to Texas," Clark says. "You just have so many different areas and places, each one with a special sensibility, and being in those places gives songwriters so much material. When I was working with Jerry and Townes, we used to see things and instantly one of us would say something and the other would say, 'Did you write that down?' or 'You've got to put that down.' It was a wonderful period, a completely different time in terms of music."

James McMurtry is part of the new breed of Texas singer/songwriter, someone whose music has ample aspects of rock and blues underneath the vivid images and delightful scenarios contained in his songs. He's also an outstanding guitarist, and sometimes includes dazzling, intricately executed accompaniment, solos or riffs to augment his creation. Backed by bassist Ronnie Johnson and drummer Daren Hess, McMurtry's trio can sometimes sound like a '50s rockabilly act, then smoothly shift to honky-tonk or folk situations. He was born in Fort Worth but now resides in Austin. McMurtry ranks among the musicians who would rather play music than talk about it, and he

Ron Wynn

doesn't go into as much detail about the creative process as some others. However, he's just as animated about the importance of emotion and energy in his songs.

"I think that most songwriters get ideas from life, from what they see and try to communicate that," McMurtry says. "I don't usually think in terms of melodies or lyrics so much as I do in terms of ideas and stories. A lot of my songs kind of write themselves in terms of the arrangement, and will just come together once the lines are down. I don't think I've ever just sat down and said, 'Let me find a melody for these words.' There have been times when songs changed, or when we started doing them live, we found out that this word didn't really fit, or that we needed to speed something up or slow it down. But I've never really thought about what I guess you would call the mechanics of songwriting."

McMurtry's first three releases were issued on Columbia, with *Too Long In The Wasteland* arguably being the best of the trio. His 1996 Sugar Hill debut, *It Had To Happen,* was the first of a fine trio for that label, the last being *St. Mary of the Woods* in 2002. But his 2004 release, *Live in Aught-Three* (on Compadre), really spotlights how McMurtry and his bunch—known as "The Heartless Bastards—truly sound in concert. It has both rough, edgy numbers and some lighter material, though McMurtry's playing and singing throughout are intense and animated.

"For me, one of the most important things about Austin is the openness of the audiences," McMurtry says. "They encourage you to try things, they respond, and it is a challenge for the musicians to remain creative and not get locked into anything. There's also room here for many styles, and there's less concern about what might or might not work commercially. I think that's probably been true of Texas for a long time, and that is something that is really inspiring to a songwriter."

Nanci Griffith says she knew she wanted to be a songwriter as a young child, which is no surprise since she learned guitar from a Saturday morning show on public television. "For me, it became easier to start writing songs than trying to learn someone else's music," Griffith laughs. Although she was born in Sequin, near San Antonio, Griffith grew up in Austin and began singing professionally as a teenager. Griffith moved from the local club circuit into national

A Tribute to Texas Songwriters

prominence in 1978, with *There's A Light Beyond These Woods*. Since then, her releases for such labels as Philo, Rounder, MCA, Elektra, and her current label [Universal] have spotlighted her own special musical brand she calls "folkabilly."

Besides being blessed with a gorgeous, instantly identifiable voice, Griffith has proven an exceptional songwriter whose songs have been cut by Lyle Lovett, Dwight Yoakam, Steve Earle, Kathy Mattea and Suzy Bogguss. "For me there is no separation between the music and the lyrics. I think they're equally important and I usually try to work on both of them at the same time," Griffith says. "There are some songs where maybe a musical idea came first, and others where I had an idea and thought about the words to illustrate it before starting on the music…but I think you have to pay attention to both of them, because a song is a complete unit. If you don't have lyrics that fit, it doesn't matter about the music. You also have to have music that works within the structure of your story. All the people that I admire, from Emmylou Harris and Dolly Parton to Johnny Cash and Willie Nelson, are performers whose songs are always fully developed. That's a challenge for songwriters, to try and think about the completed song and the best way to develop it."

Griffith has won Grammys as both a solo artist and in joint-ventures with the famed Irish band The Chieftains, but she's now focusing on her forthcoming new release, *Hearts In Mind* (Universal). Her first studio date since 2001, the 14-cut disc includes the spirited "I Love This Town" duet with Jimmy Buffett, and another stirring shared number "Rise To The Occasion" with Mac McAnally. Such songs as "Big Blue Ball of War" and "Hanoi" reflect Griffith's staunch anti-war views, but the disc shouldn't be pegged as simply a protest or political work. Indeed, tunes like "Love Conquers All," "Last Train Home," and "Before" are numbers with beautifully voiced, superbly written reminders that Griffith's a topflight wordsmith whether she's discussing romance or foreign policy.

Pat Green has emerged from the Texas underground to both surprise and amaze many Nashville observers. That's because Green isn't reluctant to express his disdain about some of what airs on contemporary country stations, yet his music has consistently exceeded commercial expectations. His early material was hugely popular on the regional circuit, and Green dabbled in blues, folk and bluegrass, as well as

Ron Wynn

country before shifting to the New York-based Republic label in 2001. But his most recent releases, coupled with frequent joint appearances with Willie Nelson and the pair's splendid duet "Threadbare Gypsy Soul," have now boosted Green from being a critically-acclaimed but relatively obscure figure, to someone whose appearances are increasingly being elevated to the upper echelon of modern country performers.

"The song is everything to me," Green says. "That's what I'm always doing out here, trying to make my songs better. One thing when you work as many dates as I have, you find out real quick what works and what doesn't. There have been times when I thought I had something really special and it just fell flat. Then you have a song that you think is nothing special, and then the people just love it. If I've learned anything over time, it's that you must perform the material before audiences. It doesn't mean anything for you to sit there and think you've got something great, then never put it out there. I'm really trying to write songs that will stand the test of time, because that's what the people I admire have always done. Willie Nelson has written so many songs that people will still be signing in the next century. The same thing is true about Waylon Jennings. I don't think you can say that about a lot of what's on the radio now, but I'm not concerned with that as much as I am with constantly improving my own songs."

"If you got out and just listen to people, you can always get ideas," Green continues. "I can't tell you how many times on the road a conversation or just something someone said hit a spark, and there's a song right there. I've written on the bus, backstage before the show, at home, whenever and wherever the idea occurs. I don't try to do anything fancy or slick...just sing about how I feel or what I'm thinking at a particular time."

His latest, *Lucky Ones* (Republic), includes a fine duet with Brad Paisley titled "College," plus the tender "My Little Heaven," and a more somber "Temporary Angel." "I guess the biggest thing that I've gotten from coming up in Texas is the courage to be honest and direct in my songwriting," Green concludes. "Every great songwriter who ever lived that was from Texas always told it straight, and that's what I try to do in my songs."

THE RESURRECTION OF KEITH URBAN

Artist survives failure of The Ranch, depression, and self-destructive behavior to become one of country's hottest acts.

By Peter Cooper
From *The Tennessean*

Fourteen years ago, Keith Urban got a letter in the mail.

"I listened to your music and really enjoyed it," is how Urban remembers the note from Mary Martin, the legendary talent scout who championed Emmylou Harris, Rodney Crowell and others. "Unfortunately, country is enjoying a traditional time at the moment. I feel that your music doesn't fit, but I hope you come back to Nashville and find a home here."

Urban's home at the time was in Australia. He was undaunted by the rejection.

"Out of all the people I shopped my music to in America, she was the only one who actually wrote back to me," said Urban, who has since become the latest member of country's upper echelon. He's up for prizes, including Entertainer, Male Vocalist and Single of the Year, at Tuesday's Academy of Country Music Awards.

"What I read from her letter was, 'Come here, and when the pendulum swings you'll be in the right place,' " he said. "I thought about that letter a lot over future years. To me it meant, 'Stick to your guns and be patient.'"

Whether that's what Martin meant or not, the lesson has served Urban quite well. After years of struggle, the 37-year-old is now

Peter Cooper

among country's hottest acts. No matter if the ACM Awards work out well for him, he has gone from anomaly to star, from multi-talented to multi-platinum.

"We saw something similar happen with Kenny Chesney and Toby Keith a few years back," said Wade Jessen, country chart director at *Billboard* magazine. "I really think this is Keith's time to get that kind of notice and that kind of ink. He's due the crown of country's new groove king."

The big fish/small pond thing can be quite nice, if the pond is as temperate as Urban's was in the early 1990s. He was in Australia, where the sun shone a lot of the time and where he could tour regularly and play in front of big crowds.

"We had a record out, and it sold pretty good," he said. "We were selling merchandise. And I'd seen artists who were having a lot more success in Australia - people like Jimmy Barnes - go over to the states and have to start all over again. They had a great living in Australia and such comfort, but their success didn't translate. To me, though, I had a want to see if I could be significant in a larger place."

Olivia Newton-John had some hits, but before Urban's ascendance no Aussie had achieved prolonged country music success in America. With confidence bolstered by Mary Martin's letter and by a sense that he was fated for a Nashville career, he moved to Music City in 1992. Like most others, his arrival was treated with indifference.

After awhile, the indifference melded with criticism: His hair was too long, some of the record executives said. Or he needed a hat. Or he was too pop. Or too rock. Or his voice wasn't as convincing as his guitar work.

"I thought I'd wander in, do some showcases, get signed, do a record and go on the road," he said. "Seriously. The constant rejection thing . . . I wasn't expecting that. They were like, 'What are you doing here?' I was like, 'What do you mean? This is what was meant to be.' It was so obvious to me, and so not obvious to every other person I met."

At home on stages since he was 7, Urban was discombobulated by his infrequent gigs in Nashville.

"A huge part of my confidence came from audience reaction," he said. "I'd had that throughout my life, but when I got to Nashville I realized that I didn't know who I was offstage. I hadn't spent a lot of time with that guy, and I didn't like him very much. I found him geeky and a nerd. He was schizo and unorganized. The guy onstage was

The Resurrection of Keith Urban

focused, with everything centered. The guy offstage was just a wreck."

Urban didn't react to that lack of balance by shoring up his off-stage self. Instead, he figured out ways to put himself back in the spotlight. He led a band, The Ranch, which was intended to be a five-piece unit but was whittled to three players because of economics. If Urban was the only guitarist, augmented only by a drummer and a bass man, money went a lot farther.

"Capitol Records (the label that released The Ranch's album in 1997) loved the idea that we were a three-piece, self-sufficient band," Urban said. "They were like, 'You guys are lean and mean. It's working for you. You love that van. You're paying your dues and learning your craft!' I was going, 'Hey, I've been paying dues and learning craft for 15 years.' We needed more support from the label."

His time with The Ranch earned Urban a reputation as one of Nashville's finest guitar players, but it didn't earn him a place as a country radio hit-maker. The group's debut album was also its swan song, and Urban was a wreck.

After a young life spent trying to "make it," he felt himself a failure. Alcohol and drugs exacerbated Urban's depression in what he now calls his "self-destructive time." He had relative youth, prodigious guitar skills and a slew of potentially marketable songs, but he was drained, dark and bitter. One dark 5 a.m., he found himself crawling around the floor in a decrepit Nashville drug house, looking for rocks of cocaine.

"The hardest thing I've dealt with was figuring out what to do after The Ranch," he said. "I thought, 'I'm lost out in the ether.' "

In late 1998, Urban checked himself into Cumberland Heights, a Nashville treatment center. It was the beginning of the process that found him re-evaluating his life and his habits. Urban's self-worth always had been bound up in audience response. That wouldn't be an easy mindset to break, but an upturn in his career would mean he wouldn't have to break from it entirely.

About 10 years after receiving Mary Martin's letter, Keith Urban was exuberant. Signed to Capitol Records as a solo act, he'd tried unsuccessfully to develop a distinctive in-studio sound. But a session with keyboard player Matt Rollings at the production helm yielded something he thought could work. "Where The Blacktop Ends" was a groove-based song, with a recurring guitar riff, yet fiddle, banjo and steel guitar kept it rooted in country.

Peter Cooper

"It was the first time in my life in the studio when I thought, 'I think this is really good,' he recalled. "I called up my girlfriend from the studio and she asked how the session was going. I said, 'I'm gonna be a (expletive) star!' That's exactly what I said. It was sheer jubilation, from feeling like I'd been in the wilderness for so long. I was grateful to be alive and happy to be healthy again, and I started to have back a little bit of the confidence that I'd lost."

Thus began the personal and commercial resurrection of Keith Urban. When "But For The Grace Of God" — a track from the Rollings-produced *Keith Urban* album — hit the radio in the fall of 2000, he was once again designated as an up-and-comer.

"If there was a temptation to pigeonhole Keith as a rock guitar player who looks great but may not be able to deliver vocally, 'But For The Grace Of God' put that theory to rest," said *Billboard's* Jessen. "People knew what a great guitarist he was, but they'd never heard him sing with that kind of intensity."

Since then, Urban's career has built steadily and deliberately. He's notched ten Top 10 records on the *Billboard* country chart, with half of those going to No. 1 (his current "Making Memories of Us" will likely become his sixth chart-topper). Aided by a stint opening shows for Kenny Chesney, his drawing power has increased to the point where he's now headlining his own shows. Industry prizes, including a 2004 CMA Vocalist of the Year trophy and two CMT Music Awards this year, underscore his place as a top-drawer attraction.

"As we track what our audience is interested in, Keith is consistently one of our top five artists," said Chris Parr, CMT's vice president of music and talent. "And when he plays live, there's almost a teen-idol shrillness in the audience response."

The result of all this has been a solidification of Urban's professional and personal life. He's building a house in Nashville, and it will be the first home he's owned in the United States. His personal life — which has been marked by an on-again, off-again relationship with a fiancé, and by another much-gossiped-about, now-dissolved relationship with supermodel Nikki Taylor — has been headline-free of late. Asked about whether the theme of love as redemption he often repeats in his songs rings true to him, Urban said, "I still believe that. Sometimes it takes awhile. I'm a late bloomer."

If Urban wins anything at Tuesday's Academy of Country Music Awards show, he won't be walking to the winner's podium. Instead,

The Resurrection of Keith Urban

he'll be in Ireland, performing with rock singer Bryan Adams.

"Keith is a global priority for (Capitol's parent company) EMI," said Fletcher Foster, Capitol Nashville's senior vice president for marketing. "We're launching an international album this month, and it's a combination of songs from (his multi-platinum selling 2002 album) *Golden Road* and (2004's) *Be Here*. We think he's going to be a great ambassador for country music."

That would be a happy ending, were it an ending at all.

"Hearing Bruce Springsteen sing 'Born To Run,' you know what his goal was," Urban said. "A man on a mission is a great thing to witness in any form. That's fantastic and inspiring. I have had moments of worrying about this: I don't have a mission that has a real focus. I didn't have a plan when I got into this. My only plan was to tour successfully and be on radio. Now that it's happening, I've thought, 'I need a new plan.'"

214

SAMMI SMITH
The Art of Inauthenticity

By David Cantwell
From *The Oxford American*'s *Southern Music Issue 2005* (Issue 50)

Listen to "Help Me Make It Through the Night," and you'll hear a stunning set piece for Sammi Smith's unique vocal strengths: her headache moan and cigarette sigh; her humid, forlorn hum; the shuddering catch in her husky alto; the slow, considered drawl that feels like she is whispering her most intimate secrets—and the way Smith uses all of these touches to create an illusion of vulnerability that's at once inviting and harrowing. "Oh, it's sad to be alone," she weeps before gulping, "Help me make it through the night." Such a simple request, but she makes it plain that the stakes are life or death.

Smith was just sixty-one when she died this past February. Her passing barely registered in the media, an oversight that was disheartening but hardly unexpected. There are all sorts of reasons Smith isn't as widely remembered today as her friends Waylon Jennings (who nicknamed her "Girl Hero") and Kris Kristofferson (who wrote "Help Me Make It Through the Night") or her chart contemporaries like Loretta Lynn, Johnny Cash (whose bassist Marshall Grant helped land Smith her first, short-lived record deal with Columbia), and Dolly Parton.

The most obvious reason Smith remains all but unknown is that she didn't have much of a chart career. "Help Me Make It Through the Night" was named the Country Music Association's Single of the Year in 1971, and was a Grammy winner as well, but her label at the time, Mega Records, was new and far too underfinanced to capitalize on Smith's out-of-the-gate success. She scored just two more Top 10 country hits during the remaining decade and a half of her recording career.

She never had a comeback, either—she only had one of her classic Mega albums reissued on CD—and I think I know part of the reason.

David Cantwell

Sammi Smith just wasn't the sort of singer that contemporary listeners on the prowl for cool old country were going to latch onto. For one thing, she lacked a key requirement for the "alternative country" resurrection: With few exceptions, she didn't write her own songs. For another, her style was countrypolitan—subdued, lush emotionalism. And there you have it: Her words were borrowed, and her sounds were orchestrated. Those two traits all but guarantee that she'd be considered inauthentic for those whose model of country artistry includes Hank Williams, say, or Merle Haggard, but does not include Eddy Arnold, Marty Robbins, or Conway Twitty.

Like all of those singers, Sammi Smith was a brilliant vocal interpreter. Indeed, Smith was such a remarkable talent, and such an overlooked one, that my instinct isn't just to proclaim her greatness but to proclaim it outrageously. For example: Her first Mega LP, *Help Me Make It Through the Night*, is as potent as any other album from the era you can name, and I don't care which genre you choose from, either.

Anyone who claims to know the definitive versions of such standards as "Sunday Mornin' Comin' Down," "Fire and Rain," "The Last Word in Lonesome Is Me," "Lonely Street," "Today I Started Loving You Again" or, of course, "Help Me Make It Through the Night," but is not familiar with Smith's versions, needs to start over.

Among Smith's most remarkable performances was her recording of "The Toast of '45," a Mega single that barely charted in the winter of 1972. In the song, a salesman "in town for the day" recognizes the singer, a former Hollywood star and current barfly, and buys her a couple of drinks, lights her cigarette, and encourages her to reminisce. It's not as though she needs prodding.

Smith chooses to deliver her lines more like she's speaking than singing, yet every syllable is musical, and she's working in a higher key than usual, which invests her voice with a controlled but nervous excitement. Smith is using her voice and her phrasing to fill in all of the emotional details that the song's lyrics leave undecided. The effect is to create for us a woman simultaneously eager for this unexpected close-up and weary of such unsolicited contact. She is now struggling not to let either emotion show.

This is a tough (and necessary) trick for any actor—revealing emotions when the character being portrayed does not want emotions revealed—but it's especially hard when the actor is a singer on a record with no props, set, or costume to work with, no facial expressions or gestures, just her voice and some music. When the narrator of the song remembers her golden years, Smith sounds as if her lower lip has begun ever so slightly to tremble. Her voice fluttery and fragile, the character seems a little embarrassed to be seen like this, though she also sounds pleased to be recognized after all this time. Smith plays her like a musical Blanche DuBois, except that Smith makes this woman genuinely elegant and never pathetic. When the man to whom the aging actress is speaking excuses himself, the one-time Toast of '45 sips her drink alone and hums to herself wistfully. And…scene.

Every great singer is a great actor. This isn't just a metaphor. We accept that the actors of stage and film are playing roles, pretending to be someone they are not, but we often resist admitting that singers do much the same thing, especially the ones who sing songs they've written themselves. Actors should be believable, we insist, but singers must be "authentic." They must not only seem real but be real.

This insistence upon a singer's "authenticity" is commonplace today, but it misunderstands how art works. It especially underestimates the art of the singer. Art is artificial, it's human-made, and even art that is what we call realistic is capturing not what is real but an illusion of the real.

This isn't to say Sammi Smith didn't draw upon her experience when creating a performance any more than it means actors don't use sense-memories. Nor does it mean Smith wasn't feeling emotions associated with the lyric while in the recording studio; it doesn't mean Smith's lip didn't tremble. I would have loved, and would have hated, too, to hear Smith sing "The Toast of '45" in the last years of her life, when she knew firsthand what it was like to be forgotten.

Still, even then, Smith necessarily would have been portraying feelings within the context of the song, using her imagination and not merely offering up to us the pangs of her own true heart. Smith's heart, like anyone's, was hers alone to know.

When we demand authenticity of what is essentially inauthentic, we disrespect the singer's art. We diminish the very artistic powers that make us empathize. It's our own responses, finally, that hold the only authenticity that matters.

The album that included "Help Me Make It Through the Night" was originally titled *He's Everywhere* after the track the label was promoting as its first single. But when it became plain that "Help Me Make It Through the Night" was going to be more than successful,

David Cantwell

the album was quickly renamed. By any name, Smith's first Mega LP is a masterpiece of inner desolation.

The album begins with Smith at "Saunders' Ferry Lane," watching autumn die away in winter's grip, and mourning the death of a lover. In "With Pen in Hand," she pauses to plead for one last chance with her husband, then she goes ahead and signs the papers. In "There He Goes," she realizes, too late, that the man her unfaithfulness has driven from her arms is the man she can't live without. On every track but one, she is alone. Usually she is by herself, engaged in soliloquy, but even when there is someone there beside her, she remains alone, crying to characters who have already made their exits. The one holdout to this litany of alienation, the one chance at possible human connection, is unexpectedly one of the loneliest singles ever made, "Help Me Make It Through the Night."

The album ends with "This Room for Rent." In contrast to most of her other sides, this rhythm track is on the fast side of mid-tempo and seems to hurtle her about the apartment that her landlady character is showing to a prospective tenant. Smith's words come in a rush, but there's a beaten-down flatness to them all the same. She speaks of the previous occupants, a young couple in love who left the room a mess, but it becomes plain from the agonized way she's telling the tale that she's singing about her own time there and her own departed lover. With each new detail of this grand tour—"There's the kitchen table where she sat and tried to dry her eyes on the corner of a scratchy paper towel; she cried to God and asked Him if that man had ever loved her anyhow"—her misery mounts, until finally she's drifted away from us entirely, and there is no one there now to whom she can plead for help.

"She's heard no word from God," she admits, "and nothing seems to matter anymore." The record just halts then, Smith's unvarnished voice trailing off, the music suddenly dead.

I don't know if Sammi Smith ever knew that kind of hopelessness, but the dread and isolation she captures here sound more than real enough.

CONTRIBUTORS

Bob Allen is the author of *George Jones: Life and Times of a Honky Tonk Legend*. He was a longtime contributor writer for *Country Music* magazine and was a contributing editor to the *Encyclopedia of Country Music* (Oxford University Press and the Country Music Foundation). He currently writes for the *Towson (Maryland) Times*.

Ralph Berrier, Jr. is a member of the Black Twig Pickers bluegrass band, a songwriter and bluegrass music reporter. He is a feature writer for the *Roanoke Times* and a reporter for the "The Crooked Road" series that explores Virginia's musical heritage.

David Cantwell is the co-author of *Heartaches by the Number: Country Music's 500 Greatest Singles* (Vanderbilt University Press). His features have appeared in *Oxford American, No Depression, The Nashville Scene*, and other publications. He lives in St. Louis, Missouri.

Nancy Cardwell works for the International Bluegrass Music Association. She is also a freelance writer and musician, and lives in Owensboro, Kentucky.

Peter Cooper covers music and entertainment for the *Nashville Tennessean*.

Francis Davis is the author of *History of the Blues: The Roots, the Music, the People from Charley Patton to Robert Cray*; and *In the Moment: Jazz in the 1980's*. He is a music critic for the *Atlantic Monthly*.

Bill DeMain is the author of *In Their Own Words: Songwriters Talk about the Creative Process*. He lives in Nashville, Tennessee.

Contributors

Benjamin Filene is author of *Romancing the Folk: Public Memory and American Roots Music* (University of North Carolina Press).

Thomas Goldsmith covered country music for the Nashville *Tennessean* for many years and edited *The Bluegrass Reader* (University of Illinois Press). He is now a features editor for the *News and Observer* in Raleigh, North Carolina.

Dave Hickey is the author of *Air Guitar: Essays on Art and Democracy* and *The Invisible Dragon*. A former engineering student, a short-story writer, music journalist, Austin gallery owner, New York editor, and Nashville songwriter, Hickey is an art and music critic and now lives in Long Beach, California.

Martha Hume is the editor of *The Journal of Country Music* and the author of several books on country music.

Paul Kingsbury is the author of *The Grand Ole Opry History of Country Music* and the editor of *The Encyclopedia of Country Music* (Oxford University Press and the Country Music Foundation).

Michael McCall was a Senior Editor with *Country Music* magazine. He now writes for *The Nashville Scene* and other music publications.

Edward Morris is the author of *Garth Brooks: Platinum Cowboy* and a former editor at *Billboard* magazine. He is now a freelance writer and lives in Nashville.

Nick Shave studied music at Keble College, Oxford and now writes for music publications such as *The Strad, The Gramophone* and *BBC Music Magazine*. He lives in London.

Contributors

Eddie Stubbs is a popular DJ on WSM radio in Nashville, host of the Grand Ole Opry, and a mighty fine fiddle player. Stubbs was a member of the Johnson Mountain Boys bluegrass band.

Phil Sweetland publishes the *Country Insider* and is a contributing writer for several publications, including *American Songwriter* and *The New York Times*.

Alec Wilkinson is the author of *A Violent Act*, *Moonshine Midnights*, and *Big Sugar*. A recipient of a Lyndhurst Prize, a Robert F. Kennedy Book Award, and a Guggenheim fellowship, he is a regular contributor to *The New Yorker*, *Esquire*, and other magazines. He lives in New York City.

Ron Wynn has written for *The Nashville Scene*, *The Nashville City Paper*, *American Songwriter*, *The Memphis Commercial Appeal*, and other publications. He lives in Nashville.

PERMISSIONS

"God's Lonely Man," written by Francis Davis, originally appeared in *The Atlantic Monthly* in the March 2004 issue. Reprinted by permission of the author.

"Unsinkable: Is Loretta Lynn Country Music's Scarlett O'Hara?" written by Martha Hume, originally appeared in *The Journal of Country Music*, Volume 24.2. Reprinted by permission of the author.

"Proud to be a Redneck Woman," written by Peter Cooper, originally appeared in the Nashville *Tennessean* on June 6, 2004. Reprinted by permission of *The Tennessean*..

"James Henry 'Jimmy' Martin (August 10, 1927–May 14, 2005)," written by Eddie Stubbs, originally appeared in *Bluegrass Unlimited* in the July, 2005 issue. Reprinted by permission of the author and publication.

"From Down-home to Big Time," by Michael McCall, originally appeared *in The Nashville Scene* on June 9, 2005. Reprinted by permission of the author.

"Iris DeMent: All That Living Will Allow," written by David Cantwell, originally appeared in *No Depression* magazine in Issue #54 (November/December 2004). Reprinted by permission of the author.

"Kris Kristofferson: The Hemingway of Songwriters," written by Phil Sweetland, originally appeared in *American Songwriter* in the September/October issue, 2004. Reprinted by permission of the author.

"The Celebrity Two-Step," written by Paul Kingsbury, originally appeared in *The Journal of Country Music* in Volume 24.1. Reprinted by permission of the author.

"The Ghostly Ones," written by Alec Wilkinson, originally appeared in *The New Yorker* on September 20, 2004. Reprinted by permission of the author.

"Through Fifty-Year-Old Eyes," written by Thomas Goldsmith, originally appeared in *Bluegrass Unlimited* in the April 2005 issue. Reprinted by permission of the author and publication.

"His Mickey Mouse Ways," written by Dave Hickey, originally appeared in *Texas Monthly* in the June 2004 issue. Reprinted by permission of the publication.

"Rhonda Vincent: Enjoying theView," written by Ralph Berrier, Jr. originally appeared in *Bluegrass Unlimited* in the July 2004 issue. Reprinted by permission of the author and publication.

"The Big Show," written by Edward Morris, originally appeared in *The Journal of Country Music* in Vol. 23.2. Reprinted by permission of the author.

"Dwight Yoakam: Hillbilly Redux," written by Bill DeMain, originally appeared in *Performing Songwriter* in the July/August 2005 issue. Reprinted by permission of the author.

"Voice of America," written by Nick Shave, originally appeared in *The Strad* (Orpheus Publications, Ltd., London) in the November 2003 issue. Reprinted by permission of the publication.

"O Brother, What Next? Making Sense of the Folk Fad," written by Benjamin Filene, originally appeared in *Southern Cultures* (University of North Carolina at Chapel Hill) in the Summer 2004 issue. Reprinted by permission of the publication.

"Lost Notes and Myriad Blessings," written by Michael McCall, originally appeared in *The Nashville Scene* on April 28, 2005. Reprinted by permission of the author.

"They're Back," written by Nancy Cardwell, originally appeared in *Bluegrass Unlimited* in the June 2004 issue. Reprinted by permission of the author and publication.

"Fame From the Tips of His Fingers," written by Bob Allen, originally appeared in *The Journal of Country Music*, Vol. 24.1. Reprinted by permission of the author.

"A Tribute to Texas Songwriters," written by Ron Wynn, originally appeared in *American Songwriter* in the March/April 2005 issue. Reprinted by permission of the author.

"The Resurrection of Keith Urban," written by Peter Cooper, originally appeared in the Nashville *Tennessean* on May 15, 2005. Reprinted by permission of *The Tennessean*.

"The Art of Inauthenticity," written by David Cantwell, originally appeared in *The Oxford American*'s *Southern Music Issue* (Summer 2005). Reprinted by permission of the author.

Randy Rudder has an M.F.A. in creative writing from the University of Memphis, an M.A. in literature from Tennessee State University, and a B.A. in communications from Mount Union College in Ohio. His articles have appeared in *The Nashville Scene*, *The Washington Post*, *The Nashville Business Journal*, *Home Life Magazine*, *Country Weekly*, and *American Songwriter*. He has also published articles in the academic journal *Southern Crossroads* (Mercer University Press), and the anthology *Country Music Goes to War* (University of Kentucky Press). He lives in Nashville with his wife Clare and daughter Abigail.

Doug Kershaw *(The Ragin' Cajun)* became a member of the Grand Ole Opry in 1957. He began his career as a fiddle player early in life and soon was a regular on such shows as the Louisiana Hayride, The WWVA Jamboree (Wheeling), and the Opry. He and his brother Rusty toured together in the 1950s before they went their separate ways. Over the past fifty years, he has recorded 29 albums. Kershaw's autobiographical tune "Louisiana Man," became the first song broadcast back to Earth from the Moon by the astronauts of Apollo 12.

224